Arms Akimbo: Africana Women in Contemporary Literature

Arms Akimbo

Africana Women in
Contemporary Literature

EDITED BY JANICE LEE LIDDELL AND YAKINI BELINDA KEMP

University Press of Florida

Gainesville · Tallahassee · Tampa · Boca Raton
Pensacola · Orlando · Miami · Jacksonville

Copyright 1999 by the Board of Regents of the State of Florida
Printed in the United States of America on acid-free paper
All rights reserved

04 03 02 01 00 99 6 5 4 3 2 1

Library of Congress Cataloging-in-Publication Data

Arms akimbo: Africana women in contemporary literature / edited by
Janice Lee Liddell and Yakini Belinda Kemp.
p. cm.
Includes bibliographical references and index.
ISBN 0-8130-1728-9 (acid-free paper)
1. American literature—Afro-American authors—History and
criticism. 2. Caribbean literature—Women authors—History and
criticism. 3. Women and literature—Caribbean Area—History—20th
century. 4. Women and literature—United States—History—20th
century. 5. American literature—Women authors—History and
criticism. 6. African literature—Women authors—History and
criticism. 7. Women and literature—Africa—History—20th century.
8. Afro-American women in literature. 9. Women, Black, in literature.
I. Liddell, Janice. II. Kemp, Yakini Belinda.
PS153.N5A87 1999
810.9'352042'08996073—dc21 99-38712

The University Press of Florida is the scholarly publishing agency for
the State University System of Florida, comprising Florida A & M
University, Florida Atlantic University, Florida International
University, Florida State University, University of Central Florida,
University of Florida, University of North Florida, University of South
Florida, and University of West Florida.

University Press of Florida
15 Northwest 15th Street
Gainesville, FL 32611–2079
http://www.upf.com

To Mama and Daddy, Euneda and Lee Liddell, who instilled in me the dedication and endurance it took to bear this fruit; to my husband, Allan Alberga, who understood its importance.

—*Janice Lee Liddell*

To the memory of my father, Cleveland "Daddy Boyd" Kemp, for his life of hard work, quiet love, and steadfast support; to Mama Rosetta, for the faith, and to my daughter, Nzinga, for her inspiration.

—*Yakini Belinda Kemp*

balancing their lives on their heads
betting you they can make it across
by dangling an extra hand on their hip
threading themselves into sweetgrass baskets
akimboing one arm
through another sister's
and walking their own paths
and be together in going home

—*Nikky Finney from "Permittable Thunder"*

CONTENTS

FOREWORD

Arms Akimbo: Africana Women in Contemporary Literature, edited by Professors Yakini Kemp and Janice Liddell, makes a significant contribution to our understanding of the complexity of contemporary writers of the African Diaspora, who are still largely ignored by mainstream literary scholars and Western feminist literary critics. This literary anthology is situated by the editors, as it should be, within the larger field of Black Women's Studies and employs both Afrocentric and feminist/womanist critical perspectives. Kemp and Liddell's comprehensive and grounding introductory essay, a praise song for the intellectual legacy of Black Women's Studies, provides the appropriate lens through which we might examine a diverse group of Africana women writers in the Americas and around the globe.

Within the past three decades, this new field of study—Black Women's Studies—emerged in part because of the failure of both Black Studies and Women's Studies to address adequately the unique experiences of women of African descent (Africana women) in the United States and throughout the world. The first critical publication in this newly emerging field was a collection of works by and about Black women, which Toni Cade (Bambara) edited in 1970. Cade's (Bambara's) *The Black Woman* was significant because of the value it attached to hearing the distinct voices of Black women, arguing that their experiences were different from both Black men and white women. Cade's

(Bambara's) work preceded by two years Gerda Lerner's 1972 documentary history *Black Women in White America,* which is often erroneously cited as having ushered in Black Women's Studies. Another pioneering work neglected by early feminist historians was Rosalyn Terborg-Penn and Sharon Harley's 1978 anthology, *The Afro-American Woman: Struggles and Images.* The groundbreaking anthology of Filomina Chioma Steady, *The Black Woman Cross-Culturally,* which appeared in 1981, was particularly significant because of its diasporan focus and its cross-cultural approach to the experiences of Africana women. Five years later, Rosalyn Terborg-Penn, Sharon Harley, and Andrea Benton Rushing's edited collection, *Women in Africa and the African Diaspora,* signaled the transformation of Black Women's Studies from a narrow U.S. focus by providing a much-needed theoretical framework for dealing with Africana women globally. Steady's essay on African feminism also enlarged the discourse on Black feminisms around the world, as would Stanlie James and Abena Busia's anthology, *Theorizing Black Feminisms: The Visionary Pragmatism of Black Women* (1994).

Kemp and Liddell remind us again that Gloria Hull, Patricia Bell Scott, and Barbara Smith were the first scholars to define Black Women's Studies; they also traced its development and provided a rationale for its existence in their 1982 foundational publication, *All the Women Are White, All the Blacks Are Men, But Some of Us Are Brave.* "Women's studies courses . . . focused almost exclusively upon the lives of white women. Black studies, which was much too often male dominated, also ignored black women. . . . Because of white women's racism and black men's sexism, there was no room in either area for a serious consideration of the lives of black women" (x).

To be sure, a critical component in the development of Black Women's Studies was the emergence of Black feminist literary criticism. Barbara Smith's essay, "Toward a Black Feminist Criticism," which appeared in the 1977 edition of *Conditions: Two,* was the first theoretical essay on Black feminist criticism. Three years later, Deborah McDowell's "New Directions for Black Feminist Criticism," which appeared in the October 1980 issue of *Black American Literature Forum,* called for a clearer definition of a "black feminist aesthetic," and delineated the major tasks that would confront the Black feminist critic over the next decade. Earlier, the pioneering work of Mary Helen Washington called attention for the first time to the distinctive vision of Black women writers in her pioneering essay "Black Women Image Makers," which appeared in the August 1974 issue of *Black World.* Her two important anthologies, *Black Eyed Susans: Classic Stories By and About Black Women* (1975) and *Midnight Birds: Stories by Contemporary Black Women Writers* (1980), marked the importance of Black women writers, as did *Sturdy Black Bridges: Visions of Black Women in Literature,* the first anthology of Black women's literature, edited by Roseann P. Bell, Bettye J. Parker, and Beverly Guy-Sheftall in 1979; its diasporan focus is reminiscent as well of new directions in Black Women's Studies. Similarly, Barbara Christian's *Black Women Novelists: The Development of a Tradition, 1892– 1976* (1980) was the first full-length study of the novels of Black women. It is also important to underscore the importance of Alice Walker's essay, "In Search of Our Mothers' Gardens" (*Ms.,* May 1974), which posits a theory of Black female creativity, and the fact that Walker designed the first course on Black women writers, which she taught in 1972 at Wellesley College.

Arms Akimbo now joins a larger body of work under the rubric of Black feminist/womanist literary discourse about which there is considerable interest in scholarly circles and literature classrooms. Its most recent diasporan "sister-texts" are Carole Boyce Davies's *Migrations of the Subject: Black Women, Writing, and Identity* (1994) and *Moving Beyond Boundaries: Black Women's Diasporas, Vol. 2,* (1995); Susheila Nasta's *Motherlands: Black Women's Writing from Africa, Caribbean and South Asia* (1992); Margaret Busby's *Daughters of Africa: An International Anthology of Words and Writings by Women of African Descent from the Ancient Egyptian to the Present* (1992); and Gay Wilentz's *Binding Cultures: Black Women Writers in Africa and the Diaspora* (1992). Kemp and Liddell's collection of critical essays on the fictions of Africana women writers will certainly broaden our understanding of global women's issues, particularly in the African Diaspora. Its analyses of the most significant women writers of the African Diaspora, a few of whom are relatively well known in literature classrooms, such as Paule Marshall, Ama Ata Aidoo, Mariama Bâ, Buchi Emecheta, and Jamaica Kincaid, are fresh and textured. As important are essays on writers such as Sherley Anne Williams, Sylvia Wynter, Beryl Gilroy, and Bessie Head, who have received less scholarly attention.

Texts such as *Arms Akimbo* will contribute, no doubt, to the transformation of the literature classroom and feminist scholarship on women writers transnationally. Like many Black Studies and Women's Studies humanities professors, I am looking forward to sharing this anthology with my students and colleagues.

Beverly Guy-Sheftall

Introduction

Black Women's Studies and the Intellectual Legacy—
A Praise Song

As women, we must also resist any attempts at being persuaded to think that the woman question has to be superseded by the struggle against any local exploitative system, the nationalist struggle or the struggle against imperialism and global monopoly capital. For what is becoming clear is that in the long run, none of these fronts is either of greater relevance than the rest or even separate from them.

Ama Ata Aidoo

Arms Akimbo is a logical culmination of the sociopolitical and academic experiences of women of African descent over the past quarter century. During these twenty-five years, women of African descent, or Africana women, in the United States and other parts of the world participated in correlative sociopolitical movements that would change the course of their history. And from this historic social period, Black Women's Studies evolved. As indicated by the above quote from writer, teacher, and social activist Ama Ata Aidoo, the interlocking components of economics, politics, race, and gender comprise the platform or battlefronts for Africana women in social struggle. Yet Aidoo's second and perhaps more profound point—that all areas of struggle are equal—is one that continues to confound and divide those involved in the community and in academe.

One illustration of the interlocutory and conflicting appositions that provided the impetus for Black Women's Studies is the movement initiated within the United States during the 1960s and '70s that has come to be known as the Black Power Movement. Evolving from the Civil Rights movement, or perhaps responding to it, the Black Power Movement was a demand by a younger militant group for freedom, justice, and equality for the Black man in America. While leaders of the various militant groups, such as the Student Nonviolent Coordinating Committee (SNCC) and the Black Panther Party, attempted to persuade American Black women of the inclusiveness and universality of the term "Black man," the movement itself belied the arguments. From their initial involvement, most Black women in these organizations thought themselves more than capable of performing the same duties as their male counterparts, including facing physical danger (Giddings 278). Before long, however, these women saw that the movement that supposedly embraced the needs of all African American people rendered no promises for women's revolution. The notorious remark of the young SNCC leader, Stokely Carmichael, that the only position for women in the movement "was prone" indicated the degree to which the work of the women activists was devalued and contradicted the rankings of women within his own organization (Giddings 302). The Black Power Movement, which was ostensibly formulated through independent group coalitions, could not fulfill the needs of Black women because of the inherent male authoritarianism within its formal and informal organization.

The second radical movement of this era was the Women's Liberation Movement. Like the Black Power Movement, which was one of the catalysts for the modern Women's Movement, there existed potential for an inclusive response to discrimination and oppression. In reality, the Women's Liberation Movement, with its white middle-class agenda, fell far short of including the concerns of women who were Black, working class, or poor. Integral to the major white women's organizational platforms was the unspoken need to preserve their class interests and racial privilege, which prevented the possibility of effective, large-scale alliances between white women and Black women. Consequently, many Black women, some working within the women's groups, came to agree that the Women's Liberation Movement would end up using the "black movement as a stepping stone for white women's advancement" in a highly competitive economy (Giddings 309). And as Black women, we assessed that we would be excluded from the rewards gained from such a liberation struggle. Thus, through active participation, Black women concluded that involvement with Black male-directed and white female-directed liberation organizations was an important aspect of the overall struggle for democratic rights in the society. However, for our issues and experiences as Black women to be addressed productively, we knew that our own efforts would forge the progression. Responding to this realization, African American women intellectual activists fomented one vehicle designed to speak to our needs as Black women—Black Women's Studies.

What follows is an overview of the intellectual and social climate that produced Black Women's Studies in the United States and its influence on the development of programs in other countries. Our overview notes particularly that from its earliest stages, Black Women's Studies incorporates works that included or were solely devoted to critical and/or historical analysis of Africana women's writing.

The rise of institutional Black Studies and Women's Studies programs during the decades of the '80s and '90s did not ensure the development of programs that gave specific focus to the study of Black women's histories and traditions. In fact, as Patricia Morton explains, African American women in the context of modern historical texts were cast as either invisible or amazonian. Thus, "Given the casting of this group of women [Black women] overwhelmingly as *other,* it becomes more explicable that in the midst of the explosion of women's studies, the concept of black women's studies continued to face a wall of apathy or hostility" (122). In the introduction to their crucial work, *But Some of Us Are Brave: Black Women's Studies* (1982), Gloria Hull, Patricia Bell Scott, and Barbara Smith further address the complex philosophical, bureaucratic, and psychological hurdles they faced when compiling the first Black Women's Studies resource book. Notably, they viewed the paths of Black Women's Studies as politically charged areas and believed that "the bias of Black women's studies must consider as primary the knowledge that will save Black women's lives" (xxv). In recent years, the fight in this politically charged arena has taken the form of funding battles for marginally supported programs, misogynistic media attacks on Black female authors/scholars, or even the naming/philosophical struggle of womanism versus feminism that has emerged in academic discourse and programs. However, these struggles directly configure or, perhaps, reconfigure the nature of struggles that resulted in the origins of Black Women's Studies. As Beverly Guy-Sheftall argues, "Though theoretical problems are inherent in Black Women's Studies, scholars in the field are in a unique position because of their ability to explore the intersection of race, sex, and class as experienced by black women in ways that are impossible for other segments of the population. They are also in a position, as Black studies scholars have always been, to challenge accepted scholarship" (39).

Black Women's Studies began informally in various venues throughout the country literally to study Black women. Wherever conclaves of African American women scholars existed, we accepted the challenge to find, study, and disseminate the works of earlier Black women. Nellie Y. McKay, literary scholar and critic, recounts how she and sister graduate students early in the 1970s unearthed "neglected Black women writers like Lucy Terry, Phillis Wheatley, Harriet Jacobs, Frances Harper and Zora Neale Hurston" and set about to learn a new trade as teachers-critics. (89)

These intellectual/activist women of the early '70s formalized their efforts by taking them into the environment that validates all intellectual traditions—the college campus. McKay recalls, "[The] career lives [of the Black women teacher-critics] depended on making themselves and the writers whom they were seeking out significant to the emerging discourse. This was not easy; and there were casualties along the way. Some, especially those in white colleges and universities, cut off from supportive communities, did not survive" (90). But fortunately, many of these pioneers and their selfless efforts not only survived, but thrived and opened doors for what must have then been viewed as a radical course of study.

The involvement of these sister-scholars in their "self-initiated, self educating sessions" and their formalized presentations in the college classroom certainly demonstrate their understanding of their own pioneering efforts in the intellectual context. The sister-scholars also recognized the principle of what bell hooks identifies as their reconstruction of the Black female intellectual tradition. Whereas they may not have used hooks's words to articulate their sense of purpose, they must have at least viscerally recognized that "sustained ongoing work that recovers Black women's intellectual legacies can take solace in the context of black women's studies. The purpose is not simply to resurrect forgotten traditions but to establish meaningful links between past and present to create a living foundation—a continuum of ideas and scholarship" (54).

In reviewing the pioneer works of intellectual activists, we do witness the conscious reconstruction, uncovering, and recovering of the Black women's intellectual tradition. Toni Cade Bambara states in the preface to *The Black Woman: An Anthology* (1970) that one of her early intentions was "to delve into history and pay tribute to all our warriors from ancient times to the slave trade to Harriet Tubman to Fannie Lou Hamer to the woman of this morning" (11). She acknowledges that the collection, the first popularly circulated cross-disciplinary collection edited and written by African American women, developed out of "impatience with the fact that in the whole bibliography of feminist literature, literature immediately and directly relevant to us wouldn't fill a page" (Bambara 10). Whereas *The Black Woman* covered many disciplines, the 1979 groundbreaking publication, *Sturdy Black Bridges: Visions of Black Women in Literature*, offered its hungry, primarily Black and female audience the first extensive examination of literature written by Black women. Through critical essays, interviews and the literary works themselves, the collection offered insightful (and some feminist) perspectives of the Africana woman as image, subject, and author.

The intellectual continuum of Black Women's Studies, initiated by the unearthing of neglected Black women writers and their works, would reach an institutional milestone in 1981 when Spelman College established the Women's Research and Resource Center, the first academic center dedicated to Black Women's Studies. Its three initial goals established it as a beacon for Black Women's Studies: (1) The center would engage in the development of women's studies curricula and related resources with particular emphases on the intersection of race, class, gender, and cross-cultural perspectives on female experiences; (2) The center would conduct or sponsor research in various academic disciplines related to Black women; (3) The center would engage in community outreach programs related to Black women locally and regionally.

In 1982 scholars of Spelman's graduate sister institution, Atlanta University, who had been actively or tangentially involved in the inception of Spelman's Women's Center, initiated what remains the only cross-cultural and interdisciplinary graduate program to focus on Black women. With its primary resolve being to develop and forward research on women of African descent and to implement and design courses focusing on these women, Atlanta University's Africana Women's Studies Program began as a federally funded program whose emphases were on developing bibliographies and course outlines, piloting new courses in Africana Women's Studies, and integrating Africana women's content

into established curricula. Despite the challenges imposed by patriarchal apathy and elitism, the program continues to attract serious women
scholars who validate it as a credible course of graduate study.

Since the early 1980s a number of Black Women's Studies programs/
courses have been developed in various geographic areas, in the United
States, the Caribbean, and Africa.[1] Inevitably, however, the battles Africana women intellectual activists face are similar: assaults against the
credibility and validity of Africana women-centered intellectual activity.
The battery against these activities is manifested in the overt racist, elitist
and sexist attitudes and statements. Often, however, the assaults are in-
sidiously subtle, but more institutionally damaging, taking such forms as
underfunding and understaffing.

Attempts to sabotage Black Women's Studies' efforts out of existence
are an ongoing reality. Equally real and ongoing are the attempts of
Black women on predominantly white and historically Black campuses
throughout the African Diaspora to solidify their presence. Following an
established tradition, inherited from decades of struggle, intellectual
activists promote education as an expedient method to implement
change. In *But Some of Us Are Brave,* Gloria Hull and Barbara Smith
emphasize the need for a "feminist and pro-woman perspective," which
would lead to Black Women's Studies as "the transformer of consciousness it needs to be" (xxi). They believe, as does bell hooks, that "Black
Women's Studies must educate about feminism while simultaneously
critically analyzing the link between racism and sexism, points of convergence and separation, the particular social construction of Black female
identity; the unique expression of gender paradigms among Black
people; as well as critiquing the racial biases which inform scholarship
on gender, including feminist work" (55).

Given the history of Black Women's Studies, the editors of *Arms
Akimbo* acknowledge their place in the unbroken continuum of feminist
scholarship. This volume of literary criticism from what we consider
feminist perspectives—that is, "perspectives which encourage critical
examination of sexist biases and the construction of new and different
epistemologies, ways of knowing" (hooks 55)—places the editors and
the anthology itself securely in the evolution of Black Women's Studies.

The legacies of the Black Women's Studies movement emanate from
this anthology in a number of ways. First, we the editors possess deep
and sustained connections to the Black Women's Studies movement in

our academic backgrounds and careers through teaching, research and administrative activities.[2]

Second, the legacies of Black Women's Studies are apparent in the purpose for which the anthology was compiled. As text, we offer *Arms Akimbo* to the growing body of resources that have enabled Black Women's Studies to persist in its struggle of supporting the intellectual climate of academic activists seeking change in the conditions of Africana women. As with the editors of *The Black Woman, Sturdy Black Bridges* and the myriad other texts that have emerged since, we view as a primary goal of this text the examination of issues that affect the lives of Africana women as they surface in literary works. Creative and critical texts are the tools of the intellectual activist, and those written from Black and gynocentric perspectives inevitably will explore intricacies of race, sex, and class biases that continue to define the world order.

Third, *Arms Akimbo* is spirited by the legacy of focus. Following the impetus of the first academic course and academic text on Black women, this anthology examines imaginative literature. The struggle for the Africana woman writer to gain her rightful place in the literary world is a continual one. To have her voice in print and to have access to the books that she "wanted to read," as Toni Morrison says, and the books that "she should have been able to read," as Alice Walker states, are concomitant goals of the Africana women writers. The women writers themselves created portraits of women who were beyond stereotype, beyond the limitations posed by patriarchal imagination. The fictional women created by Africana women display remarkable variations in lifestyle and life strategies, which are representative of the range of real women's experiences.

While *Arms Akimbo* holds much in common with its literary and critical predecessors, this volume is thoroughly and consciously Africana in scope as only a few Black women's studies texts have been. Our choice of the term "Africana" is employed to acknowledge and to affirm the common heritage of all women writers of the African Diaspora. We use it as a singular point of identification for the writers' texts studied in this anthology without purporting the congruence of experiences found in their writings; the works themselves confer or dispute that. While several critical works focus on one or the other of African American women, Caribbean women, or African women, this anthology holds at its very core the convergences and divergences of experiences of Black women throughout much of the diaspora. Thus, this text overcomes the major boundaries of geography as does Filomina Steady's sociologically oriented *Black Women Cross Culturally* (1981); Margaret Busby's anthology of literary works *Daughters of Africa* (1992); Carole Boyce Davies and Molara Ogundipe-Leslie's collection of writers' commentary, fiction, and poetry *Moving Beyond Boundaries: International Dimensions of Black Women's Writing* (1995); and such critical works as Gay Wilentz's *Binding Cultures* (1992), Susheila Nasta's *Motherlands: Black Women's Writing from Africa, Caribbean and South Asia* (1992), and Karla Holloway's *Moorings and Metaphors* (1992). Indeed, both the forced and voluntary migrations of Africana women over the past three centuries have created a variegation—a single entity marked by difference and variety—as the essays herein attest. However, also important to these pieces are the continuities that bond Africana women by race, culture, class, and gender.

Additionally, this anthology brings to the fore women writers and works that may not be universally recognized outside particular geographic or intellectual cultures. We limited the inclusion of those few Africana women writers who might be considered literary luminaries to encourage the study of writers and works less known outside their geographical or sociocultural areas. This is in keeping with one of the aims of scholars and teachers within literary fields of Black Women's Studies: to promote and cultivate a broader audience for the works of Africana writers.

While a number of essays in the anthology center on a specific writer from a singular culture, many of the essays present comparative analyses of works, themes, and issues. In effect, these comparative essays examine the works of writers whose primary origins are as similar as the cultures of Yoruba and Ibo or Ashanti and Akan, but whose contemporary existence is as different as the cultures of Africa and Europe or the Caribbean and North America. The diversity continues as critics from Africa, Canada, the United States, or the Caribbean are moved to write about cultures not necessarily their own. Hence, the anthology offers internal and external perspectives of sociocultural experiences of Black women.

Arms Akimbo certainly does not purport to be definitive in its offering of perspectives, works or authors. During the decades of the '80s and '90s, as critical studies evolved to post-colonial studies, to African Diaspora studies and to the ever-burgeoning cultural criticism, the obvious dynamic of scholarly inquiry continued, apparent in the subtle or startling changes in focus. While we do declare this text a logical culmination of the sociopolitical and academic experiences of Africana women, we recognize it nevertheless as another step on our intellectual continuum. Certainly, we pay homage to sister-writers and scholars like Barbara Christian, Carol Boyce Davies, Gloria Hull, Barbara Smith, Beverly Guy-Sheftall, and many others who have come forth and laid the foundation for the conceptualization and realization of an anthology such as ours. We hope this anthology can strengthen the foundations for others yet to come. The inclusion here of Zain Muse's comparative study, written while she was yet an undergraduate, portends that the future for Africana women's studies, like the foundation on which it rests, is indeed solid.

We gave this anthology the title *Arms Akimbo* because as we worked, studied, and traveled with women of African descent from all over the world, we noticed many observable similarities, one of which was body language. We found one striking similarity to be the majestic, sometimes defiant, always affirming stance of arms on the hips, which Black women—whether we are from Dakar, Kingston, or D.C.—so often assume. And in that stance we found also the representation of the way Africana women—wherever we are—must face a world that denies us our rights because of race, sex, class. *Arms Akimbo,* for us, is a defiant *and* affirming assertion of our right to re/invent ourselves as Africana women.

Arms Akimbo is structured in four parts. Each of these parts focuses on issues and themes of concern to scholar-teachers throughout the African Diaspora as we engage in self-re/invention and the processes of social change. Part 1, A Birthing of Self, focuses on the self-realization and actualization processes women both encounter and undertake to reinvent themselves as whole individuated personalities within their cultures. Part 2, Relationships: Mothering, Mistressing, Marrying, and Woman-to-Woman—Disengaging the Family Romance, centers primarily on the relationships women hold dear with the "significant others" of their lives and the impact these relationships have on the women as well as on "the others." Part 3, War on All Fronts: Race, Class, Sex, Age, and Nationality, examines those primary differentials that drastically affect the status of women in these concomitant struggles and their coping or proactive mechanisms developed to face the challenges. Part 4, Invention and Convention: Womanist Gazes on Literary and Critical Traditions, the final section, explores texts that display women's impact on cultural manifestations and traditions in both literature and society. Using varied critical approaches, the critics analyze the impact of literary and cultural traditions on the lives of women in folklore, novels, and in filmmaker Julie Dash's *Daughters of the Dust.*

Notes

1. The Black Women's Studies programs at Medgar Evers College in New York and Southern University in Louisiana and the Women and Development Program (WAND) at the University of the West Indies, Cane Hill, Barbados, are the other established academic programs known to the authors. The non-academic African Association of Women and Development in Senegal can also be considered a research organization. As well, several African universities are in the developing stages of African(a) women-focused programs—universities in Zambia, Namibia, and Zimbabwe, to name a few.

2. Janice Liddell, former chairperson of the department of English at Clark Atlanta University, served on the original task force for the Atlanta University Africana Women's Center, precursor of the CAU Africana Women's Studies Program. Presently, she is a member of the Africana Women's Studies task force and teaches courses in the program. Atlanta-born Yakini Kemp, a Spelman graduate, was a student at Wellesley College and was enrolled in the African American literature course taught by Alice Walker, one of the first college courses to focus on Black women's writing. Kemp is former Dean of Humanities at Talladega College and now professor of English at Florida A & M University, both historically Black institutions. Both Liddell and Kemp have taught, written, and researched widely in areas of Black Women's Studies.

Works Cited

Bell Scott, Patricia, Beverly Guy-Sheftall, and Bettye Parker, eds. *Sturdy Black Bridges: Visions of Black Women in Literature.* New York: Anchor, 1979.

Boyce Davies, Carole and Molara Ogundipe-Leslie, eds. *Moving Beyond Boundaries: International Dimensions of Black Women's Writing. Vol. 1.* New York: New York University Press, 1995.

Cade, Toni. *The Black Woman: An Anthology.* New York: New American Library, 1970.

Giddings, Paula. *When and Where I Enter: The Impact of Black Women on Race and Sex in America.* New York: Bantam, 1984.

Guy-Sheftall, Beverly. "Black Women's Studies: The Interface of Women's Studies and Black Studies." *Phylon* 49, Nos. 1, 2 (1992), 33–41. See also, "Ethnic Studies, Women's Studies, and the Liberal Arts Curriculum: Retrospect and Prospect." *Transforming the Curriculum: Ethnic Studies and Women's Studies.* Ed. Johnella Butler and John C. Walter. Albany: State University of New York, 1991. 305–12.

hooks, bell. "Feminism and Black Women's Studies." *Sage: a Scholarly Journal on Black Women* 6.1 (Summer 1989): 54–56.

Hull, Gloria, Patricia Bell Scott, and Barbara Smith, eds. *All the Women Are White, All the Blacks Are Men, But Some of Us Are Brave: Black Women's Studies.* Old Westbury, N.Y.: Feminist Press, 1982.

McKay, Nellie Y. "Black Women's Literary Scholarship: Reclaiming an Intellectual Tradition." *Sage: A Scholarly Journal on Black Women* 6.1 (Summer 1989): 89, 90.

Morton, Patricia. "Black Studies/Women's Studies: Discovering Black Women's History?" *Disfigured Images: The Historical Assault on Afro-American Women.* New York: Praeger, 1991. 113–24.

Steady, Filomina. *The Black Woman Cross-Culturally.* Cambridge: Schenkman, 1981.

Wilentz, Gay. *Binding Cultures: Black Women Writers in Africa and the Diaspora.* Bloomington: Indiana University Press, 1992.

PART 1

A Birthing of Self

Not long ago I needed to contact a colleague for a rather important matter concerning a project on which the two of us were working. I had never needed to call her at home before and, hence, had not thought to ask for her home telephone number. On this particular evening, I tried calling two other colleagues who I knew would have her number; neither of them were at home. Since I go to bed fairly early, I certainly didn't feel like waiting on my prospective informants, so I broke down and used the telephone book. It dawned on me by then that the number was no doubt in her husband's name—and for the life of me I could not remember his name. Even if I'd known where the couple lived, the number of Smiths in the directory was too great to search by address. Indeed, for that moment, my colleague was totally lost to me. Hidden between the lines of over twelve thousand Smiths was my wonderful, hardworking colleague, and I could not find her. I wondered how many of the Smiths listed concealed the identity of a fully grown, productive woman person. How many names in the entire directory did? I shuddered.

Of course, as a feminist scholar, I had discussed, read about and even written about invisibility; however, it had never been as stark and as absolute as it was for me at that moment. I literally could not find my colleague, who has earned three degrees, including a Ph.D.; is an accomplished scholar; and has birthed and raised three children. I could not find her *because I did not know her husband's name.* Patronymics: one of the many tools used by patriarchal/patrilineal societies to marginalize or even "invisibilize" one half of their population.

In African societies names and naming are so important that it is often said that "the name is the person" (Mbiti 154). However, legal marriages, which throughout Africana societies have become the ideal, if not the norm, have stripped women not only of symbolic identities—"their" names—but almost completely of material and personal identities as well. A Nigerian woman writer has written, "[I]n marriage men are like amoeba. They embrace, absorb, and entirely devour the entity of their partner, her name, state of origin, private property and a whole lot more" (*Women in Nigeria Today* 177). Even where marriage is not the single devouring culprit, Africana women are effectively invisibilized in both private and public sectors. Other patriarchal "tools," often coupled with the identity-devouring tools of racism, conceal the true selves of so many Africana women, even from themselves. This is especially true in the "new world," where patronymics for Blacks are not only motivated by gender but also by race; where for those of African descent, naming itself becomes one primary legacy of slavery.

The essays in part 1, "A Birthing of Self," focus on works by Africana women in which respective women characters undergo some transformative process, an epiphany of sorts, and who, after various successful challenges, emerge with a newly found sense of who they are and of their capabilities within their social and/or cultural milieus.

Until recently, in nearly all works about "new world" slavery, with the exception of Margaret Walker's *Jubilee,* slave women have been rendered voiceless except as their voices have filtered through the biases and stereotypes of detached "others," white women and white and Black men. In Emma Waters-Dawson's essay, the focus is on the liminal and black womanist vision of slavery and slave women as offered by Sherley Anne Williams's inclusionist historical novel, *Dessa Rose.* Waters-Dawson explicates the true self of the enslaved Dessa Rose in her thorough analysis of the novel that importantly bears this slave woman's name.

The odyssey of this charted course to freedom and self-fulfillment in the lives of three "new world" women is the focus of Janice Liddell's essay. Here, another invisible and voiceless sector, postmenopausal women, is given voice. Caribbean women in Sylvia Wynter's *Hills of Hebron* and Beryl Gilroy's *Frangipani House,* and the African American protagonist in Paule Marshall's *Praisesong for the Widow,* all demonstrate the quest for self as it continues beyond the woman stages of "lust and lactation."

Carol Marsh-Lockett's essay asserts the relevant importance of women's art forms as symbolic and actual manifestations of women's evolving selfhood. Weaving, music, and dance form the locus of Marsh-Lockett's dialogical reading of Ntozake Shange's *Sassafras, Cypress and Indigo* and serve as facilators for the essential quest as experienced by three southern African American women. As with the other chapters in part 1, Marsh-Lockett's analysis of Shange's work focuses on the varied strategies used by Africana women and writers of Africana women to deconstruct prevailing stereotypes and to reconstruct culturally imposed women's experiences in order to (re)invent identities meaningful to Africana women.

Often the voices of African women can be heard dismantling stereotypes and reordering experiences; however, in many African societies—contemporary Igbo society, for example—a woman whose voice is "too strong" is often identified as a "he woman." In her essay, Australia Tarver examines Flora Nwapa's Amaka of *One is Enough,* who, like Sherley Williams's *Dessa Rose,* is not only strong voiced but strong willed. Tarver's examination of the self-conscious process of awakening and transformation agrees with the premise central to Waters-Dawson's essay and the others in this section: Women will have to chart their own course to freedom.

Works Cited

Editorial Committee Women in Nigeria. *Women in Nigeria Today.* London: Zed Books, 1985.

Mbiti, John. *African Religions and Philosophy.* New York: Praeger, 1969.

Psychic Rage and Response

The Enslaved and The Enslaver in Sherley Anne Williams's *Dessa Rose*

EMMA WATERS DAWSON

In her 1986 neo-slave narrative *Dessa Rose,* Sherley Anne Williams examines the psychic rage and response of both the enslaved and the enslaver. Like Toni Morrison's *Beloved,* published the following year, the enslaved Black woman's psychic response to her condition becomes central to the plot. *Dessa Rose* also relates the complexities of recording the enslaved Black woman's narrative for, as Jean Fagan Yellin states: "Most Black women . . . lacked access to polite letters, their literary contributions were made within the oral tradition" (xxxiii). Yellin's comments introduce the actual slave narrative of Harriet Jacobs, a Black woman who could render her life story in written and spoken words. For the slave woman, words evidence her existence. They also signal betrayal when they record her experiences from the perspective of and in the words of those not sensitive to her being who she simply is—woman, wife, mother, slave—Black. For the slave woman, the ability to speak words and to have others actually hear them is a record of the inner emotions. Also, there is a generally acknowledged assumption that history belongs to those who can speak for themselves.

In *Ar'n't I a Woman,* Deborah Gray White observes that although the historical material on slavery in general exists in abundance, similar material on the slave woman is scarce. White states, "Slave women were everywhere, yet nowhere. They were in Southern households and in Southern fields but the sources are silent about female status in the slave community and the bondwoman's self-perception" (23). Sherley Anne Williams's novel *Dessa Rose* is one example of contemporary fictional responses to the existence of this interaction. Hence, this discussion emphasizes the view of the slave woman that others have as well as the slave woman's perception of herself and others.

The telling of the stories within a story in *Dessa Rose* is quite significant, for it represents those Black women who did escape slavery, yet did not acquire formal literacy. Thus, my examination of *Dessa Rose* comprises two levels; though the theme of the psychic rage of both the enslaved and the enslaver is present, I also see the novel itself as a finished text or product of controlled rage by the novelist. Specifically, Williams's innovative narrative technique in itself is a response to previous ways that the historical slave narrative has been recorded. Williams views the transcribing by both the white male and female as being changed in the process and not fully conveying the intensity of the emotion the slave actually felt, structuring *Dessa Rose* in such a way that the reader sees points of view from the perspective of the enslaved Black woman, the white man, and the white woman. Given these viewpoints, the reader then must decide whose point of view or combination of points of view is most valid. Artistic control, thus, mutes the author's personal rage.

The basis of *Dessa Rose* is Williams's adaptation of the true stories of two women. A pregnant Kentucky slave, Dessa, was charged with helping to lead an insurrection on a slave coffle in 1829. Sentenced to die, she was not to be hanged until the birth of her baby. With these historical events as fictional seeds, Williams incorporates the story of Rufel, an allegedly eccentric white woman, rumored to harbor runaway slaves, who lived in North Carolina around 1830.[1] She structures her narrative around events that might have occurred had Dessa and Rufel actually met.

The Prologue, told in Dessa's altered subconscious, is a cogent exploration of Dessa and Kaine's love relationship. Williams, in this section, is able not only to offer the reality of romantic love among slaves, but more importantly, she is able to articulate the passionate emotions through the voice of the slave herself. Although she endures backbreaking, hot, and tiresome work as a field hand, Dessa still fulfills her role as willing lover. About the relationship between Dessa and Kaine, Williams notes, "I really wanted to say that slavery had not killed the passion and tenderness in black men and women" (Greene 34). The intensity of Dessa's memory of lovemaking with Kaine is compounded when the reader realizes that the master has already killed him. Thus, Dessa's dreaming of her dead lover highly magnifies her loss.

The novel is divided into sections called "Prologue," "The Darky," "The Wench," "The Negress," and "The Epilogue." The "Prologue" presents Dessa, the protagonist, whose personal history and relationships with others are the crux of the novel. Adam Nehemiah, the insensitive recorder of Dessa's story, is central to the first section, "The Darky." While he desires to sensationalize Dessa's tale for commercial success, he nevertheless manages to greatly understate Dessa's true affection for Kaine. Nehemiah's transfiguration of Dessa's version of Kaine's death not only misrepresents the severity of the event but undermines Dessa's emotional attachment to it: "These are the facts of the darky's history as I have thus far uncovered them: The master smashed the young buck's banjo. The young buck attacked the master. The master killed the young buck. The darky attacked the master—and was sold to the Wilson slave coffle" (35). Sterile, cold facts void of passion, love, or even the understanding of such emotions are the basis for Nehemiah's almost journalistic recordings. Yet Nehemiah restores the significance of words, since the violence in the connotations of *attacked* and *killed* is meaningful. Nehemiah's language conjures images of a brutal slave and completely dismisses the motivations behind the attack and murder.

When Nehemiah queries Dessa as to why she kills the master, he records her verbal response to him: "'I kill white mens' . . . 'I kill white mens cause the same reason Masa kill Kaine. Cause I can'" (13). Cheryll Greene observes that Dessa "recognizes that she has some choice, even if it's nothing more than the choice between destroying somebody else and destroying herself" (34). Her response also reveals more about the power of the slaveowner in a patriarchal society than it does about her "power." Dessa's killing rage, resulting from the murder of her unborn child's father, establishes a relationship between enemies and reveals the rage and response of both the slave and the enslaver. It reclaims Kaine's initiative and creativity in making his banjo out of good parchment and seasoned wood that he had gathered. When the master breaks Kaine's spirit by destroying the banjo, Dessa attempts to comfort him, encouraging Kaine to make another banjo by gathering wood and horsehair. He tells her, "'Masa can make another one'. . . 'Nigga can't do shit. Masa can step on a nigga hand, nigga heart, nigga life, and what can a nigga do? Nigga can't do shit. What can a nigga do when Masa house on fire? What

can a nigga do when Masa house on fire? Bet *not* do [*mo'n yell, fire, fire.*]
[*Cause a nigga can't do shit!*]'" (34). Thus, when Dessa speaks of the pain
she shares with Kaine after the destruction of the banjo, she articulates
his ultimate powerlessness as a Black man in an inhumane system.
Nehemiah, however, in attitudinal alliance with the patriarchal system,
writes, "*This was the 'fiend,' the 'devil woman'* who attacked white men and
roused other niggers to rebellion" (13). He completely dismisses Dessa's
explanation.

In presenting the relationship between slave woman and plantation
owner from the perspective of Nehemiah, Williams selects an alleged
nonpartisan observer. As such, she explores the effects slavery had on
those not directly connected to the system, yet who profited, as did
Nehemiah, from the misery and human suffering of the slave. "The
Darky" section also investigates via the omniscient narrative voice the
conditions of slavery as they affected family relations and even longevity.
Human possessions themselves, the slaves, therefore, had no right to
stake ownership to something as simple as a banjo. "If they lived, they
lived long. But the toll of those who did not, who died or were permanently debilitated by the annual fevers . . . that walked through the Quarters with agonizing regularity, from punishments or their aftereffects.
. . . Increasingly, they were sold away. Even in dreams that threat had
haunted her" (55, 56). Though the experience sounds realistic enough,
the narrative voice is clearly in control here; but even more noticeable is
the language Nehemiah uses. Nehemiah records Dessa's description in
words that *he* would use. Nehemiah literally badgers Dessa "back to life
by an onslaught of questions" he poses in "researching a book about
insurrections for the enlightenment of the slaveholder" (Gillespie 1), yet
she "exists on a level which is incomprehensible to" him (Davenport
337). Perception for Dessa comes in narrating her experience, giving
meaning to her existence.

In this relationship between Dessa, the Black slave woman, and Nehemiah, the white author, Williams responds to the volatile event of a
slave insurrection and creatively counters "the travestied as-told-to-
memoir" (336). Doris Davenport describes Nehemiah as an "ambitious
nineteenth-century yuppie [who] callously interviews Dessa" (336).
Marcia Gillespie notes that "his questions and blind assumptions force
Dessa to confront her history, count her losses, give voice to all she

intuitively has come to know" (1), for Nehemiah bases his beliefs and thoughts of Dessa upon a condescending and arrogant view of the slave woman. There is no space in his white male patriarchal psyche for the concept of a Black woman's committing murder because she could; he blindly and falsely assumes that Dessa attempts to murder the mistress because the latter discovers an alleged affair between Dessa and the slave master, responding to the conventions of his time and the generally accepted images and stereotypes of the slave woman in her relations with others. Ernece B. Kelly states, "Such a deep experiential gulf divides Williams's black characters from her white ones that each doubts the others' stories. . . . Paradoxically, these very stories reveal the profound influences they had on each others' lives" (18).

Deborah White uses the term "Jezebel" and Barbara Christian, "the loose Black Woman," to characterize images of Black women as promiscuous and immoral. In the chapter "Jezebel and Mammy: The Mythology of Female Slavery," White discusses the problematic nature of these two dominant myths the slaveholding class fostered about the slave woman, saying that they are actually private and public versions of the same conceptual problem. Other feminist critics also respond to the prevalence of these myths, stereotypes and images,[2] and Williams creates both the image of the loose Black woman and the mammy in the characters of Dessa—Dessa's own "mammy" and Dorcas, Rufel's "mammy."

"The Wench" explores more prevailing images of the slave woman. In this section, the narrative voice focuses on Dessa and her history from the perspective of Ruth Elizabeth or "Rufel," the white woman who takes in runaway slaves. The segment also questions the roles of both Black and white women in nineteenth-century Southern society, questioning "the safety of a pedestal" for white women. Through the characters of Dessa and Rufel, Williams presents images of the slave woman and the slave mistress that are in stark contrast to the nineteenth-century conception of women. For example, Gillespie describes Rufel as "a pampered daughter of the plantocracy" who is a slave to class and privilege (2). Rufel rejects the explanation the runaways give her of the circumstances surrounding Dessa's conditions. Though Rufel orders the Blacks to put the ill and post-partum Dessa into the only bed available on the estate, the Mistress's own featherbed, she still blindly assumes that the victim is really the aggressor. She thinks that Dessa's mean behavior of kicking and hitting may be attributable to a cruel master, but seeing Dessa's scarless back, she acknowledges she has heard that "No white man would do that" (94). Only Mammy is able to provide insight into Rufel's hastily drawn conclusion about the slave woman's obvious complicity in whatever misfortune she had suffered. A conversation in which Mammy informs Rufel about the realities of miscegenation ensues, and Mammy admonishes her that "men can do things a *lady* can't even guess at." Acknowledging this point to herself, but failing to concede to Mammy's truth, Rufel retorts, "Everyone know men like em half white and whiter" (94).

"'Miz Rufel,' Mammy had snapped. 'Lawd know it must be some way for high yeller to git like that!'"(94). Mammy's response indicates that the images of the loose slave woman and the mammy have just enough grounding in reality to lend credibility to stereotypes that would profoundly affect the slave woman and the white woman; consequently, the scene illustrates rather well Williams's creative rejoinder to the issues of racial and sexual stereotypes and miscegenation in her characterizations of Dessa, Rufel, and Dorcas, for Rufel assumes Dessa is a loose woman. In doing so, she projects "the conventional wisdom . . . that black women were naturally promiscuous, and thus desired such connections" (White 38). In *Dessa Rose,* the myth of the loose Black woman is an archetypal Eve and the mammy, a parallel to the Virgin Mary. On one hand, the loose woman appears obsessed with carnality; on the other, the mammy is asexual, yet maternal. Though the images are apparently inverse, they existed in conventional Southern thought and also in Williams's adaptation of the peculiar history of the relationship between the slave woman and the slave mistress.

The development of Dessa, perceived as the loose Black woman, and of Dorcas, as Mammy, is consistent with the maternal or Victorian ideal of womanhood prevalent in the nineteenth century. The mammy in *Dessa Rose* takes care of Rufel and the latter's children, performs and supervises household chores, and advises Rufel on her personal affairs. At her death, Rufel mourns deeply, but is rudely awakened from her grieving and discourse about "Mammy" at Dessa's sickbed. Dessa becomes enraged at the endless, apparently senseless chatter about Rufel's Charleston past and angrily utters, "Wasn't no 'mammy' to it." Though Rufel and Dessa obviously refer to different "mammies," and Dessa is aware of that point, her litany continues:

"Mammy ain't made you nothing! . . . You don't even know mammy . . . Mammy live on the Vaugham plantation near Simeon on the Beauford River, McAllen County . . ."

The white woman gaped, like a fish, Dessa thought *contemptuously*, just like a fish out of water. Anybody could make this white woman's wits go gathering . . . "Your 'mammy'! . . . You ain't got no 'mammy' . . . Didn't you have no peoples where you lived? 'Mammy' ain't nobody name, not they real one . . . See! See! You don't even not know 'mammy's' name. Mammy have a name, have children . . . What was her name then?" Dessa taunted. "Child don't even know its own mammy's name. What was mammy's name? What—." (124, 125)

Despite Rufel's spluttered response—which indicates she really does not know—Dessa wins the argument when Rufel tries to state Mammy's name but is unable to do so.

In this incensed exchange, Williams gives voice to the slave woman's history. In her angry response, Dessa represents multiple voices: for herself, for her mother, and for the nameless "mammies" in the history of the slave woman. Indeed, Williams pays homage to her maternal ancestors by exposing justifiable rage in the characters. Their characterizations, thus, reveal the author's muted, controlled rage. Davenport cites this exchange as a major turning point in the nature of the relationship between the two women, observing that "[j]ust as Dessa let Nehemiah know that he did *not know* her, she lets Rufel know . . . . Relatedly, Williams lets types like these two whites know again and again, that *they* do not know" (339). Davenport's italicizing of "*not*" and "*they*" interprets Williams's creation of the scene as a form of controlled rage. In other words, Dessa "has the last word," and Williams, as the creator of Dessa's story, is the medium of this enraged voice.

Greene notes that *Dessa Rose* is "an exciting adventure, full of fine, complex characterization, historical authenticity and lessons for today about empowerment, courage, love, friendship and family" (34). Though Greene's observation is quite perceptive, the novel also grapples most poignantly and specifically with interrelationships. The exchange between Rufel and Dessa, according to Davenport, "indirectly drives Rufel into the arms—the blue-black arms—of Nathan" (339), one of the men on the coffle with Dessa who escapes while she is captured and imprisoned to await the birth of the baby. But Nathan, Cully, and Harker, runaways whom they meet in the woods, rescue Dessa from her imprisonment and take her to Rufel's ramshackle plantation. Deserted by her gambling husband, Rufel has only her two children, Mammy (Dorcas), and the other runaway slaves. These runaways, ironically, become "*slaves*" on her plantation and actually run the household in which Rufel unwittingly allows them to stay. Her eccentricity also leads her to turn to Nathan to learn about the other runaway slaves on her plantation, particularly about Dessa's history in order to abate her own rage and resentment toward "the Wench." Rufel begrudgingly becomes more sympathetic, though not approving of Dessa's running or attacking the master. She secretly admires the courage that made Dessa's actions possible and emphasizes Dessa's color in her amazement that Dessa "had helped to make herself free" (158).

In the unfolding relationship between Rufel and Nathan, Williams grapples with the myth of the Black man's lust for white women. White remarks, "Black men and women were thought to have such insatiable sexual appetites that they had to go beyond the boundaries of their race to get satisfaction" (38). Williams creatively juxtaposes these generalizations, for Rufel learns about Nathan's personal history as a paramour of white women. Barbara Christian observes, "[A]cknowledging that white women would willingly be sexually involved with Black Men was opposed to white women's sacred position—that they were a treasure to be possessed only by white men. . . . *Dessa Rose* . . . illustrates the longevity of this taboo. For many readers, Black and white, are stunned, sometimes offended by the sexual relationship between Miz Rufel . . . and . . . Nathan despite the historical evidence that such relationships existed" (331). Nathan tells Rufel of a former slaveowner, Miz Lorraine, who "took her bedmates young, saw that they learned some more conventional trade, and, about the time their fear of discovery and their awe of her abated, about the time they found their tongues with her and might have boasted to others, about that time she got rid of them, sold them off" (169). In her controlled artistic rage, Williams engrossingly inverts the stereotypes of Blacks' sexual longing for whites so that the latter are the aggressors in such liaisons.

In a rejection of the perpetuated historical lie that casts Black men as agents of miscegenation, Williams develops an interracial love relationship between Rufel and Nathan. The relationship's development seems almost inevitable. It first begins when Nathan angrily explains to Rufel the sense of family he has for Dessa, in response to her teasing him about "being sweet on Dessa." Visibly annoyed, Nathan rebuts Rufel's teasing with a comment on the history he shares with Dessa and the other slaves. He explains their common plight and history as slaves altered and dehumanized by their conditions and expresses his admiration for Dessa's survival from the system without destruction of her spirit. Nathan feels pride in their new common experience of freedom while others fared worse. From her friendship with Nathan—despite their positions as runaway and mistress—Rufel begins to realize the drastic effect the runaways have on her sense of self and doubts whether her husband would share the crops with the slaves in response to Nathan's inquiries. Her painful understanding that she would have no more rights than the slaves when or if Bertie returns is a turning point in the novel, for Rufel is no longer the arrogant, condescending mistress that Dessa still perceives her to be. Her accidental viewing of Dessa's body also influences Rufel's change in attitude. To her, Dessa's "bottom was so scarred that Rufel had thought she must be wearing some kind of garment . . . The wench's loins looked like a mutilated cat's face. Scar tissue plowed through her pubic region so no hair would ever grow there again" (166). Ironically, another accidental viewing of bodies—Dessa's walking in on Rufel who was in bed with Nathan—increases the schism between the two as far as Dessa is concerned.

The next section of the novel, called "The Negress," is omnisciently narrated and explores Dessa's perspective on the liaison between Rufel and Nathan: anger and rage toward an interracial relationship. Dessa perceives Nathan's affair with Rufel as a personal rejection of her. She angrily seethes within and expresses to herself the rage she feels by thinking: "I never *seed* such a thing! Nathan—laying cross that white woman—Black as night and so—so *satisfied*. It was like seeing her nurse Mony for the first time all over again. . . . All the while I was yelling at her . . . And something inside me was screaming, Can't I have nothing? Can't I have nothing?" (175) Williams explores the psychic rage Dessa feels at seeing Nathan with Rufel, the woman who represents for her the power in whiteness and her own powerlessness as a slave woman. Denied both family and lover, Dessa shares with the men on the coffle a bond of family fostered in their common adversity. She sees Rufel's consorting with Nathan as yet another denial of her limited existence. Dessa is hurt even more when she realizes that Ada and the other runaways think she wants Nathan for herself, assuming that is why she calls Rufel "Miz Ruint."

Still enraged, she begins to ponder Rufel's motives in allowing the runaways to stay on the plantation. She questions Rufel's role as a "good master," since her experiences as a slave woman have not prepared her for such an image. Williams emphasizes Dessa's rage to examine miscegenation between the white woman and the slave man. As novelist, she subverts so-called realities and stereotypes. Whereas slave women had been nursemaids for white infants, Williams juxtaposes this historical reality with Rufel's nursing a Black infant. She becomes a white "*mammy.*" White states, "White women also played a role in slave child care, and while a legend has been built around the Black nurses who helped raise Southern white children, the role that white women played in raising slave children has largely been ignored" (53). Williams explores this historical ignorance and foreshadows Rufel's lovemaking with Nathan. Though Williams explores the tenderness involved in Rufel's nursing of Mony, Dessa's son, she emphasizes the rage Dessa feels not only at the nursing, but also at Rufel's association with Nathan. Despite such conflict, Williams states, "I wanted to see whether there was a basis on which Black women and white women could relate to each other, with respect, despite the fact of interracial liaisons between white women and Black men" (Greene 34).

The realization of commonalities on the part of both Rufel and Dessa is a slow and painful process, which Williams appears to accomplish more quickly through Rufel's character than through Dessa's. Rufel knows that she will not have any rights as a person upon her husband's return, yet Dessa still resents her intrusion. She imagines the slave-master's rage toward a Black man's consorting with the mistress, an act punishable by death, and contrasts that image with her simultaneous fear for Nathan's life and her rage at Rufel's risking Nathan's life.

The bond Dessa shares with the men, having escaped slavery together, prompts them to form an ingenious plan to leave slave territory before Rufel's husband returns. Yet Dessa initially refuses to comply with the resourceful plan of the runaways, who conspire to obtain money by having Rufel pose as an unfortunate slave mistress who must sell her much-loved slaves to settle family debts. The scheme of serial sale of slaves, their escape, and their resale, would be repeated in regular intervals in different towns. Yet the rage still smothers within Dessa, and she has serious problems conceding to the plan. When Nathan asks Dessa why she is so angry, she thinks that he should already know: "White folks had taken everything in the world from me except my baby and my life and they had tried to take them. And to see him . . . wallowing in what had hurt me so—I didn't feel that nothing I could say would tell him what the pain was like . . . I could've hit him, he was making me so mad . . . I couldn't put into words all this that was going through my head" (186–188). The runaway Dessa in "The Negress" section is almost as inarticulate as the Darky and the Wench that Nehemiah and Rufel, initially, perceive. Still, the narrative voice emphasizes Dessa's feelings— her sense of betrayal even though she does not possess the words to convey her rage.

Nathan and the others eventually convince Dessa that there is no other way to go west to California without money, and she resentfully complies despite her reluctance to be around Rufel, who agrees to participate in the scheme to raise enough money to return to Charleston. These circumstances—the women in constant company with each other—lead to Dessa's "rage and resentment and fear gradually [succumbing] to guiding acceptance and understanding" (Gillespie 2).

After she helps Rufel repel the advances of a drunken white man, Dessa painfully realizes something startling. As women in a man's world, she and Rufel share certain bonds. She perceives that the white woman was subject to sexual assault also, and the thought obsesses her. Dessa acknowledges that "they would kill a black man for loving with a white woman; would they kill black man for keeping a white man off a white woman?" (220) She begins to be more sympathetic toward Rufel. "Ultimately, Dessa retains her silence because she realizes that knowing white mens wanted the same thing, would take the same thing from a white woman as they would from a black woman. Cause they could" (220).

The novel continues with the flimflam recurring in various towns. Dessa even halfheartedly accepts the relationship between Nathan and Rufel. She states, "I don't mean to say that I ever got so's I liked the idea, black man, white woman. I don't think none of us ever liked the idea; and we was uneasy situated as we was, had to be uneasy" (225). Her thoughts hint at the shared adversity involved in their scheme of duplicity using the runaways and in the sense of family the Black runaways and white mistress share. Dessa begins to notice a change in Rufel's attitude and language and responds to it. On occasion, Rufel would startle Dessa with her comments, hinting her desire to continue west with the former slaves to escape the hatred of slaveholding whites and expressing her reluctance to live around slavery in complicitous silence.

So engrossed is Dessa in thought about Rufel's comments that Nehemiah captures her by complete surprise when she hears someone call, "Odessa." According to Mary Kemp Davis, Nehemiah's referral to Dessa as "Odessa" indicates that "it never occurs to [Nehemiah] that Dessa's mother knew what she wanted to name her own child and so named her" (548). "Odessa" is the name Nehemiah has given Dessa, not the one given to her by her mother. Furthermore, Nehemiah has become so obsessed with Dessa that he devotes his life to recapturing her, for he feels her escape is a personal affront to him. He is obviously enraged and literally mad to embark on such an all-consuming search. At his command, she is knocked down, beaten, and jailed when she runs away.

This second episode that Dessa has with Nehemiah allows Williams to question "theories of inequality that women were weaker than men and that their physical and mental constitution suited them only for domestic duties" (White 14). Rufel is a trickster mistress, and Dessa poses as the mistress's maid. They are at the center of the bilking scheme as they handle and keep on their persons at all times the money from the sale of the runaways, and Nehemiah certainly tests their mental constitution when he demands that the Sheriff search Dessa's body to verify the scar tissue on her genitals.

His insistence to the Sheriff to have Dessa reveal her scars to the men present recalls the nineteenth-century experience of Sojourner Truth. The men in the audience in Silver Lake, Indiana, in 1850 challenged the famous abolitionist to prove she was a woman by demanding that she bare her breasts. They questioned her womanhood, since her physical strength and oral ability as an abolitionist had led to rumors that she was a man. Truth's experience serves as a metaphor for the slave woman's experience. Michelle Wallace observes, "Slave women were the only women in America who were sexually exploited with impunity, stripped and whipped with a lash, worked like oxen. In the nineteenth century when the nation was preoccupied with keeping women in the home and protecting them, only slave women were so totally unprotected by men or by law. Only black women had their womanhood so totally denied"

(162). In this powerful scene, Dessa confronts her personal history. The very evidence of her past as a slave woman, the visible scar tissue, appears to indict her as a runaway. However, the invisible "scar tissue" that the Sheriff and Nehemiah cannot see is the impetus that compels the women to continue the trickery they have mastered so well in the bilking scheme. The memory of the keloidal scars on Dessa's body becomes for both Dessa and Rufel a symbol of male inhumanity that unites them against the threat of intimidation and, possibly, abuse. Both women have escaped the "sanctity of the home" and entered the male sphere of trickery and deceit, and their participation in the swindle reveals that women were not as naive and guileless as they were perceived to be. The possibility that they could be discovered requires that they continue their resourcefulness.

After the Sheriff summons Rufel to the jail, she takes him aside to confide that she and Dessa were women traveling alone, carrying a great deal of money for the hiring of hands; therefore, she could not have Dessa undress in front of someone like Nehemiah, whom she could not trust. The Sheriff accepts Rufel's explanation and sends for Aunt Chloe, an old Black woman, to have her examine Dessa. Enraged, Nehemiah howls, "You can't set no darky to check a darky, catch a darky; that's the mistake they made at the last place. You can't take no darky's word on this" (253). The Sheriff, however, dismisses Nehemiah's accusations despite the truth present in his statement. Thus, Rufel, Dessa, and Aunt Chloe outwit the power structure when the latter tells the Sheriff that Dessa has no scars. Aunt Chloe's role as a loyal, devoted servant enables her to dupe and deceive the Sheriff under a mask of docility and submissiveness in order to protect a part of the slave woman's life from white *and* male invasion. Nehemiah recognizes the women's complicity as a scheme of womanhood against the patriarchal system of power, for when the Sheriff releases Dessa from jail, and Rufel and Dessa move to leave, he states, "You-all in this together. . . . [W]omanhood . . . All alike. Sluts" (255).

His raging statements reveal a view of the patriarchal system of the nineteenth century that almost always conceived of women in terms of their gender. He fails to acknowledge that women could be aggressive, superordinate—or even his mental equals. Thus, the experience of Dessa and Rufel contradicts antebellum assumptions about woman's limited ability and even suggests that such conjectures were intentionally hypo-critical. Indeed, Nehemiah's exhibition of a lack of respect for the sex of women emphasizes this rather well.

Williams juxtaposes the myths of the emotional nature of the female against the relatively calm demeanor of the male in times of crisis and duress, for Dessa and Rufel exhibit calm astuteness and inventiveness in contrast to Nehemiah's very emotional hysteria. Finally, the epilogue presents the perspective of Dessa as the free woman years later as she recounts her story to her granddaughter—the rightful heir to her story—so that it may be written down. Hence, through innovative narrative strategies in *Dessa Rose,* the novelist Sherley Anne Williams controls her pattern of rage so that her characters contradict historical assumptions about the general nature and behavior of men and women.

Notes

1. In an author's note, Sherley Anne Williams states: "I read of the first incident in Angela Davis's seminal essay, 'Reflections on the Black Woman's Role in the Community of Slaves,'" *The Black Scholar* (December 1971): 2–15. In tracking Davis to her source in Herbert Aptheker's *American Slave Revolts* (New York, 1947), I discovered the second incident. How sad, I thought then, that these two women never met."

2. Barbara Christian, *Black Women Novelists: The Development of a Tradition, 1892–1972* (Westport, Conn.: Greenwood Press, 1980); C. Minrose Gwin, *Black and White Women of the Old South: The Peculiar Sisterhood in American Literature* (Knoxville: University of Tennessee Press, 1985); Anne Firor Scott, *The Southern Lady From Pedestal to Politics, 1830–1930* (Chicago: University of Chicago Press, 1970); and Carolyn Alpine Watson, *Prologue: The Novels of Black American Women, 1891–1965* (Westport, Conn.: Greenwood Press, 1985), are a few critics who discuss the corresponding images of the Southern white lady and the loose Black woman and the mammy as they appear in fact and in fiction in American history and literature.

Works Cited

Christian, Barbara. "'Somebody Forgot to Tell Somebody Something': Afri-can-American Women's Historical Novels." *Wild Women in the Whirlwind: Afra-American Culture and the Contemporary Literary Renaissance.* Ed. Joanne M. Braxton and Andree Nicola McLaughlin. New Brunswick, N.J.: Rutgers University Press, 1990. 326–41.

————. *Black Women Novelists: The Development of a Tradition.* Westport, Conn.: Greenwood Press, 1980.

Davenport, Doris. *"Dessa Rose." Black American Literature Forum* 20.3 (1986): 335–40.

Davis, Mary Kemp. "Everybody Knows Her Name: The Recovery of the Past in Sherley Anne Williams' *Dessa Rose." Callaloo* (Summer 1989): 544–58.

Gillespie, Marcia. "The Seraglio, The Plantation—Intrigue and Survival." *Ms.* (September 1986): 20, 21.

Greene, Cheryll Y. "A Conversation with Sherley Anne Williams about the Impact of her New Novel *Dessa Rose" Essence* (December 1986): 34.

Gwin, Minrose C. *Black and White Women of the Old South: The Peculiar Sisterhood in American Literature.* Knoxville: University of Tennessee Press, 1985.

Kelly, Ernece B. "Slave Life Recalled in Moving Tale." *New Directions for Women* 16.3 (May/June 1987): 18.

Morrison, Toni. *Beloved.* New York: Knopf, 1987.

Scott, Anne Firor. *The Southern Lady from Pedestal to Politics, 1830–1930.* Chicago: University of Chicago Press, 1970.

Wallace, Michelle. "Slaves of History." *Women's Review of Books* (1986): 1.

White, Deborah Gray. *Ar'n't I a Woman: Female Slaves in the Plantation South.* New York: W. W. Norton, 1985.

Williams, Sherley Anne. *Dessa Rose.* New York: Berkley/William Morrow, 1986.

Yellin, Jean Fagan. Introduction to Harriet Jacobs, *Incidents in the Life of a Slave Girl: Written by Herself.* Ed. L. Maria Child. 1861. Cambridge: Harvard University Press, 1987. xiii–xxxiv.

2

Voyages Beyond Lust and Lactation

The Climacteric as Seen in Novels by
Sylvia Wynter, Beryl Gilroy, and Paule Marshall

JANICE LEE LIDDELL

The older woman is a strong and pervasive presence in both Caribbean life and literature. She is often the steadfast stabilizing force in many Caribbean homes, both real and fictive. As African American critic Gloria Wade-Gayles writes of African-American older women, Caribbean women are also "the bridge between generations, the perpetuators of . . . culture, the griots (reciters) of family history, the disciplinarians, housekeepers, cooks and repositories of wisdom and strength" (58). Unfortunately, however, the literary role these women have traditionally held has been more singular. In fiction, the Caribbean woman over sixty is generally relegated to the strong, sacrificing, "no-nonsense" grandmother figure—a postmenopausal archetype. Myriad Caribbean authors have found little else to do with her than to commit her to this singular women's destiny. In the literature, she is rarely the focus; she inevitably plays a supportive role or makes a few cameo appearances. Few readers undoubtedly have even wondered about the possible complexities of this older woman's life. Though perhaps one of the most well-known fictional characters (nearly every work has a grandmother or grandmother figure), the postclimacteric or postmenopausal woman may, in fact, be the least understood character in Caribbean literature.

Although the grandmother role may be the predominant social function of the older Caribbean woman, for many it is most certainly not the only one. For a significant number of postclimacteric women, different and challenging destinies are inevitably in the offing. According to sociologist/novelist Erna Brodber, until this century, if women were able to expand their social functions beyond those of mothering, they were able to do so after menopause. After the era of what African American writer Toni Morrison calls "lust and lactation" (Morrison 110), a number of women were able to obtain and maintain a freedom in some areas known only to men. Often, according to Brodber, these women rose in the community as religious or secular leaders. Perhaps as they were "neutered" by time, the capacities of these women to produce both life and sustenance no longer intimidated men; hence, men could view them more as equals. Unfortunately, however, the names and deeds of most of these women leaders have gone unrecorded and remain a hidden part of Caribbean history.

Trinidadian Clotil Walcott, mother of five and grandmother of even more, has emerged in real life as one of these Caribbean "sheroes." Saved from the scrap heap of historical oblivion by Trinidadian scholar Rhoda Reddock, the prodigious activities of this older woman who served as industrial relations officer of the Union of Ship Builders and Ship Repairers and Allied Workers, as chairperson of the Bank and General Workers Union, and as member of the Women's Arm of the Bank and General Workers Union, are well documented (Walcott). And thanks to at least three age- and gender-conscious women writers—Sylvia Wynter, Paule Marshall and Beryl Gilroy—the fictive lives of three postmenopausal women have been shown to be filled with the complexities usually reserved for younger and/or male characters.

Indeed, the works written by these novelists—respectively, *Hills of Hebron* (*HH*), *Praisesong for the Widow* (*PW*), and *Frangipani House* (*FH*)—all portray classic journey motifs wherein the postmenopausal women, as in the case of the archetypal hero, complete a series of ordeals during some psychological and/or territorial odyssey. As with the archetypal—most often male—hero, these rites of passage of the postmenopausal women are also distinguished by the classic archetypal pattern of departure, initiation, and return. In *The Hero with a Thousand Faces,* Joseph Campbell adroitly describes this pattern, one that I believe fits so closely to the journeys taken by the protagonists of the above-cited works. He says the journeys "are distinguished by formal and usually very severe exercises of severances whereby the mind is radically cut away from the attitudes, attachments and life patterns of the stage being left behind. This follows an interval of more or less extended retirement during which are enacted rituals designed to introduce the life adventurer to the forms and proper feelings of [her] new estate, so that when at last the time has ripened for return to the normal world, the initiate will be as good as reborn" (10).

The three aging female protagonists from these novels—Gatha Randall Burton, Avey Johnson, and Mama King, respectively—are certainly reborn. They are reborn into individuated older women who proceed into new inner and outer landscapes less informed by their predetermined woman destinies than by their own realized potential and desires.

Sylvia Wynter's Gatha Randall Burton in *Hills of Hebron* appears as the first postmenopausal woman in Caribbean literature to receive serious and sustained attention. Gatha, indeed, is an indomitable older woman figure. Although her age is not given, she is presumably over sixty during the novel's action. That Gatha has married in her forties and birthed her only son, now grown, even later, assists in this estimate and contributes significantly to her complexities.

Miss Gatha is a paradox. Rearing her first child when most women her age would be assisting with grandchildren, this indomitable woman finds herself caught in the throes of self-sacrificing motherdom. As the totally self-sacrificing mother, all the responsibilities and burdens she undertakes are for her self-centered and "crippled" son, Isaac. While in this regard she is mother-ideal, she is at the same time a pillar of fortitude, resourcefulness, and wisdom as leader of the small community of Hebron. The primary thematic concern in the novel is not the life of this rather stoic figure; it is the rites of passage of Hebron, a poor, rural Jamaican community, from post-slavery oppression and poverty toward physical and psychical freedom. The text does not belong to Gatha, although she does ultimately seize the focus. The narrative is based on the deliverance by Prophet Moses Barton, Gatha's husband, of his people out of physical and psychological bondage. Within the context of the patriarchal and patrilineal community of Hebron, the tenacious Gatha Randall Burton, widow to the now-deceased Moses, emerges. Her emergence is into the indomitable shero—as by Campbell's definition of hero, Gatha is "able to battle past [her] personal and local historical limitations to the generally valid, normally human forms" (19, 20). But whereas Campbell does accord such valiant heroic victories to both men and women, Gatha's rise is above the prescribed limitations of an entrenched patriarchy; hence, her battles must be considered inherently womanist or "sheroic."

Gatha's journey is essentially from her silent psychical sufferings as the wife of a fanatical prophet to her position as a forceful outspoken leader in her own right. Her transformation occurs abruptly upon the sudden death of her husband by the sheer necessity of securing for her only son what she perceives as his legacy. Initially, the Church of the New Believers of Hebron is embroiled in dissension over new leadership. Gatha, however, is quietly awaiting Isaac's ostensible return from boarding school to assume the leadership.

While the leadership is nearly snatched by another contestant, Gatha—the only member of the poor community with material resources—is able to secure the leadership for Isaac by assuming the position herself. Her ascent to power, though of little surprise given the abject circumstances of the community, is nevertheless no small accomplishment in such a patriarchal/patrilineal environ as Hebron. The narrator tells us, "[She] emerged from her anonymity, stamped herself upon their consciousness. Whilst her husband was alive she had been something of a spectre at a feast, someone whose inability to laugh made them uneasy. But they had no more positive notice of her than a man takes of his shadow. Then all at once she was there, enforcing respect" (*HH* 13).

Gatha's journey to the position of leader, albeit a temporary position for her, indeed serves as her rite of passage. Gatha does proceed through what might be called classic ordeals to become ostensibly the first self-actualized woman of African descent in Caribbean literature. Gatha, in effect, creates herself. The death of Moses Barton serves as her preparation—an opportunity if not an obligation—to secure the leadership for her son. This motivation is certainly not unknown to most women in the world and contributes to Wynter's womanist vision of the whole heroic quest motif. Gatha pledges to give her all to create a world worthy of her son's leadership as she portends it. In creating this world, she also creates a woman self, the likes of which has never been seen in Hebron.

The prevailing attitude toward women in Hebron, as in most patriarchies, is that they should maintain their prescribed woman places and woman roles. When the wife of an influential Hebronite announces her pregnancy to her husband, his response is, "So what? What else God make women for?" (*HH* 91). When the wife of Obadiah, Prophet Moses' hand-picked successor, is impregnated by an adulterer who turns out to be Gatha's son Isaac, the same Hebronite, Hugh denounces Obadiah for

his inability to control his wife. Hugh tells him, "You let down Hebron
. . . bring down God's wrath and the drought on us and all because of a
woman whom you weren't man enough to keep in order" (*HH* 61).

Gatha, however, emerges to the fore to demonstrate "what else God
make women for"; she emerges as one woman whom none is "man
enough to keep in order." Gatha, the narrator tells us, is almost dictato-
rial in her commands, "giving peremptory orders to the men," assigning
each to special tasks, which they all complete for the refortification of
their community (*HH* 55).

Gatha's objective of making ready the community before the arrival of
her heir-son is accomplished; however, the now educated heir-son has
decided not to return to what he considers a backward community. This
knowledge disorients the seemingly indomitable woman, but she is even
more devastated when she discovers that not only will he not assume the
leadership, but he has also stolen the money left to her by her late husband. Gatha's entire sense of purpose has been snatched away. The tragedy of Gatha's sheroic journey is that the actualization of her own importance is never considered "the prize" of her odyssey; hence, she never
recognizes the personal and historic success of her journey. Instead, she
perceives her son's recalcitrance to be her personal failure. Her journey,
a linear one, ends not in "the classic return and reintegration with society" (Campbell 36); rather, it ends in a kind of retreat into depression
and pathos.

But all is not lost. At the novel's end, Gatha's hopes are renewed by
the illicit child of Isaac and Obadiah's wife: "Only in her [Gatha's] lap
was there any warmth. She put her hands under the shawl, traced the
outlines of the child's body. It was perfect . . . The sins of the father, then,
had not been visited on the children? The fabric of her foreboding dis-
solved and she wept" (*HH* 305). For Gatha, the child's physical perfec-
tion portends him as the true redeemer of Hebron. The reader leaves the
work recognizing that Gatha's journeys as older woman are incomplete.
As grandmother-ideal she is bound to find new reasons to meet new
challenges and inevitably to commence new sheroic journeys.

While the realities of the older women in Wynter's novel are secondary
in the context of individual to community, Caribbean-American Paule
Marshall's *Praisesong for the Widow* focuses exclusively on both the symbolic and literal journeys of the postmenopausal woman. Marshall's
Praisesong may, in fact, be said to be an Africana woman's novel come of

age. Certainly, it is the first full-length novel to focus completely and consciously on the physical and psychic quests of an Africana postmenopausal woman character. Indeed, this novel, Marshall's fourth, explores what African American psychologist Jacquelyn Johnson Jackson refers to as the three major adaptive tasks of aging: (1) adapting to loss, (2) remaining active so as to retain life functions, and (3) reviewing one's identity (Jackson 94). It is this last adaptive task, a "delineation of 'an identity which integrates the diverse elements of an individual's life and allows [her] to come to a reasonably positive view of [her] life's worth'" (Jackson 94), however, that becomes the primary goal of the protagonist, Avey Johnson. This goal is achieved through Marshall's use of archetypal patterns, particularly the rites of passage inclusive of the classic heroic departure, initiation, and return.

Christine Downing, author of *Journey Through Menopause,* distinguishes the classical linear or semicircle journey as defined by Joseph Campbell from the more rare circular voyage that he also cites. Downing asserts that for the cultures in which the linear or semicircular pattern is conceived, the "magnification [seems] to fall more on separation and initiation than on return." She goes on to say, "Traditionally in the literature of quest and pilgrimage, the focus is on the faraway goal and on the dangers and difficulties of the approach. Arrival at the goal represents a climax and a turnaround point; the return voyage is almost anticlimactic, easy, swift and quickly told" (62). But in the circular odyssey that Avey undertakes, the return journey is equally important. In fact, as Downing says, "The circuitous journey that returned home was thus combined with the one-way pilgrimage that symbolized life" (63). Such is Avey's convoluted pilgrimage.

Avey's own ethnicity as African American serves as a significant metaphor in this circularity. Historically uprooted from Africa, her people have completed the departure phase of the journey via the Middle Passage and have undergone four centuries of racism, discrimination, slavery, Jim Crowism, and so on, which serve as the tests and ordeals of initiation. Avey's personal odyssey culminates not only in her own psychic return to Africa, but in the symbolic return home of all African Americans. Yet the novel itself is as much Caribbean as it is African American. Avey's aborted cruise to the Caribbean with her two longtime friends, her own personal trek through the remote regions of Carriacou, and her almost forgotten past in Tatem, South Carolina, demonstrate the author's facility to function almost simultaneously in what might be called two African Diasporic realities. Marshall adroitly reveals the vital connections between Avey's historical family homespace of Tatem, her transplanted homespace of New York, her spiritual homespace of the Caribbean, and ultimately the entire African Diaspora.

The novel is certainly an analysis of the archetypal journey of Africana people and a study of the vincula connecting them. However, it is even more a conscious and womanist examination of the liberation process—itself an odyssey—of Africana women living in racist, sexist, and ageist environments. The liberation process as experienced by Avey is purely and dramatically orchestrated by a deeper consciousness than she is aware of and also by a collective consciousness born from centuries of common experiences between Africana peoples, particularly Africana women.

Threads that have surreptitiously maintained for Avey what sociologist Joyce Ladner has called "the connection of common ancestry and oppression" (Ladner 15) have appeared slack throughout her and her husband's tortuous climb to a comfortable plateau of American middle classdom. The overt attempt by her husband Jerome Johnson to sever the threads to his inglorious past are virtually complete. Upon his arrival to this plateau, he cannot even bear to mention by name the street on which their upward climb had been the most intense and painful.

This odyssey from Brooklyn's Halsey Street, the sanctuary turned emotional abyss, to North White Plains, New York, culturally neuters the couple. Their White Plains destination is spiritually and culturally vapid, with its manicured lawns, self-contained neighborhoods, and Avey's own ostentatious "sterling silver tea and coffee service on the buffet, her special crystal and china in the break front, the chandelier above the great oval table" (*PW* 26).

The odyssey taken by Avey and led by Jerome is a significant one in Avey's liberation process. For it is this vapid existence from which she will be liberated after his death to find her true identity as an Africana woman. This, however, is not Avey's only odyssey. In fact, Avey takes a number of different treks throughout her life that lead to seemingly disparate ends but which have a significant and accumulative impact on who and what Avey Johnson ultimately becomes. Joyce Pettis observes, "The extensive criss-crossing of literal and metaphysical journeys in *Praisesong* comprises a metastructure within the narrative. Her travels intervene with dream, symbol, and ritual to establish motifs of circularity characterized by progress and completion. Avey's journeys signify the physical and cultural displacement of the African diaspora" (125). However, Avey's essential reversal of the journey(s) her African ancestors took as they trekked across the Atlantic from Africa to the New World, from the Caribbean to North America, and later from the southern United States to the northern United States, reconnects her culturally and physically to her past and prepares her for the regeneration about to occur.

Marshall's deconstruction of Avey's life through several past odysseys is revealed through a series of flashbacks, dreams, and surrealistic visions. These "delusions" emerge from what Dorothy Denniston calls Avey's "subconscious search to regain her lost identity" (125). They are, in fact, part of the "subterranean current that flows throughout the novel, [the] current [that] keeps the heroine afloat in her literal and symbolic travels over water" (125). The delusions indeed prove dangerous to the Odyssean Avey, as they "carry keys that open the whole realm of the desired and feared adventure of the discovery of the self. Destruction of the world that [Avey and her husband Jerome] have built and in which [they] live, and of [herself] with it" (Campbell 8). This deconstruction and destruction of Avey's "man" (Jerome)-made world contributes to the reconstruction of her liberation process, or what amounts to her convoluted trek toward individuation.

One particular past odyssey, perhaps her first one, haunts Avey through a recurring dream, which Downing describes as a primary vehicle for rites of passage preparation (34). In the dream, Avey relives her childhood travels from Harlem to "Tatem Island just across from Beaufort on the South Carolina Tidewater." In the dream, Aunt Cuney violently attempts to force Avey back into the road chosen for her.

It was eccentric Aunt Cuney who so long ago introduced Avey—whom she insisted on calling by her birth name, Avatara—to Ibo Landing, the legend of the flying Ibos, and her African connections. Aunt Cuney, family griot and sage, has followed the footsteps of yet another Avatara, Aunt Cuney's grandmother for whom Avey is named. As their names suggest, both Avataras represent avatars or incarnations of ancestral spirits. Avey's legacy to follow Aunt Cuney as family sage and griot is assigned to her even before her birth. "There was the story of how [Aunt Cuney] had sent word before her birth that it would be a girl and she was to be called after her grandmother who had come to her in a dream with the news. 'It's my gran done sent her. She's her little girl'" (*PW* 42).

Yet another odyssey—perhaps Avey's most significant—is about to begin at the novel's opening. Avey has already made her irreversible decision to abort the annual excursion she takes with two contemporaries. Her leave-taking is prompted by a number of strange and symbolic events, one of which is the dream in which Aunt Cuney attempts to coax an adult Avey back to Ibo Landing. This dream and the series of other events all serve as subliminal signals designed to redirect and reconnect Avey's consciousness to her past and future destinies as well as to her individual and collective fates. Here her physical departure is indeed the initial step of her personal rites of passage. Her leave-taking is that about which Campbell speaks (10).

Avey abruptly departs the cruise ship and the company of her two friends ostensibly to return to White Plains; however, a layover in Grenada and a chance meeting with Mr. Lebert Joseph, the rum shop owner who becomes her spiritual guide, alters her destination considerably. Even before introductions, Lebert Joseph and others seem to recognize Avey. This case of "mistaken identity" is in actuality a recognition of Avey's true identity and her introduction into an African Diasporic relationship. With this connection fused, Avey can begin what amounts to both a psychic and territorial journey toward individuation.

Her territorial journey takes her to Carriacou in a rickety, overly peopled boat to participate in the Big Drum Ceremony, a kind of cultural and spiritual reunion. Spiritually and psychically Avey is launched into recognition of the African aspects of herself. During the trip she experiences, with the help of a sisterhood, a ceremony of purgation, which enables her to eliminate much of her inner baggage as she prepares for the final stages of her arrival. The circle of older women on the boat who assist in her spiritual cleansing—and later Rosalie Parvay, who conducts her physical cleansing—help Avey to reestablish her forgotten communal and integrative memories. As well, these rituals prepare her for her induction into the "bonds of sisterhood with all women who participate in [the same] rhythms" (Downing 31).

The climactic Big Drum Ceremony provides the cosmic connections of geography, history, and kinship for Avey. Lebert Joseph, in the spirit of Legba, Voudon god of the crossroads, guides Avey to the crossroads of her life and points her in the direction of liberation and her pre-birth destiny. When Avey leaves Carriacou, she leaves as a whole individuated personality. She has indeed returned to her original cosmic wholeness, the one recognized by Aunt Cuney even before Avey's birth. Her psychic circle is complete. But her return is also territorial. En route back to her physical home, New York, she resolves to fulfill the destiny bequeathed her by her ancestress, Avatara. She will return to Tatem and teach her grandchildren and other young ones of the old ways left as legacies by their ancestors.

Indeed, *Praisesong* explores the rites of passage of the postmenopause for the Africana woman as it follows Avey's physical and psychical quests of self-liberation. Yet another novel that holds the postmenopausal woman at its center is Guyanese Beryl Gilroy's *Frangipani House.* Set in Guyana after World War II, the work becomes a discourse similar to *Praisesong* of the postmenopausal woman's attempts to regain a place for herself within her society and within her family. Essentially, the protagonist of this novel must undertake all three of the adaptive tasks cited by Jacquelyn Johnson Jackson as she undergoes her own rites of passage.

Mabel King, called Mama King by all who know her, must adapt to the loss of her husband, who has been deceased now for nearly two decades, and subsequently to the loss of her distorted memories of him. She must adapt, too, to the loss of the social and family roles important to virtually communal and integrative memories.

As with Avey in *Praisesong,* Mama King's story is primarily that of the older Africana woman's quest for identity. Presently, her place in her society and in her family is questionable. She has seemingly exhausted all her primary social and biological mother functions. No longer able to bear children, her husband deceased and her children both grown, Mama King is also unable even to fulfill the anticipated social function of grandmothering. Both daughters have migrated to America and taken with them all of Mama King's grandchildren. Without any of these important social roles and relationships, Mama King as older woman proves to be socially and psychically displaced.

But as well, Mama King is physically displaced. Frangipani House, one of the country's few homes for the elderly, has become Mama King's home. Run by capable, middle-aged Olga Trask, this refuge for elderly women is initially a rather pleasant confinement. In fact, "the strangeness of the routine, the ordered rhythm of life and the cleanliness of everything excited her" (*FH* 4). However, after a short time, the lack of both variety and freedom begins to affect the independent aging woman. This forced retirement from all that is important provides Mama King with the opportunity for "reflective interpretation." Herein she, like Avey, begins to experience a delusional past. Her daydreams, night dreams and memories, however, become distortions of her experienced reality. They create, for example, a handsome caring husband who "looks after his family" in place of the actual abusive and alcoholic Danny. These fantasies, again as Downing asserts, serve as a preamble to or a preparation for her rites of passage.

When her only remaining friend, Ginchey Thorley, reminds her of more harsh realities and makes the remarkable confession to killing Mama King's incurably misogynist husband, Mama King banishes her friend from her life. Even though the deed was done over two decades earlier to protect her from the violent abuse, Mama King even now cannot forgive her lifelong friend. With Ginchey's confession and subsequent death from cancer, Mama King is left devastatingly alone. Without her biological and social woman roles, without her memories or her friend, and without the bonds of sisterhood that Avey encounters at every turn, Mama King becomes an aging specter.

A brief surprise visit from one of her returning grandchildren inevitably sparks new memories and new life into the old woman. Her subsequent escape from Frangipani House, like Avey's leave-taking, serves as her abrupt detachment from the stage of life she is putting behind her. Her initiation takes place in a world vastly different from any she has known. She is "rescued" and adopted by a bevy of young beggars who serve as her surrogate kinship group. With them she is able to reactivate the all important sharing/caring elements of her life and to restore a sense of purpose.

Mama King's territorial journey takes her into the underbelly of the town with her young vagabonds. There, she is viciously mugged by a youth unknown to her, an event that requires her to be hospitalized and that necessitates her family's return to Guyana to attend to her and her return to the "normal world." But what is now the normal world is one with which she is unaccustomed. The culturally alienated youth of the changing Guyana, represented by the muggers and her own daughters, are preoccupied with material goods and themselves; old values and traditions have no place. As most of her kin prepare to leave, Mama

King's daughter Token best exemplifies the selfish lack of understanding of the younger generation: "I am going back to where I am—to where the life that is mine exists. This place is the past—the painful past. Mama never wanted more than this. This is her life, not mine. I never never wanted to be like her—her altruism sickened me. Her patience—her low, low goals. Just look at her. Worn out—worked out for nothing" (*FH* 98). The irony, of course, is that Mama King *is* "worn out—worked out" because of her lifelong efforts to be the "good mumma." Sadly, her daughters are not able to form the surrogate sisterhood that will enable Mama King to make her smooth transitions. They themselves are wandering aimlessly on their own journeys and are unable to synchronize their steps to the rhythms of their mother's journey.

But all is not lost. Mama King's youngest granddaughter represents hope for traditional values. It is a pregnant Cindy who is able to make the now vital connections with the displaced matriarch. Cindy and her husband remain to care for the elderly woman and ostensibly to urge her to move with them to America. The young couple values the old woman as nucleus of their family, and while their views toward family tend toward the romantic, they exhibit a tradition that Mama King recognizes, thus enabling her to begin the return journey to her status as matriarch and individuated woman. Also, the young husband Chuck comes closest to Mama King's romantic images of Danny. By now, however, she has faced the reality of Danny's violence and chased the "beat-crazy man" out of her daydreams. Still, Chuck represents all of what she would have wanted Danny to be.

The birth of the couple's twins in Mama King's home with a midwife and Mama in attendance forges a renewed bond of youth and traditions. The twin's births are also a "rebirthing" of a temporarily displaced grandmother. Mama King herself recognizes the tenuousness of this unaccustomed grandmother experience. She tells her granddaughter, "I will do the best I can but . . . my heart brittle—like eggshell. It easy to break" (*FH* 109). Her return is complete as she assumes the respected tradition.

Frangipani House, a short but intensely provocative work, perhaps comes closest of the three novels on postmenopausal women to provide a sociopolitical statement. In fact, Gilroy's novel may be the protest novel for older Caribbean women. While it is not strident or overbearing in its attempt to make its point, a position is nevertheless clear. *Frangipani*

House poignantly attacks institutions and attitudes that strip aging women of their identities and self-respect as it adamantly supports the need for maintaining traditional family values. In the end, Mama King is able to engage in a very important reconstruction of her own life, appreciating "the number of times that life had reconstituted her—first as child, then as woman, wife, mother, grandmother, mad-head old woman, beggar and finally old woman at peace at last" (*FH* 104). In so doing, Mama King, like Avey, is able to return with her "life-transmuting trophy" (Campbell 193). The trophy is a new self.

While *Frangipani House* is the most explicit in its statements about the plights of older women, all three works and all three protagonists are affirmations of the abilities of older women to direct their own personal journeys to fulfillment and selfhood. Downing speaks to the experiences of all three characters when she says of her situation, "[T]he journey brought me home and at home I found myself a postmenopausal woman engaged in the tasks of the reincorporation phase: assimilation, integration and finding a way to share what I had experienced" (18). Additionally, these three novels together weave the experiences of older women into the complex tapestry of human experiences. The common themes of and quests for gender and group identity, for independence and self-fulfillment—for whatever purposes—are themes and quests inherent in the experiences of humans throughout the world and throughout time. Wynter, Marshall, and Gilroy, as Caribbean women, indeed, show through the adventurous personal journeys of their aging but vital characters "what else God make women for" as they demonstrate also the vitality of life after lust and lactation.

Works Cited

Brodber, Erna. Interview with Janice Liddell. Atlanta, Georgia, 1989.

Campbell, Joseph. *The Hero with a Thousand Faces.* New York: Ballinger Foundation, 1949. Princeton: Princeton University Press, 1968.

Denniston, Dorothy Hamer. *The Fiction of Paule Marshall: Reconstructions of History, Culture, and Gender.* Knoxville: University of Tennessee Press, 1995.

Downing, Christine. *Journey Through Menopause: A Personal Rite of Passage.* New York: Cross Road Publishing, 1987.

Gilroy, Beryl. *Frangipani House.* London: Heinemann Educational Books, 1986.

Jackson, Jacquelyn Johnson. *Minorities and Aging.* California: Wadsworth, 1980.

Ladner, Joyce. *Tomorrow's Tomorrow: The Black Woman.* New York: Doubleday, 1972.

Marshall, Paule. *Praisesong for the Widow.* New York: G. P. Putnam's Sons, 1983.

Morrison, Toni. *The Bluest Eye.* New York: Washington Square Press, 1970.

Pettis, Joyce. *Toward Wholeness in Paule Marshall's Fiction.* Charlottesville: University Press of Virginia, 1995.

Wade-Gayles, Gloria. *No Crystal Stair: Visions of Race and Sex in Black Women's Fiction.* New York: Pilgrim Press, 1984.

Walcott, Clotil. *Fight Back Says a Woman.* The Hague: Institute of Social Studies, 1980.

Wynter, Sylvia. *The Hills of Hebron.* 1964. Essex: Longman Group, 1984.

3

A Woman's Art; A Woman's Craft

The Self in Ntozake Shange's *Sassafras,*
Cypress, and Indigo

CAROL MARSH-LOCKETT

"If Black women don't say who they are,
other people will and say it badly for them."
(Christian xii)

In the last lines of her choreopoem *for colored girls who have considered*
suicide/when the rainbow is enuf, Ntozake Shange's characters declare the
ultimate affirmation of their personhood: "i found god in myself / & i
loved her / i loved her fiercely" (63). Such a potent utterance posits a
viable solution to the problematic spiritual and psychological existence
of African American women who have been forced to confront the vicis-
situdes of life in America and their particularly hostile implications for
African American women from the seventeenth century to the present.
Marginalized, therefore, by the triple hazard of gender, race, and class,
the African American woman has continually been forced to define herself, to struggle against the stereotypes of mammy, matriarch, and jezebel to name herself and her place in society—indeed, the universe.

Ntozake Shange is one of several African American artists and intellectuals who have deconstructed the stereotypes. Confronting the inherent contradiction between the ideologies of womanhood and the devalued status of African American women, she has created works ultimately
undergirded by a troubling and painful realization that in spite of the
western patriarchal myth that women are supposed to be on a pedestal,
African American women, left to the devices of larger society, are mis-
treated and assigned, as Zora Neale Hurston has written, the status of
mules. She has, however, like the earliest of African American literary

foremothers, continued in the tradition of countering the negative impact of life in America by developing or defining an African American female self—one that is not constricted by the influence and dictates of a white male power structure or its shadow, African American male prescriptions and assumptions. Thus, by defining and describing in her own terms an African American female experience and identity, Shange, who claimed her own power and personhood by renaming herself from Paulette Williams, suggests through her art that the African American woman derives her power through loving and claiming the divine in herself and expressing herself in her own terms. Shange's choice of the Zulu names—*Ntozake* ("she who comes with her own things") and *Shange* ("she who walks like a lion")—attests to her embracing and affirming her own power. More significantly, however, her name change and general aesthetic herald an evolution in the empowerment of African American women writers from the nineteenth century, when the polemic of the novel sought to appeal to the moral sense of white readers, to the current trend in the late twentieth century when African American women's novels address the African American community and a large African American female readership. For, like most contemporary African American female writers, Shange renders a distinct African American female self in all of its idealized and flawed dimensions.

Shange's *Sassafras, Cypress, and Indigo* is an example of an African American female text that identifies as its locus of power an African American sisterhood rather than white readers. Centered on a family of Charlestonian women, the novel is a verbal mosaic and a study in lyricism that celebrates womanhood, life, and art. As Barbara Christian observes, Shange "consciously uses a potpourri of forms primarily associated with women: recipes, potions, letters, as well as poetry and dance rhythms, to construct her novel" (185). In addition, she laces the novel with Afrocentric motifs and incorporates lush, powerful, and utilitarian vegetation imagery (sassafras, cypress, and indigo) in naming her major characters and in so doing shapes reader expectations of the strength, rootedness, and value of African American womanhood.

The novel has, moreover, a middle-class focus. The omniscient narrative voice is middle class and would seem to reflect cadences of Shange's own Paulette Williams background. Shange has, therefore, been able to easily portray the artistic and middle-class orientation of Hilda Effania and her three daughters as they discover themselves, define their womanhood, and work through the dynamics of the mother-daughter relationship. Further, the work is middle class in that it subordinates working class concerns to the artistic experience and at points in the text approaches but never embraces art for its own sake. But in so doing, the novel examines the quality of African American women's lives in the face of racism and sexism. For throughout the novel, despite their heightened spirituality and artistic sensibilities, the Effania women encounter instances of racism and sexism. Nevertheless, we can contrast the vivid portrayal of proletariat issues raised in much of African American literature, such as Richard Wright's *Native Son* or Ann Petry's *The Street*. A great achievement in the novel, then, is Shange's ultimate displacement of the European notion of art for art's sake with the traditional African perception of art's serving a functional and spiritual purpose in people's (here, Black women's) lives.

The artistic expression of the middle-class ethos comes through a triple plot structure in which there are three centrally linked stories, each exploring a sister's voyage into self-discovery through the medium of art. The three plots, in turn, are linked through the return structure of the mother-daughter relationship that is reminiscent of the pattern described by Myer Abrams in *Natural Supernaturalism*. This, according to Abrams, is a pattern that takes its philosophical origins from Hegel and Schelling, a structure that is aided in its support of the narrative by Shange's use of the arts, in this case, three—weaving, music, and dance. It is Shange's use of the arts metaphor in the exploration of African American female selfhood that I intend to examine in this essay.

In the novel, weaving occupies a central position, for it is the symbol of the mother-daughter relationship, and it maintains the unity of the novel. It also functions, as it has in much of Western literature, as a symbol of creation and life, of multiplicity and growth. We are reminded of the three fates: Atropos, who carried the shears and cut the thread of life; Clotho, who carried the spindle and spun the thread of life; and Lachesis, who carried the globe and scroll and determined the length of life. Weaving is a universal activity found also, for example, in African culture where, as opposed to European culture, it is not a gender-specific activity. However, in this instance, Shange transforms the motif and makes weaving a distinctly African American female activity and a means of exploring the essential self.

Early in the novel, weaving is a symbol of maturity or womanhood. It is, for example, an activity pursued by Hilda, Sassafras, and Cypress and does not include the prepubescent Indigo. We are told, "If the rhythm was interrupted, Sassafras would just stare at the loom. Cypress would look at her work and not know where to start or what gauge her stitches were. Mama would burn herself with some peculiarly tinted boiling water. Everybody would be mad and not working, so Indigo would be sent to talk to the dolls" (7). Weaving, here, becomes a nonverbal expression of sisterhood and a shared activity between women.

In the symbolism of weaving, we also find an exploration of Hilda Effania's consciousness and value system. For her, weaving is a source of joy and is the dominant motif of motherhood. Weaving features largely, for example, in the Christmas celebration in the Effania household. When the girls are home for Christmas, Hilda is weaving and enjoying the fullness of life. We are told that her most precious time "was spinning in the kitchen, while the girls did what they were going to do" (55). In this context, weaving is also associated with gift-giving and spiritual, psychic, and intellectual bonding between women. Her gifts to Sassafras and Cypress are handmade and consistent with each daughter's interest. To Sassafras she gives a woven blanket and eight skeins of "finest spun cotton dyed so many colors" (68), and to Cypress she gives a tutu. In turn, Sassafras's gift to Hilda is "a woven hanging called 'You Know Where We Came From Mama' & six amethysts with holes drilled thru for her mother's creative weaving" (70).

Juxtaposed to Sassafras's aesthetic preoccupation with weaving is Hilda's practical concern. Just as each daughter has artistic and spiritual dreams based on which she seeks to shape her being and her destiny, so we are told, "Hilda Effania had some dreams of her own. Not so much to change the world, but to change her daughters' lives. Make it so that they wouldn't have to do what she did. Listen to every syllable came out of that white woman's mouth. It wasn't really distasteful to her. She liked her life. She liked making cloth: the touch, the rhythm of it, colors. What she wanted for her girls was more than that. She wanted happiness, however they could get it. Whatever it was. Whoever brought it" (57). In her pragmatism, Hilda, like many women in Western literature—Penelope and Anna come to mind—sees weaving as a means of constructing and maintaining a life-support system for the family and preserving the integrity of the kinship group. While she enjoys the craft, it is for her merely an occupation—a means of survival, and her desire for her daughters is a means of survival that would allow them their own direction and liberation from the dictates of the prevailing white power structure. This desire is especially clear in her reaction to Miz Fitzhugh's monetary gift to the girls. The annual gift comes with specific constraints, and we are mindful of Miz Fitzhugh's bigoted view of Hilda and her children and their "gall" as she sees it to seek existences as African American women outside of traditional "Negro" roles. Like the crafty Penelope, Hilda has a hidden set of motivations. While she preserves her positive relationship with Miz Fitzhugh, she also maintains her central position in her daughters' lives. That they have only one mother and that they will not be defined by white America is evident in Hilda's allowing the girls to spend the money exactly as they please.

Also significant to Hilda's identity as a mother is that, just as she literally weaves, she figuratively weaves a blanket of spiritual and emotional protection for her daughters. We are told, for example, of her concerns for Indigo, because the child even early in life pursues her own direction and defines for herself an identity and code of values out of deeply traditional southern folk beliefs and practices. The child, according to Hilda, "has too much of the South in her." We see this ever-spreading blanket of protection in her letters to the girls in which she expresses concern and passes judgment on their lifestyles, but pours out an incessant supply of loving support for them and their directions while expressing her desire that they acquire traditional American success in fine husbands and professions.

Weaving is also the axis of Sassafras's development as an African American woman. As a weaver, Sassafras comes into spiritual and emotional fruition through plying the craft she learned from Hilda. Ironically, Sassafras is the only one of Hilda's children whom Miz Fitzhugh attempts to appreciate. Out of this appreciation, she is motivated to finance Sassafras's prep school education. Her view of Sassafras and her weaving, however, is warped, since for Sassafras weaving is more than a mere honorable trade but is instead an affirmative merging of her artistic imagination and her womanhood. Miz Fitzhugh's presence, then, is significant to the dialogical relationship existing between the reader and the text, for she serves to remind the reader that for all their insulation, not even privileged African American women are immune to the intrusions of race and class; that only determination like Hilda's and firm self-definition like that of Sassafras can protect the African American woman from such intrusion.

Although Sassafras is eventually successful in her quest, her affirmation is not to be achieved without difficulties and frustrations as she finds herself thwarted and tested in the pursuit of her craft and in her attempt to reconcile her artistic and psychosexual beings. Sassafras endures these tests at the hands of her lover, Mitch, a musician who in his chauvinism seeks to undermine her talents and self-esteem and to denigrate her womanhood. Ignorant of the worth of her weaving, which she has to hide from him, he is by implication and deed insensitive to the full measure of her being. Weaving, then, is associated with Sassafras's assertion of selfhood as the activity becomes a retreat from the misogyny of Mitch and his two friends, Howard and Otis. Her weaving also allows her to absorb herself in the sanctity of her African American female heritage, which enables her to see herself in a positive light. We are told, "Sassafras had always been proud that her mother had a craft; that all the women in her family could make something besides a baby. . . . She had grown up in a room full of spinning wheels, table and floor looms, and her mother was always busy making cloth . . . but Sassafras had never wanted to weave, she just couldn't help. . . . It was as essential to her as dancing is to Carmen de Lavallade, or singing to Aretha Franklin. . . . Making cloth was the only tradition that Sassafras had inherited that gave her a sense of womanhood that was rich and sensuous, not tired and stingy" (91,92). This insightful acknowledgment of her identity as a weaver is significant and necessary to her total well-being. It connects her to the larger tradition of womanhood. It ultimately creates for her a niche in the Black artists' and craftsmen's commune just outside New Orleans, and it allows her to merge spiritually with the Yoruba practices and value system of the commune. More important, it underlies her realization that she and Mitch can never reconcile their arts and spirits because they have divergent orientations and absolutely incongruous and disparate views of themselves and the world. Finally, in keeping with the association of weaving with reproduction, life, and growth, we find that this same realization, reinforced by the Afrocentric ethos of the commune and the growth Sassafras experiences there, gives her the strength she needs to shake the bonds of male dependency by ridding herself of Mitch, returning to Charleston to have a baby (the symbol of a new and healthy self), and, in Hilda's discourse, to "find the rest of [herself]" (220).

Like weaving, music in the novel is central to female development and identity. In the novel the music motif bears both positive and negative connotations as it assists in shaping the women's worldview and in defining for the reader and for the women themselves their place in the world.

First, music is the metaphor for Indigo's identity and her passage from childhood into African American womanhood. After her first menstrual period, Uncle John gives her a fiddle for which she demonstrates a natural love and talent. At the lower end of the socioeconomic scale, Uncle John sees the fiddle as a means of connecting Indigo with her past and with the folk tradition. At this time, Uncle John becomes her mentor as he explains to her the link between music and the psychic survival of slaves:

> Them whites that owned slaves took everything was ourselves. . . . Just threw it on away. . . . Took them drums what they could . . . but they couldn't take our feet. Took them languages we speak. Took off wit our spirits & left us wit they Son. But the fiddle was the talkin one. The fiddle be callin' our gods what left us/be giving back some devilment & hope in our bodies worn down & lonely over these fields and kitchens. . . . What ya think music is, whatchu think the blues be, & them get happy church musics is about but talkin' wit the unreal what's mo' real than most folks ever gonna know. (27)

Here, Indigo learns that knowing the past is central to understanding the present, and music is integral to this lesson. Uncle John's influence remains dominant in Indigo's psyche as she continues to learn to play the fiddle with a view to retaining her link to the past and to the folk tradition. We also find that as she matures she remains steeped in the folk tradition and so defines her personhood.

Indigo's fiddle playing further facilitates her entree into local folk tradition when, as a result of her playing and the accompanying near mystical power, she acquires the friendship of Spats and Crunch, two Junior Geechee Captains, and is accepted and initiated as a Junior Geechee Captain herself. This evolving sense of folk identity also serves to shepherd Indigo out of childhood, as witnessed by her willingness to relinquish the childhood companionship of her dolls and pursue her music under the auspices of Sister Mary Louise, Uncle John, Spats and Crunch, and Pretty Man, the owner of a local tavern with a working-class clientele. It is this element of society that can relate to Indigo and her music. While they can perceive her genuine efforts to "play her own mind" and thus become increasingly steeped in the local folk tradition and her allegiance to the folk, Hilda, consistent with her middle-class dreams for her daughters, wants Indigo to have a conventional experience with music and encourages her to take traditional violin lessons. We note that at this stage of her development, Indigo's music lacks harmony; but as she becomes more personally integrated, her music becomes more melodious and less resembles the sounds of "banshees."

Music also becomes the metaphor for Indigo's maturation as she contemplates the meaning of womanhood. This is evident, for example, when Pretty Man's girlfriend, Mabel, fails to fully understand the implications of Indigo's experience with music and thus receives a beating from him. The reader is aware that Mabel and Indigo are motivated by two widely divergent sets of influences, Mabel by the profit motive and Indigo by the ancestral and folk spirits. Indigo, however, realizes only that she is responsible for Mabel's suffering. Through the medium of music she comes to understand the need for bonding between women, particularly African American women, because "the Colored had hurt enough already" (49). Later in the novel, music becomes the symbol of Indigo's full maturation and true identity as a midwife and folklorist on Difuskie Island, where she goes to live and study with her Aunt Haydee. There, Indigo studies and plays the violin and is able to contribute to and find her place among the folk. Music becomes the metaphor for Indigo's mode of expression and mystical powers—indeed, her psychic connection with her ancestral and folk past. Initially her fiddle playing serves to "soothe" the women in childbirth. Later, however, Indigo and her music become an institution as mothers and children seek spiritual refuge in her. Ultimately, Indigo and her music merge with the folk tradition on Difuskie Island. Through her powerful fiddle playing she is linked with the legend of the indomitable slave woman, Blue Sunday, who, as no one except Indigo had since done, moved the sea. Thus, armed with her talents and her spiritual and psychic connection with her folk past, Indigo assumes an easy and natural place among the folk and later inherits a position of responsibility when Aunt Haydee dies.

Shange also uses the music metaphor in her portrayal of African American male-female relationships. She demonstrates the developmental role of these relationships in the lives of African American women through the stark contrast between two significant relationships. On the one hand, there is the liaison between Sassafras and Mitch, in which music bears the Dionysian associations of destruction. In addition, just as in literature music has been associated with war, so the motif is used here to depict the battle between the sexes.

Mitch, a former juvenile delinquent, now a prison parolee, and worse yet, a junkie, is a musician. While he perceives himself to be an artist, music is, in his hands, a weapon and a means by which he can act out his brutally misogynistic tendencies. Part of this brutality is psychological, which we see in his efforts to negate Sassafras's creative impulses. He is, for example, intolerant of her weaving, for he does not fully understand its value as an art form. In addition, he does not allow her to display a sequin and feather hanging shaped like a vagina because, in his view, "it wasn't proper for a new African woman to make things of such a sexual nature" (78). He also tries to intimidate her into writing. The result is that she has to conceal her natural talents; but when, on one occasion, she does attempt to write and is meeting with success, he disrupts her first with sexual overtures and then by playing the Looney Tunes theme. He thus drives Sassafras into the kitchen to begin cooking. Perhaps, however, the most graphic example of the association between Mitch, misogyny, and music lies in the vivid scene in which Sassafras is subjected to Otis's poem "Ebony Cunt," which he reads, musically accompanied by Mitch and Howard. The poem celebrates African American men's sexual exploitation of African American women. When Sassafras voices her intolerance, she indicates in her rage the men's connection with African American women, and, consequently, embarrasses Mitch in front of his friends. His solution is violence. He beats her after the others leave and then plays the solo from Eric Dolphy's "Green Dolphin Street."

Because, as we can infer, Mitch is, for any number of reasons, detached from the feminine in himself; because he cannot see equality and harmony between the sexes; because, further, his consciousness is not Afrocentric, he lacks creativity. We note that the music he plays is not his own and that when he does offer love to Sassafras, it comes in the form of a "bewitched and tortuous mermaid song" (123). Music, then, becomes the metaphor for the cacophonous, nightmarish element of the male-female relationship that threatens the possibility of harmony and ultimately personhood.

In contrast, music celebrates the possibility of wholesomeness and fullness of life, the possibility of personhood, of light and hope, of union and harmony, as it shapes the context and structure of the relationship between Cypress and Leroy, which stands diametrically opposed to the lack of union between Sassafras and Mitch. Again, it is the music motif that establishes the dichotomy between Leroy and Mitch and their impact on the women's lives. Whereas Mitch has no worthwhile origins, no constructive present, and, hence, no potential for the future, Leroy is moral and disciplined, spiritually and emotionally integrated, and genuinely creative. He is well grounded in a past that has given him direction for a well-structured present and a productive and successful future. Moreover, throughout graduate school Leroy has endured the struggle to legitimize African American music and meets ultimately with success, as seen in the progress of his European tour. More important, as opposed to Mitch, Leroy is not misogynistic and sees in Cypress his chance for intimacy. He serves, then, as an enhancement to Cypress and an essential aid to her burgeoning selfhood.

Interconnected with the music motif is that of dance, which, like both weaving and music, bears an important association with female development and identity. Central to Cypress's existence, dance is the means by which she is able to assert her African American heritage, explore her womanhood, and eventually find her niche in the African American, albeit avant-garde middle class. Like Sassafras, however, Cypress finds that the pursuit of self-actualization is not an easy one. Initially, even Hilda is caustic about Cypress's heavy backside and suitability for ballet, but she eventually agrees to support Cypress's study of dance. In this context, dance features in the mother-daughter relationship and is the metaphor for psychic connection and shared values between Hilda and Cypress. It is significant that Hilda's initial views reflect the Euro-American view of the African American woman's body being unsuitable for the "high culture" of ballet. As Hilda grows in her relationship with Cypress, the reader would expect her to overcome the Euro-American view of the Black female body. On this point, however, the text remains silent. On the one hand, this silence underscores the generational distance between the two women, but on the other it reinforces the totality of Hilda's unconditional love and support for Cypress. Later, as Cypress begins to mature as a dancer, she benefits from the African influences brought to dance by Ariel Moroe and the Kushites Returned and the feminist interpretations brought by the lesbian troupe Azure Bosom. Both these troupes offer her options for self-definition. But her experiences with them leave her scarred, for she suffers as a result of Ariel's misogyny and Azure Bosom's emotional cannibalism.

Nevertheless, just as dance is associated with the pain necessary for

Cypress's growth, so it is also the means by which she achieves affirmation. The reader is made aware of this affirmation through the combined motifs of music and dance, which are worked out through the perfect harmony she shares with Leroy. In this context music and dance converge into a cathartic, healing experience when, in a drunken, brokenhearted state after her lesbian affair with Idrina of Azure Bosom, Cypress finds herself in the Golden Onk. It is there that she enters a new realm and experiences a new universe where all is cosmic harmony. She hears Leroy's music and becomes "a dance of a new thing, her own spirit, loose, fecund, deep" (156).

In addition, the combined motifs of dance and music serve to dramatize the healing, restorative power of love as we follow the relationship of Cypress and Leroy and Cypress's increasing empowerment. Leroy inspires Cypress to dance, and she, in turn, learns through dance that she need not learn to read music—that she can "just climb into it" (196). As a result of Leroy's presence and influence, Cypress is able to expand her horizons through dance and resolve her questions about the ills of her past associations with Ariel and Idrina. Similarly, Cypress's presence and influence enable Leroy to face and dismiss the bitter memories of past racial injustices. In short, music and dance in the novel become symbols of the growth and emancipation of the human spirit. Such liberation can culminate only in joy and harmony, which in the novel is manifested in Leroy's proposal of marriage and Cypress's acceptance.

In what traditional American critical discourse might term this "highly experimental novel," each woman's voyage into self-discovery constitutes her story. Each woman's journey necessitates a return to the place which, for good or for ill, whether she will stay there or not, she must call home. Each returns to Charleston—Sassafras to give birth, the symbol of a new life, assisted in the act by her sisters; Indigo to carry out last rites for Aunt Haydee; and Cypress to begin a new life with Leroy. Facilitated by the arts motif, the return or circular plot structure is complete as each sister finds herself back in her Charleston origins, having explored her womanhood in distinctly African American terms through the medium of art.

In her construction of a narrative that outlines the development into womanhood of these three sisters, Shange has employed a dominant theme that surfaces in much of African American women's fiction: the quest theme that, according to Claudia Tate, is "a character's personal search for a meaningful identity and self-sustaining dignity in a world of growing isolation, meaninglessness, and moral decay" (xix). And in so doing, Shange, like many of her counterparts, has reconstructed the traditional Euro-American female bildungsroman, which typically depicts female growth *down* into womanhood and its life of privilege. Shange's novel gives us a new form that depicts one of several African American female patterns of growth into selfhood. These are, however, patterns that frequently challenge traditional American expectations. Their depiction involves the reader in a dialogical process with the reality external to the text that necessitates the reader's resistance of traditional Euro-American values, which have not only given rise to negative stereotypes of African American women but have also mandated an ideal African American female identity: a middle class, darker skinned, sometimes victimized, but otherwise identical version of a white woman. Shange's female characters, however, are far more than blackfaced white middle-class women, for they represent a distinct and affirming Afrocentric experience and value system that result from a successful fusion of African sensibilities and western culture.

Works Cited

Abrams, M. H. *Natural Supernaturalism: Tradition and Revolution in Romantic Literature*. New York: W. W. Norton, 1971.

Christian, Barbara. *Black Feminist Criticism: Perspectives on Black Women Writers*. New York: Pergamon Press, 1985.

Shange, Ntozake. *for colored girls who have considered suicide/ when the rainbow is enuf*. New York: Macmillan, 1975.

———. *Sassafras, Cypress, and Indigo*. New York: St. Martin's Press, 1982.

Tate, Claudia. *Black Women Writers at Work*. New York: Continuum, 1983.

4

 Coming Home to Herself
Autonomy and Self-Conversion in
Flora Nwapa's *One Is Enough*

AUSTRALIA TARVER

As Nigeria's first woman novelist, the late Flora Nwapa[1] will be remembered for themes of female transformation that create a feminine space in an arena dominated by African male writers. Indeed, the impact of Nwapa's presentation of emerging women characters is comparable to the Igbo female's relatively recent encroachment into mask cult ceremonies, a tradition among the Izzi clan of Igbos historically reserved for men.[2] As the symbolic female mask wearer, Nwapa assumes control of the identity construction of African women characters, creating in the whole of her fiction lives that change and grow both within and outside of the social, economic, and moral/spiritual traditions of Igbo society.

Although the focus of this paper is Nwapa's third novel, *One Is Enough* (Tana, 1981; Africa World, 1992), it is important to view this work in the evolving context of her other novels and short stories in order to see the progression of her theme of autonomy.[3] As Brenda Berrian observes, the themes of "self-autonomy and choice" (62) were treated in earlier novels, *Efuru* (1966) and *Idu* (1970). In both novels the women protagonists initially view their community as a "collective other," which serves as a predetermined guide for women's roles. These women transform their dependence on traditional roles into a manipulation of these roles to achieve their respective needs. In short, Efuru and Idu ultimately feminize the traditions within their communities. Efuru undergoes female circumcision according to community standards, but when she is abandoned by her first husband, she defiantly leaves his house, and after yet another unsuccessful marriage, turns to the power of the Igbo lake goddess, Uhamiri. Marie Umeh maintains that Idu challenges "the cultural ethics of wife inheritance, male dominance, and the primacy of the child" (118). Thus, Idu's wish to join her husband in death is not an adherence to the dominance of Igbo tradition but rather a rejection of that dominance.

While Nwapa continues the conflicts of the widow and her in-laws in "The Delinquent Adults" (in *This is Lagos and Other Stories*, 1971), the seeds for *One Is Enough* are more obvious in *Wives at War and Other Stories* (1980). Unlike Efuru and Idu, who remain in their village community, the women in *Wives at War* are urbane and toughened by their experiences in the Nigerian civil war. In such stories as "Wives at War," "Man Palaver," "Mission to Lagos," and "The Chief's Daughter," women engage in a battle similar to Nwapa's artistic/literal war against the marginalization of women. Nwapa's interest in female city life in *One Is Enough* extends beyond the ideas planted in *Wives at War* to those advocating the primacy of female economic independence over marriage and the value of female sexual pleasure outside of marriage.

Florence Stratton maintains that *One Is Enough* is a novel of awakening, as are all of Nwapa's novels (86); it displays the emergence of a feminine ego from self-abasement and alienation to personal empowerment and reconciliation. As a female bildungsroman, the novel offers the multiple stages that are peculiar to the self-decolonizing process of an African woman character. To "arrive at her own coherent self" (Stratton 13), Amaka ultimately challenges patriarchy and tradition, but her journey to this point involves alienation, self-doubt and belittlement, renewal and, finally, reconceptualization.

Nwapa clearly articulates that the progression of a woman in the Igbo society of which Amaka is a part is linear and predictable: A woman is meant to bear children, or as Helen Ware puts it, woman means wife (15). Personal independence within a value system that ultimately supports the community and the men who live within it must be limited to the good of the family. Even a woman's money from her own trade business, which Amaka has, may benefit family members. Initially, Amaka accepts these values. They control, and are the cause of, her negative self-image and her willingness to maintain her marriage to Obiora despite his cruelty and arrogance.

Critic Molara Ogundipe-Leslie complains, "The theme of childlessness has been explored by African female writers so much that one would wish they would seek other themes" (9). Nonetheless, Nwapa's treatment of her childless protagonist at the beginning of the novel assists in deconstructing her low self-esteem and her concomitant servility. Amaka's childlessness serves as a symbol of her societal and ultimately her own self-abasement. Having no child relegates her to the level of infant in the eyes of Obiora's family. Cursed by her in-laws for having had no child in six years of marriage, Amaka kneels in front of her mother-in-law as if seeking forgiveness from an angry parent. At this stage in her development, Amaka displays qualities central to the colonized mind: She accepts the truncated image given to her by those she deems more powerful than herself; she subsumes her own talents in order to appear more acceptable to those she feels are in control; and she allows herself to be materialized for the benefit of those in control. Additionally, her usefulness as a "phallic receptacle" (Ogundipe-Leslie 6) takes ultimate precedence over her qualities as a human being.

This pre-coherent stage of Amaka's development is both ironic and subtextual. Her efforts to assimilate—to be the wife that the community sanctions—are met with violence and physical abuse from her husband and derision from her mother-in-law. Amaka's attempts to avoid the curse of being a "he" woman, one who challenges her husband in an argument, results in the confirmed belief that she is this dreaded social pariah. Amaka's victim status does not, however, prevent her from pondering questions related to a woman's identity and empowerment in a society in which development is viewed in masculine terms (Abel 7): "Was a woman nothing because she was unmarried or barren? Was there no other fulfillment [sic] for her? Could she not be happy . . . just by having men friends who were not husbands?" (Nwapa 22). Although these questions are an index to Amaka's self-doubt and alienation, they are also the subtext that emerges as the guidepost for her gradual self-actualization in Lagos as an economically independent, single woman.

Although Nwapa has said in an interview that Amaka's circumstances as a heroine are different from those of earlier heroines Efuru and Idu because Amaka lives in a faster, more modern Nigeria (James 115), her subtext of the single woman who transcends the contempt and indifference of her society only reinforces the challenges in the journey to wholeness that Amaka must make. Even modern African responses to the single, urban woman appear as traditional as those in Amaka's home village of Onitsha. Citing J. C. Caldwell's study, *Population Growth and Family Change in Africa,* Maria Cutrufelli observes that Ghanaian men

and women disapproved of Western women who were single and childless, and more women than men viewed the single woman as immoral.
Songs were used to deride a woman's single status: "Young woman, go
and seek some drug / You have been ill long / Get yourself some drug / So
that somebody may marry you" (70, 71). Attitudes toward the single,
urban woman in Nigeria take more stringent forms. In her discussion of
the obstacles to single female migration from rural Nigerian towns to
urban areas such as Iwo and Lagos, Lai Olurode lists "religious, sociocultural, political, legal and academic" barriers (299). Olurode explains
that in Iwo, while general attitudes toward female migrants were tolerant
because of economic growth, male migrants were the obvious choice as
home builders in new housing developments, and landlords could be
arrested for renting to single women (300). The concern over the negative impact of the female migrant on the town's women was also reflected in the location of the train depot, which was "five kilometers
south of Iwo." Olurode explains that, according to this story, the "chiefs
of the town were opposed" to having the train pass through Iwo "because
they feared the train would take away their women" (301). This fear and
abhorrence of the single urban female reflects the patriarchal need to
keep women in traditional roles, and, as Carolyne Dennis puts it, to
target them in Nigeria's "War Against Indiscipline" as one of the groups
of women responsible for the corruption of the Nigerian character (19–
24).

Nwapa's depiction of Amaka interrogates and revises the sociocultural treatment of single women presented above, but even literary
critics differ on how Amaka's single life should be read. Chimalum
Nwankwo, on the one hand, empresses a view close to that of the above-
mentioned Ghanaian men and women censors, and, on the other, critics
Chikwenye Okonjo Ogunyemi and Brenda Berrian view Nigerian urban
life philosophically. For Chimalum Nwankwo, there is a "rupture" between Nwapa's first two novels and her remaining works, a fault that
does not occur with Ngugi wa Thoing'o, Wole Soyinka, or Chinua
Achebe. Nwankwo believes the problem is that Nwapa fails to ground
One Is Enough in cultural, historical traditions. The "beauty" that Nwapa
loses in this novel is that of the power of the Igbo woman's expressing
herself in childbirth and marriage. Unlike *Things Fall Apart, One Is
Enough* leaves few Igbo traditions intact. Western values and weak men
seem to hold sway. Nwankwo says reproachfully, "The metropolis [in

One Is Enough] has a stamina that completely swamps whatever there is in the power of tradition. Most of the author's characters are still Igbo, but the legacy of the Lake goddess and other forms of values of restraint do not give these characters the verve with which to combat metropolitan circumstances. . . . There is something ranking [*sic*] about the profligacy of women like Amaka and the unscrupulous Madam Ojei and the Cash Madam Club" (50). Nwankwo limits his discussion of *One Is Enough* to a few paragraphs while devoting most of his essay and reserving most of his somewhat muted praise to *Efuru* and *Idu*. As he implies in the quote above, Nwankwo sees Amaka's singleness and her life in the city as aberrations against the idealized Mother Africa image, which upholds masculine values. In his rejection of Amaka, Nwankwo ignores the roots of his own argument supporting some aspects of Igbo tradition that help Amaka grow. He maintains that "[t]he Igbo world is a world of fluid dualities, and the pragmatic of existence derive from those dualities" (46). But Amaka's consciousness of "pragmatic" is just what Brenda Berrian feels Amaka (and Nwapa's other urban-bound women) possess. In contrast to Nwankwo, Berrian argues that Amaka's capacity to survive in "a world of fluid dualities" helps her choose "an alternative lifestyle outside of marriage" against the wishes of her community and move to an urban environment (53, 54). Similarly, Chikwenye Okonjo Ogunyemi wryly implies that the reason critics reject *One Is Enough* is because of the flexibility that Amaka's singleness affords: "Amaka represents the new mother. Ex-wife (or part-time wife, as is increasingly becoming the case), single, wealthy, and independent, the new mother prominently occupies the contemporary national space which delegitimizes the notion of illegitimacy. With female independence thus instituted, one husband is not just enough. Indeed, one might be too much. This pill is difficult for male critics to swallow as birth control gives way to husband control or the death of the husband" (9).

Amaka's journey into the single life, beyond the limited geographical and cultural space of her community, is also a spiritual and psychological journey inward. In pursuing self-created goals, Amaka achieves a clarity of inward vision that she had not explored. For the first time, she is able to act on her own behalf without the restrictions of a husband or mother-in-law. She extends her talents as a contractor in Lagos, supplying materials and equipment to government ministries and the military. Within three years she acquires land outside of Lagos and in Onitsha; she builds on both sites, hires a maid and driver, and divorces Obiora according to custom and civil law. While her wealth allows her an independence she has never known, she gradually understands that actual freedom comes from a liberation of the soul, an acceptance of the core self without pretense or influence.

This self-reckoning helps Amaka admit truths that strengthen her resolve to be guided only by her own visions and possibilities for growth. The first truth for her is that one husband is enough. Amaka becomes pregnant by Izu, a Catholic priest who has taken the name Father Mclaid. Izu acknowledges paternity of the twin boys and dutifully begins relinquishing his vows to marry Amaka. Amaka's mother and Izu press for the marriage. With characteristic forcefulness, Amaka's mother sets the date for the marriage rites. Ignoring her formidable mother and the obliging priest, Amaka cancels the marriage rites. Marrying Izu may not subject Amaka to the "soul-destroying chores," as her mother calls them, of a wife. But for Amaka, once was enough to suffer in the restrictive world of a husband who could claim that the community sanctioned his role as the one who is always right. Being a wife, Amaka tells her sister, Ado, is like being "impotent, in prison, unable to advance in body and soul" (127). The second truth follows that Amaka, finally achieving her heart's desire to have children, feels capable of rearing them herself. "There would be no one to dictate to her, to tell her what she should do and what she should not do. She would bring up her children well" (120). Nwapa's choice of twins may suggest not only approval of Amaka's self-reconstruction, but it also may be a subtle observation of the ability of Igbo traditions to change—as they must for women—from one that "threw" twins away to one that celebrates their birth to an independent woman.

For Nwapa, Amaka's spiritual reformation would not be possible without the economic security she has achieved. It allows her the leisure and luxury of thought, self-examination, and inner peace; it has helped to support her spiritual armor against the conventions and traditions that could submerge her individuality; and it provides her with the means and power to be generous to people in her home community— even those who thought she was a harlot for living single in Lagos. In Nwapa's eyes, economic independence is the axis for Amaka's self-esteem. Nwapa's endorsement of the new Amaka is reflected in Nwapa's dedication of the novel to her husband's mother: "For Ine, my husband's mother who believes that all women married or single should be economically independent." Nwapa seems to dramatize the voice of her mother-in-law through the forceful presentation of Amaka's aunt, who instructs Amaka with a warning similar to that heard by daughters (particularly those of color) the world over in their apprenticeships to womanhood: "Never depend on your husband. Never slave for him. Have your own business no matter how small, because you never can tell" (9).

As stated earlier, Amaka's awakening to spiritual independence and wealth has divided critics, whose disagreements regarding the source of her wealth demonstrate the assumptions of Western feminist critics, the appropriations of some male African critics, and the insistence of new Africanist feminist critics that African women characters should be rescued from both schools of thought. While Elleke Boehmer applauds Nwapa as the African woman writer who, in the sixties, began to concentrate on women characters in a manner that African male writers ignored, Boehmer discredits the women in Nwapa's later works because they become "exploitative and conspicuously consumerist" and they do not challenge "patriarchal law" (18). Katherine Frank is more blunt. She calls the means by which Amaka achieves self-reliance "a shrewd kind of prostitution," but she balances this statement with the realization that although Amaka sleeps with the Alhaji and then with Izu in order to get contracts, Amaka "has no illusions about her behavior" and "very little choice" (21, 22). In evaluating Frank's response to Amaka's use of lovers, Florence Stratton interjects, "Frank's perception of the kinds of transaction in which Amaka engages is clearly much closer to that of an Ekwensi or Ngugi than it is to Nwapa's. For Nwapa, who . . . takes her cue from Emecheta, revises the topos of the prostitute, subverting the authority of figures like Jagua and Wanja. . . . In Nwapa's conception, then, it is men who are the agents of social corruption. Prostitution, on the other hand, is for her a strategy women have adopted for confronting male domination" (21, 22).

The harshest criticism, extremely patriarchal and reminiscent of Chimalum Nwankwo's assertion of Amaka's "rank" character, comes from Nigerian critic Oladele Taiwo, who also sees Amaka as "little better than a common prostitute." Taiwo dismisses Amaka as one who embodies the corruption of Lagos, having abandoned her "rural virtues," which she had in Onitsha. Taiwo's denunciation of Amaka implies that she would have been better off remaining in Onitsha where she was "well domesticated" (64–68), even though it meant that her childlessness re-sulted in a status lower in the eyes of the villagers than Obiora's second wife, who "did not know her right from her left."

Such feminist critics of African literature as Tanzanian Jane Bryce-Okunlola and Nigerian Obioma Nnaemeka would take the above-men-tioned critics to task for imposing their limited perceptions of gender on Nwapa's vision of an African woman who designs her own strategy for evolving in the context of an African urban world. For Bryce-Okunlola, Katherine Frank's assumption of a universal feminism is a "serious mis-reading" of Nwapa's novel. Bryce-Okunlola's concerns about Frank's interpretation stress the importance of the feminist critic's ability to contextualize and reveal the multiple layers supporting the construction of an African female character. Bryce-Okunlola's rejoinder to Frank could serve also as an appropriate response to Boehmer and Taiwo: "[I]n her own terms, Amaka was neither a traditional woman at the beginning nor did she set out to 'liberate' herself into a life without men. On the contrary, in the last lines of the novel, she makes her priorities perfectly clear when she tells the nun, who has come to inform her of Izu's return to the church, that, 'I shall forever remain grateful to him for proving to the world that I am a mother as well as a woman' (154). . . . In the subversion of the conventional happy ending, the union of man and woman, Flora Nwapa expresses her philosophy. However unacceptably materialist it may appear, it is a response to the empirical conditions of women's lives in Nigeria" (206, 207).

Nnaemeka appears to concur with Bryce-Okunlola and extends her discussion to how insider (African)/outsider (Western) and Western feminist critics interpret African literature. Nnaemeka argues further that the position from which some feminist critics evaluate African texts is the same as that of the patriarchal privilege feminists profess to criti-cize. While Nnaemeka's focus on *One Is Enough* is limited, she uses Nwapa's works to cite the shortcomings of Western feminists like Frank, who "foreground sex/gender issues to the detriment of serious engage-ments with other issues in the literary texts, some of which may even help to increase our understanding of the sex/gender issues" (93).

Nwapa's approach to the development of a woman character is not only practical, as Bryce-Okunlola and Berrian suggest, but it is also multileveled; for she presents Amaka's generational ties to women who play a major role in her growth as well as in the self-reliance achieved in female bonding both inside and outside of marriage. Nwapa allows her older women characters a prophetic voice, informing Amaka of the truths that have helped them survive in traditional society. While these elders are problematized as women who uphold the patriarchal values of their community, the mother and aunt do not question Amaka's use of "bottom power" (sexual favors in exchange for business profits), and they reveal a pugnacity and strength that they pass on to Amaka with the hope that she will use them to advance to greater independence. The marriage advice of Amaka's mother is instructive in that it demonstrates Nwapa's depiction of the Igbo woman's creative practicality, even in the face of a male-centered world. When Amaka's childless marriage to Obiora fails, her mother reproaches her, not for being childless but for failing in what Ogunyemi calls the "marital war" (7). Winning the war in the mother's eyes would mean leaving Obiora or staying with him and getting pregnant by someone else.

While generational ties help in the transmission of beliefs about self-empowerment from older to younger women in the same family, Nwapa measures Amaka's growth against the spiritual toughness and development of other urban women and men. Nwapa shows that the female decolonized mind is open, flexible, able to form coalitions with other women of like minds and interests for spiritual and economic benefits. Amaka is an equal match for the Cash Madam Club members—aggressive, mercenary contractors who use the corruption of the city for their own survival. The solidarity among the group of urban businesswomen whom Amaka joins may be compared to the well-structured agricultural trade groups organized by African women who are the backbone of that economy. These women, the ones whom Oladele Taiwo calls "debased," are also similar to some of Nwapa's women characters in *Wives at War* (1980) who are "attack trade" participants in the Nigerian civil war, obtaining food from the enemy in order to feed their families. Nwapa exhibits obvious pride in the post–Biafran War bravery of the Cash Madams and in their ability to survive in a city that, as Chikwenye Ogunyemi implies, is suffering from "postcolonial traumatic syndrome" (7).

Nwapa's subtextual comparison of the development of Amaka and other women to men is clearly critical of men. She suggests that the world in which Amaka comes of age is one that facilitates and encourages the development of men. Yet, despite this advantage, the men demonstrate little flexibility and much less insight than the women. Even the most loving husband is not as capable of change as his wife. Mike, the husband of Amaka's best friend, is the only husband whose thoughts are revealed as he struggles to understand his wife's independence. Perhaps Nwapa shares these thoughts to demonstrate how difficult autonomy is to achieve for a woman who must live by the double standards contrived by men. Few men, except Izu, the father of Amaka's twins, display any qualities of independence. Self-reliance is not characteristic of Obiora, Amaka's former husband, who depends on his mother to eject Amaka from the marriage; nor does Mike display much ingenuity or foresight as a Lagos bureaucrat. Even with Izu, Nwapa suggests that without autonomous women, men would not be as successful as they are. Amaka's determination to live alone saves Izu from a loveless marriage and from falsely abandoning his life's work in the priesthood. As Bryce-Okunlola indicates, this novel does not suggest that the autonomous woman should forgo all relationships with men, but it does advocate that women have the right to make choices about men. Both Amaka and her mother make clear distinctions between husbands who allow a woman no independence and lovers who do. Hence, Nwapa answers Amaka's questions about the single woman by debunking the idea that a woman without a man is inadequate, weak or contemptible.

Paule Marshall's revelation to Mary Helen Washington that women writers often "expiate" their success in the world by making homebodies of their women characters (Abel 278) runs counter to Nwapa's objective in this novel. Rather, Nwapa's protagonist appears to be the hoped for, successful prototype of the African woman who, through personal fortitude and bonding with other women, accomplishes in fiction what Nwapa, perhaps wisely, did not do in reality: radically reject a system that dehumanizes women. Indeed, Amaka, in her newfound self, eclipses her outspoken mother, who insists that a wife should sacrifice virtue and fidelity to avoid childlessness. However, against her mother's wishes, Amaka rejects marriage itself because it caused doubt about her worth as a human being. Amaka arrives at the belief that marriage is expendable, but self-determination is not.

Ultimately, the self that Nwapa's protagonist comes "home" to is a reconstituted self, arrived at after an evolutionary process from submergence and disintegration to re-evaluation and recovery. These stages of homecoming, while they may seem on the surface to be antithetical to the basic communal nature of African life, are shown in the whole of

Nwapa's works to be an integral part of the experience of her women protagonists. In her introductory essay to the critical anthology *Ngambika*, Carole Davies infers from such African women as Ogundipe-Leslie and Annabella Rodrigues that in Africa it may be easier to change the external forces of colonialism and economic dependence than it is to change the internal ones dealing with the oppression of women. African women have the more difficult task, says Davies, of confronting how they are affected by their own cultures and, hence, their own self-images (8). The achievement of inner peace by the protagonist in *One Is Enough* may reflect Nwapa's hope that the African woman will continue to accept this difficult challenge, for, in Davies's words, "it is she who will have to define her own freedom" (7).

Notes

1. Flora Nwapa died on October 16, 1993, of pneumonia in Enugu, Nigeria. She was sixty-two. While she is reportedly the first Nigerian woman novelist, critic Brenda Berrian suggests there is some question as to whether she is the first African woman novelist. In a footnote in her article, "The Reinvention of Woman through Conversations and Humor in Flora Nwapa's *One Is Enough*" (66), Berrian observes that *The Promised Land* by Grace Ogot of Kenya was also published in 1966, but publishing records are not clear as to which writer was first.

2. In her exploration of the mask performance of the Izzi people, Chinyere Grace Okafor explains that although mask wearing in performance and ritual was a male province, during the Nigerian civil war (1967–1970), Izzi people accepted the oracle that decreed women's participation in mask performances. See "From the Heart of Masculinity: Ogbodo-Uke Women's Masking" (7–17).

3. A recently published critical anthology contextualizes all of Nwapa's known works, including her unpublished manuscript *The Late Goddess: Emerging Perspectives on Flora Nwapa—Critical and Theoretical Essays,* ed. Marie Umeh (Trenton: Africa World Press, 1998).

Works Cited

Abel, Elizabeth, Marianne Hirsch, and Elizabeth Langland, eds. *The Voyage In: Fictions of Female Development.* Hanover: University Press of New England, 1983.

Berrian, Brenda. "The Reinvention of Woman Through Conversations and

Humor in Flora Nwapa's *One Is Enough.*" *Research in African Literatures* 26.2 (1995): 53–67.

Boehmer, Elleke. "Stories of Women and Mothers: Gender and Nationalism in the Early Fiction of Flora Nwapa." Susheila Nasta 3–23.

Bryce-Okunlola, Jane. "Motherhood as a Metaphor for Creativity in Three Women's Novels: Flora Nwapa, Rebeka Njau and Bessie Head." Susheila Nasta 200–218.

Cutrufelli, Maria Rosa. *Women in Africa, Roots of Oppression.* London: Zed Press, 1983.

Davies, Carole Boyce. "Feminist Consciousness and African Literary Criticism." *Ngambika: Studies of Women in African Literature.* Ed. Carole Boyce Davies and Anne Adams Graves. Trenton: Africa World Press, 1986. 1–23.

Dennis, Carolyne. "Women and the State in Nigeria: the [*sic*] Case of the Federal Military Government, 1984–1985." *Women, State and Ideology, Studies from Africa and Asia.* Ed. Haleh Afshar. London: Macmillan Press, 1987. 13–27.

Frank, Katherine. "Women Without Men: The Feminist Novel in Africa." *Women in African Literature Today.* Ed. Eldred Durosimi Jones, Eustace Palmer, and Marjorie Jones. Trenton: Africa World Press, 1987. 14–34.

James, Adeola. *In Their Own Voices: African Women Writers Talk.* Portsmouth, N.H.: Heinemann, 1990.

Nasta, Susheila, ed. *Motherlands: Black Women's Writing from Africa, the Caribbean and South Asia.* New Brunswick, N.J.: Rutgers University Press, 1992.

Nnaemeka, Obioma. "Feminism, Rebellious Women, and Cultural Boundaries: Rereading Flora Nwapa and Her Compatriots." *Research in African Literatures* 26.2 (1995): 81–113.

Nwankwo, Chimalum. "The Igbo Word in Flora Nwapa's Craft." *Research in African Literatures* 26.2 (1995): 42–52.

Nwapa, Flora. *One Is Enough.* Enugu: Tana Press, 1981.

Ogundipe-Leslie, Molara. "The Female Writer and Her Commitment." Eldred Durosimi Jones, Eustace Palmer, and Marjorie Jones 5–13.

Ogunyemi, Chikwenye Okonjo. "Introduction: The Invalid, Dea(r)th, and the Author: The Case of Flora Nwapa, *aka* Professor (Mrs.) Flora Nwanzuruahu Nwakuche." *Research in African Literatures* 26.2 (1995): 1–16.

Okafor, Chinyere Grace. "From the Heart of Masculinity: Ogbodo-Uke Women's Masking." *Research in African Literatures* 25.3 (1994): 7–17.

Olurode, Lai. "Women in Rural-Urban Migration in the Town of Iwo in Nigeria." *The Migration Experience in Africa.* Ed. Jonathan Baker and Tade Akin Aina. Sweden: Nordiska Afrikainstitutet, 1995. 289–302.

Stratton, Florence. *Contemporary African Literature and the Politics of Gender.* New York: Routledge, 1994.

Taiwo, Oladele. *Female Novelists of Modern Africa.* New York: St. Martin's Press, 1984.

Umeh, Marie. "Finale: Signifyin(g) The Griottes: Flora Nwapa's Legacy of (Re)Vision and Voice." *Research in African Literatures* 26.2 (1995): 114–23.

Ware, Helen. "Female and Male Life Cycles." *Female and Male in West Africa.* Ed. Christine Oppong. Boston: Allen and Unwin, 1983. 6–31.

PART 2

Relationships: Mothering, Marrying, Mistressing, and Women to Women

Disengaging the Family Romance

In speaking of the Africana family construct, we generally mean what African American sociologist Andrew Billingsley defines as "an intimate association of persons of African descent who are related to one another by a variety of means, including blood, marriage, formal adoption, informal adoption, or by appropriation . . . and deeply embedded in a network of social structures both internal and external to itself" (28). While Billingsley is discussing the African American family milieu specifically, his definition generally encompasses the framework of families throughout the African Diaspora. What Billingsley omits here, however, is the patriarchal and patrilineal paradigms that have historically defined and prescribed family structure for "persons of African descent" and that have greatly influenced the assignment of roles and status both within the family and within the larger community. Certainly the familial connections and structures within the diaspora pose a variety of subtle and, perhaps, not so subtle distinctions based on geoculturality and economics; however, the kinship patterns suggested in Billingsley's definition remain fairly constant even considering these differences. Hence, typically, one or the other of the male/female, guardian/child, and/or sibling relationships remain central whether the family structure is nuclear, polyandrous, extended or single-parented.

It is the family and its concomitant relationships that traditionally engender the most socially significant roles for women, especially those of wife, mother, and daughter, roles that simultaneously centralize and marginalize women. These relationships, and often the romantic/sexual dynamics that contextualize some of them, consequently compel and propel the development of women from infant to mature adult. Thus, in Africana societies generally, women's identities, roles, and social status typically have been connected to whose daughter, whose wife/lover, or whose mother the women are, more so than to any other social factor. Even in what is sometimes referred to as the women-centered matriarchal or women-headed families, the ideology of patriarchal and male dominance often prevails as son, brother, uncle, or some other male relative or acquaintance assumes the surrogacy of the absent pater-power.

Within these typically patriarchal family constructs, a host of women-identified motifs related to powerlessness and pain thread through almost any given family's metanarratives, themes of subordination, marginality, exploitation, violence, silence, sacrifice, and so on. However, the corpus of fictive versions—many of which have become what can be considered Africana-classic in that they are highly read, taught, and critiqued throughout the diaspora—not only are written by men, but offer what might be described at best as a glorified, romanticized, and, at least, a rationalized explanation, examination or exploration of the less-than-pivotal roles of women in these cultures. Of course, over the past two decades significant writings of a precious few Africana women have emerged to challenge the status quo represented in the works of male writers; but the work of these males, nevertheless, continues to serve as models of the families and of the women within the respective Africana cultures.

We have but to look at, among a myriad other works, such African classics as Camara Laye's *The African Child;* Chinua Achebe's trilogy beginning with *Things Fall Apart;* the politically charged works of Ousmane Sembene and Ngugi wa Thiong'o, respectively, *God's Bits of Wood* and *A Grain of Wheat;* the enduring African American novels by Richard Wright and James Baldwin or the emerging mainstays by John A. Williams and John Wideman; and, in the Caribbean, the celebrated classic by

George Lamming, *In The Castle of My Skin,* or any of the works by Caribbean authors Roger Mais, Sam Selvon and Earl Lovelace. In this copious collection of works, all the writers, either centrally or peripherally, engage in writing the "family romance," fictive accounts of the Africana family that tend to naturalize and romanticize the positionalities of women, as they also rationalize the treatment of women.

In the group of essays in this section, however, feminist readings and interpretations of works written by Africana women writers offer the common position that "black women writers have made black women the subjects of their own family stories" (McDowell 84). Whereas the essays focus on an array of women-identified relationships—lesbian romantic, mother/daughter, and male/female—each critic, as does each work, appropriates the active centrality of Africana women within their own relationships as she also disengages the myth of the "fantasy family." Writing about this disengagement in the works of African American women, Deborah McDowell says, "This narrative of a fantasy family is unfulfilled in the majority of writings by contemporary black women. Much of their work exposes black women's subordination within the nuclear family, rethinks and configures its structures, and places utterance outside the father's preserve and control "(83). These "de-romanticized" interpretations and interrogations of Africana familial and romantic relationships unify this section. Whether the women in these relationships are viewed from their positions as mother, wife, mistress/lover, friend or some combination thereof, it is precisely the centralizing of the women within the deconstructed family matrix that serves as the critical impulse of each essay. While each of the critics in this section uses a different theoretical perspective in her approach to the issue of relationships in the novels of African, Caribbean or African American women, each, nevertheless, makes Black women the subject of the Black family story.

Yakini B. Kemp uses a feminist theoretical construct in her overarching but unstated premise that lesbian relationships constitute valid and socially redemptive familial and romantic relationships. Using Audre Lorde's groundbreaking "biomythography" in her positioning of the constant and continuous issues facing African American lesbians, Kemp demonstrates that the fiction by selected lesbian writers both de-marginalizes and de-victimizes their lesbian characters.

Brenda Berrian's critical perspective is sociopsychological as she contextualizes the theories of E. H. Erickson in her explorations of the impact of interpersonal relationships on female identity formation in two novels by Jamaica Kincaid. In a series of what Berrian calls "snapshots," which loosely mirror the structure of one of the novels, the critic centralizes the novels' female relationships—mother/daughter, grandmother/granddaughter, and pubescent friendships—and counterpoises them with a typical colonial-Caribbean and Afro-Caribbean cultural battle royal.

The disengagement perpetrated by Thelma Thompson-Deloatch results from her exploration of one of many "varied responses to the female dilemma and their varied strategies for resistance and survival." Thompson-Deloatch's analysis of the nexus of socioeconomics and romance in several male/female relationships in Elizabeth Nunez-Harrell's *When Rocks Dance* utilizes a reverse materialist interpretation of exploitation with the Caribbean woman as co-agent.

Utilizing the perspective of African feminism as forwarded by African feminist critics and scholars, Kitty Wu critiques Ama Ata Aidoo's *Changes: A Love Story* and contemporary African male-female relationships. Wu exposes the tensions that implode traditional relationships as women attempt to disengage from African family romance by ostensibly balancing their modern self-perceptions with traditional perception (and roles) of women. Like the other authors in this section, Wu portends that self-liberation will only be effected for women if they can successfully disengage their roles as mother, wife, and lover from age-old relational paradigms.

Note

See Deborah E. McDowell's essay "Reading Family Matters" for a larger discussion of the concept of family romance in the African American context. She borrows the term from Janet Beiger. See Janet Beiger, *Family Plots* (New Haven: Yale University Press, 1986).

Works Cited

Billingsley, Andrew. *Climbing Jacob's Ladder: The Enduring of African-American Families.* New York: Touchstone Books, 1992.

McDowell, Deborah E. "Reading Family Matters." *Changing Our Own Words.* Ed. Cheryl A. Wall. New Brunswick, N.J.: Rutgers University Press, 1989.

5

When Difference Is Not the Dilemma

The Black Woman Couple in
African American Women's Fiction

YAKINI B. KEMP

"Most Black lesbians were closeted, correctly recognizing the Black community's lack of interest in our position, as well as the many more immediate threats to our survival as Black people in a racist society. It was hard enough to be Black, to be Black and female, to be Black, female and gay" (Lorde 224). Audre Lorde's words summarize the emotional and social implications of being an African American lesbian in her chronicle of the late 1950s in New York's Greenwich Village society. While specifically recounting the isolated position of the African American woman in the predominantly white "gay-girl" community, Lorde's maxim holds true for the fictional portraits of African American women-loving women of the later three decades as well. Compassionate, realistic, and sometimes brutal portraits of African American lesbian relationships have been written by acclaimed writers Alice Walker, Gloria Naylor, and Ntozake Shange in *The Color Purple, The Women of Brewster Place,* and *Sassafras, Cypress and Indigo,* respectively. These writers and other successful African American women writers have been influential in forcing the U.S. literary establishment to take note of African American women's perceptions of life, love, and society. Yet novels and short story collections by African American women with central woman-loving woman plots are still primarily published by women's and alternative presses (Smith 239).[1]

Lorde's 1982 "biomythography," *Zami,* presents a profoundly poetic, existential, and political account of coming of age as an African American and as a lesbian. One of the greatest strengths of *Zami* is Lorde's self-critical perspective. While illustrating the protagonist's development (a mythologized Audre) into lesbian womanhood, she also examines the social and political interconnections of her youthful woman's life and love(s) with the immediate community and with the larger society. From this mixture of art and politics, *Zami* achieves a narrative richness that makes it unique and invaluable among the creative narratives by and about African American lesbians. This synopsis of *Zami* provides a fitting introduction to my discussion of Black women couples, since predominant issues brought forth in Lorde's autobiographical narrative about the fifties remain the same for lesbian writers' narratives of the later three decades: the development, protection, and continuation of love, commitment, and sexuality in the face of a most often hostile, sometimes disinterested, society.

The narrative focus, the story of two African American women's attempt to build a successful romantic union in the midst of the ever-present, aggressive forces of racism, sexism, classism, and homophobia, can be viewed as representative of individual quests for freedom of choice in romantic and sexual partnerships and ultimately, as microcosmic glimpses of a struggle for human (and democratic) rights. Chicana writer and activist Cherrie Moraga emphasizes the political ramifications of lesbian identity for women of color: "My lesbianism is the avenue through which I have learned the most about silence and oppression, and it continues to be the most tactile reminder to me that we are not free human beings . . . In this country, lesbianism is a poverty—as is being brown, as is being a woman, as is being just plain poor" (52).

My discussion examines the Black woman couples featured as central characters in Ann Allen Shockley's early eighties novel, *Say Jesus and Come to Me*, and in later fiction by African American lesbian writers. Fiction by Becky Birtha, Julie Blackwomon, Donna Allegra, Cherry Muhanji, and Helen Elaine Lee depicts woman-love relationships that center most often on the establishment of love and stability, which will help shore against a hostile community. The women characters created by these writers are distinct from the "tragic lesbians" as pictured in "The Two" in Naylor's *The Women of Brewster Place;* neither are they as insular as Celie and Shug in *The Color Purple* by Alice Walker; nor are they recognizable as the "emotional vultures" of Shange's *Sassafras, Cypress and Indigo.* The women's relationships created by lesbian writers vary, for as Barbara Smith states, "a realistic depiction of African American Lesbian experience would neither be a complete idyll nor a total nightmare"

(Smith 23). Overall, the novels and short stories examined here demonstrate that the Black woman couple's relationships, depicted at varying stages of commitment and intimacy, almost always serve as affirmative forces for transformation and growth in the protagonist's personhood (her self-image, lesbian-identified consciousness) and in her understanding of life and romantic love.

Published the same year as *Zami*, Ann Allen Shockley's *Say Jesus and Come to Me* details the development of an all-purpose women's march, initiated by an African American woman minister, a closet lesbian. The narrative also depicts the development of the romantic relationship between the minister, Myrtle Black, and a heretofore heterosexual rhythm and blues singer, Travis Lee. Although Shockley's novel includes the common elements of popular romance fiction, the genre in which it should ultimately be placed,[2] it provides a clear chronicle of a Black woman couple's development while it attempts to demonstrate the protagonist's unfolding lesbian-identified consciousness and what might be labelled a "monogamous" romantic consciousness. Whereas more texts by African American women can be found in bookstores now, novels about and/or written by African American lesbians are still rare. Helen Elaine Lee's 1994 novel, *The Serpent's Gift,* breaks new ground by featuring among its major characterizations a Black woman couple who share a half-century-long relationship. Yet, *Say Jesus and Come to Me* remains one of the few novels that centers its entire romantic plot on the life and love of an African American lesbian. The novelist's use of elements of the popular romance story juxtaposed with Black church ritual caused Jewelle Gomez to find *Say Jesus and Come to Me* lacking in the vital areas of cultural and social authenticity (Gomez 114). However, SDiane Bogus finds Shockley's protagonists as "not unselfconscious though they are brave, confronting life's adversities with varying degrees of grace and integrity" (Bogus 288). Citing the characterization of Travis Lee and others as "Queen B figures," Bogus also asserts that Shockley's characters fit a narrative (and real-life) lesbian cultural tradition found within the African American community (278). Although these two established lesbian critics differ on the overall contextual representation of *Say Jesus and Come to Me,* both Gomez and Bogus acknowledge Shockley as the first author to provide credible, nonstereotyped African American lesbian characterization in her novel *Loving Her* (1974).

Many of the stories written by African American lesbians convey personal narrative techniques and chronicle the formative stages of relationships rendering them reminiscent of autobiography. Explaining the preponderance of these fictional personal narratives, Patricia Duncker believes they "represent the search for definition and the search for a way to articulate and inhabit the word 'Lesbian'" (167). For the African American woman, even the term "Black lesbian" denoted a relatively new creation in the eighties, according to SDiane Bogus: "The fact is, the black lesbian is a recent incarnation of lesbian-feminist politics, and the term is used as a handy label by those who must call the woman-loving black woman something to give her presence and identify her, even at risk of separating her from the culture of which she is so integrally a part" (288).

The issue of identity, specifically lesbian identity, confronts Myrtle Davis, the protagonist of *Say Jesus and Come to Me*. She does not use the appellation "lesbian" very often in her self-reflective thoughts, and never has she voiced her identity out loud, even though her economic and social status depend on the power and charisma of her oratory as a Baptist minister. When the subject of lesbians and Black women enters the discussion at a planning meeting for her women's march in Nashville, Myrtle remains silent. Iffe Degman, a professor at a local university whom Myrtle enlists to organize the march, recounts her failed attempt to organize a feminist organization on campus: "We met a few times, then they voted to change the name from Black Feminists to the Black Women's Improvement Club. You see, the word feminist was anathema. It antagonized their black men, and men are important to black southern women, you can believe it! To top that, they equate the word feminist with man-haters, white women, and lesbians. And like wow! Lesbians are something that can't be dealt with in the black community—queers and funny people" (Shockley 133). Shockley's young professor outlines real-life attitudes that still exist within the academic and general African American community regarding use of "feminist" as an affirmative appellation.[3] Iffe's use of sarcasm to end her comment indicates her own view that despite its apparently narrow perspective, the Black community has an inherent ability to tolerate "difference." Myrtle's perspective, reflecting her internal homophobia, is perhaps more realistic. "It was such times as these, by her locked-in secrecy, she felt a traitor to herself. . . . For her to come out now, declare her lesbianism, could be disastrous for both herself and her church. The core of her existence was rooted in

Black life. Black people had not yet come fully to grips with homosexuality.... Religion and race mattered first to her" (Shockley 133). Like the "southern women" who placed their men's opinions and their own homophobia above inclusive women's issues, Myrtle chooses to remain silent about her life. Only later, after having a successful all-purpose women's march, a thriving church congregation, and a sincere love relationship, does she make her lesbian identity public. The decision, as posited in the novel, has much to do with her development as a partner in a romantic love relationship.

Perhaps equally problematic is Myrtle's characterization as a female counterpart to the philandering Baptist male preacher; she remains mentally and emotionally prepared to stay "a free-wheeling gospel spirit" (Shockley 12) even after her relationship with Travis Lee begins. Brokering the authority afforded by her ministry and the inherent freedom (albeit, a contradictory term) of same-sex encounters (her abandoned lovers were never pregnant), Myrtle's dealings with younger women have been exploitative and primarily for sexual gratification. While her social activism extends its concerns to the socially marginalized and to the entire community of women, her religious sincerity and integrity fail to promote any socially conscious assessment of her personal liaisons. In keeping with its romance fiction elements, Myrtle's sex life garners adequate erotic word space in the narrative, showing her to be an amorous and spirited lover of women. Also necessary for the genre is finding the true love that frees the heart and mind. But in this instance, finding the true love becomes a major impetus for freeing Myrtle's woman-centered identity and consciousness.

Shockley's romantic plot portrays the journey to total emotional commitment as an easy transition for Travis Lee, even in the face of the newness of her love of a woman. Her previous relationships have been with opportunistic men whom she supported financially. One factor in the ultimate success of this woman-couple may be power relations within the union; unlike Myrtle's previous encounters, Travis is famous and a "Queen B," as SDiane Bogus defines her. Thus, the two women meet on an equal social plane as religious leader and successful entertainer within the varied spectrum of the same class. Rather than brokering authority, Myrtle must learn to deal with the requisites of monogamous romantic love. Whereas Travis knows that she has loved and feels love for Myrtle, Myrtle never uses the word love with Travis and questions her own understanding of romantic love: "There was love for Jesus, love for people, love for yourself, and love for a person. The last she frowned over. Had *she* really *loved* anyone? She liked being with Travis, holding her like this with her body melting against her own like heat. Was that love?" (Shockley 183).

Characterized as authoritative, shrewd, and serious on all matters dealing with the advancement of her ministerial career, Myrtle has devoted little time to the development of her emotional life. Settling into a long-term relationship with one woman poses new issues. The resolution to her dilemma is found when she can assert her "love" for Travis and publicly announce her identity as a lesbian. These two assertions become fundamental elements of Myrtle's personhood: Through self-criticism, social activism (primarily, but not exclusively women's issues), and romantic partnership, she develops for the first time a woman-centered identity and lesbian consciousness, which bring a new level of maturity into her womanhood. From this identification, Myrtle can freely enter further intimacy in her relationship with Travis. Thus, Shockley's "romance fiction" actually posits lesbian affirmation as the key to progressive consciousness for her characters.

Shockley's novel treats the issues of the church and sexuality with didactic formality. Within the narrative, the impact of Myrtle's coming out is lessened somewhat as a significant portion of Myrtle's congregation is gay or socially marginalized. Secure with her sexuality, no longer viewing lesbianism as sin, the advice Reverend Myrtle Black gives to her church members is obviously her personal perspective on her own lifestyle: "If they are comfortable with themselves being homosexual, I tell them they have a right to their sexual preference, as long as they are not infringing upon or hurting someone else. God's heaven is open to all believers" (137).

Becky Birtha's short story, "In the Life," provides an interesting contrast to the liberal attitude of *Say Jesus and Come to Me* and demonstrates that the question of religion, lesbianism, and community acceptance can withstand humorous treatment. The story describes Jinx's (Pearl Irene Jenkins) remembrances thirteen years after the death of Gracie, her life-partner. Jinx recalls that thirty years earlier she and Gracie had gone to church at the prompting and urging of Gracie's "meddling cousin, who was always nagging us about how we unnatural and sinful and a disgrace to her family" (Birtha 144). She and Gracie attend the church dressed according to their own lesbian identities, Gracie in a dress, Jinx in her "best tailor-made suit" and "gray Stetson hat" (145). The church members are, of course, confounded. Jinx recalls an "old gentleman" admonishing Gracie to ask her "beau" to remove her hat while the church women huffed indignation because Jinx, a woman, should cover her head while "setting in the house of the lord" (145). The irony and contradictions of the situation have little to do with the attainment of religion; instead, the church members' bewilderment indicates socialized gender protocol and societal reaction to lesbian identities. Cousin Hattie does not bother the couple about coming to church again. And while Jinx views the sanctimonious church women with deep skepticism, "I ain't never known how to answer anybody who manages to bring the lord into every conversation" (Birtha 143), she views religious judgment and reckoning as an individual spiritual occurrence, beyond the power of the gossipy community. In her self-conscious reckoning of her life, Jinx, like Myrtle, has found a view of religion that allows her equality within the heterosexual domain of organized religion. Avoiding the psychological discord that could result from a different view of religion, such as Myrtle's earlier attempt to "exorcise" her demon of homosexuality, they both attain a comfortable balance by viewing a truly egalitarian God.

Becky Birtha's short story briefly outlines the "gendered" lesbian identities that appear in most of the narratives in this study, although the distinctions are muted or less relevant as in *Say Jesus and Come to Me*. Whereas Gracie and Jinx, lesbians of an earlier era, portray distinct masculine-identified and feminine-identified roles, neither Myrtle nor Travis can be solely cast in such roles. These lesbian identities may provoke immediate homophobic reaction, as Julie Blackwomon's "The Long Way Home" demonstrates.

Like Myrtle Black, Julie Blackwomon's teenage protagonist, Cat (Catherine), also experiences "coming-of-age" through confirmation of her identity and affirmation of her love for another woman. However, Cat's maturity results from painful lessons taught through her shocked reaction and incredulity when her father accuses her of forcing herself on her friend and lover, Sheila. Sheila has lied to her uncle to avoid homophobic censure after he discovered the couple making love in Sheila's bedroom. Sheila's disavowal of their reciprocal romantic affections and her refusal to acknowledge her lesbian identity sends Cat reeling because they declared their love for each other and settled the question of their sexual identity in an earlier conversation:

"We aren't bulldaggers are we Cat?"
"No, bulldaggers want to be men. We don't want to be men right?"
"Right, we just love each other and there's nothing wrong with loving someone."
"Yeah and nobody can choose who you fall in love with." (Blackwomon 8)

Their conversation affirms identity and mutual emotional attachment. Therefore, Sheila's subsequent abdication of her own identity and of her feelings ends Cat's faith in the relationship.

Though only sixteen, Cat's physical demeanor and her lack of interest in feminine trappings make her noticeably different from other girls her age. Sheila's cousin has labeled Cat a "bulldagger" after looking at her only a few seconds. However, the story's action indicates that Cat represents a woman who can handle homophobic reaction because she *owns* her identity. She will not tolerate involvement with a woman who hides or denies who she is or who she loves. Prominent among Cat's requirements for a successful love relationship are mutual acknowledgment of feelings and the bravery needed to face family and/or public denunciation. Sheila does not recognize the depth of her betrayal as she asks Cat to meet her once again in their private place in the park. Because she lacks courage and understanding, she does not realize that Cat will never meet her again. Although heartbroken, Julie Blackwomon's young protagonist develops a lesbian-identified consciousness that configures the type of romantic relationship she expects to form. "The Long Way Home" renders the issues of coming-of-age, sexual identity, and romantic love very effectively with its sketch of the Black woman couple in formative years. Notably, and true to type, Cat, the "butch"-looking teenager, is most definitive in acceptance and defense of her lesbian identity.

The issue of "butch" identity moves beyond stereotype with the two young women in Donna Allegra's "Carrot Juice." Both women, already settled in their identity, label themselves "butch" and work on construction crews. The unnamed narrator accepts the label despite its contemporary incorrectness: "The newly born feminists especially get all riled.

They claim there's no such animal: butch and femme don't exist; butch is male-identified, femininity is a social construct and so on, you know the rap" (Allegra 18,19). But she prefers "women who are at least as butch as I am" (18) because "With another butch, I feel safer to be straight-up for real. I don't have to mind my manners to impress her" (19). Khalilah, the woman whom the narrator meets as they both cycle about New York, is pretty and feminine but also considers herself "butch." As a newly developing couple, the two women form a friend-ship and move toward romantic attachment until the narrator pulls away from the budding relationship due to apprehensions about involvement with a "femme." Ultimately, the story demonstrates that the woman couple can experience difficulties in relationships due to their own pre-conceived notions of lesbian roles within romantic relationships.

The women in "Carrot Juice" might be described as women who reclaimed roles that some lesbian feminists denounced during the so-cially conscious seventies. The extent to which African American lesbi-ans adhered to this debunking of femme-butch role identification is less documented, and the trend may have been primarily class based. In her study of twentieth-century American lesbian life, Lillian Faderman ex-plains that "lesbians who wanted to identify as butch or femme in the 1980s could choose to express themselves in a larger variety of images" (265). The narrator in "Carrot Juice" eats red meat and considers "candy bars and make-up . . . perfectly natural" (18), whereas Khalilah wears no make-up, is a vegetarian, and is a health food aesthete. Living amidst cosmopolitan communities of New York, the women are familiar with feminist perspectives and varied lifestyles. Their identification with the additional gender stratification within their own lesbian community (butch-femme) is also natural for them. Bonnie Zimmerman theorizes that this "the introduction of 'gender' difference into a uniformly female lesbian community created that gap in which lies erotic desire. Butch and femme desire each other because they differ from one another" (113). Following that point, even though the narrator says that she wants a woman who is as "butch" as she, her attraction to Khalilah is particu-larly enhanced by Khalilah's "femme" appearance. The story concludes optimistically, as the two women reconcile and grapple with their role identification, that is, who will be butch, who will be femme. Neverthe-less, adherence to a single "gendered" role will not suffice for the overall success of their romantic partnership, since both women exhibit attractive and affirmative characteristics assigned as both "butch" and "femme." Their lighthearted dispute at the story's conclusion understates the real issues of power relations that are inherent connotations of the labels, and it subdues the concern that each woman must modify or refashion aspects of her present self-image in order to form a complementary and strong union. Despite their own self-labeling, the women's dispute underscores what Yin Quilter (a pseudonym) says in her autobiographical essay: "[T]he frustrations can also be great because . . . when two women are in a relationship together, everything is up for grabs. There are no predetermined roles to be filled. . . . It's simply you are two people, what do you wish to do? Without the roles that we all take on without even thinking much about it, we're on our own. As restrictive and confining as those roles can be in male/female relationships . . . they at least provide a modicum of predictability (though that too can be a problem). As a lesbian couple, we have no predictability. Nothing to rest on. It's all up to us" (224). Furthermore, while characterization of these two women demonstrates their confident self-awareness and firm ideas about their requisites for relationships, the process of forming a romantic attachment also brings them to another stage of development in their personhood. Before their friendship and romantic attachment, each disregarded the fluid and interactive aspects of their own personalities; both women learn that labeling identities and categorizing behavior will interfere with rather than suffice for human understanding and communication. They emerge with a new self-critical stance comparable to the introspection by the characters of Shockley, Birtha, and Blackwomon.

The stories and characterizations discussed thus far present women whose primary social and sexual involvements exist with women. In contrast, Cherry Muhanji's 1990 novel, *Her*, portrays two middle-aged lesbians married to men in a working-class Detroit community of the early sixties. The women, Charlotte and Ricky, live across the street from each other without speaking for over a decade. Their separation occurred just before World War II, when Ricky left New York to perform in Europe; she became a celebrity in Europe while the rest of the performance company, including her lover, Charlotte, remained in New York. Charlotte's bitterness toward Ricky's apparent abandonment results in years of silence between the two women.

Interestingly, Muhanji, like other African American women writers, demonstrates that the collective power of women's relationships (in the novel, the women on "John R Street") consolidate a women's community, which serves as a salvage or personal healing network for other women. (Ann Shockley configures the interracial women's collective so ideally in *Say Jesus and Come to Me* that it overcomes class and race conflicts, with middle-class white women marching against their own class interests with poor and working-class African American women.) In Muhanji's narrative, the women's community rallies to rescue Charlotte's daughter-in-law, who is lured into a prostitution ring by a seductive but sadistic pimp. While depicting this constructive aspect of African American women's networking, the two central characterizations in *Her* add a further accent to this discussion of the Black woman couple. For if Muhanji's premise is to be believed, Charlotte and Ricky's rekindled affections are so profound and their desire so fervent that one encounter renews the passionate intensity of their relationship decades earlier.

Muhanji's novel provides a crowded portrait of a thriving working-class community, along with its lively personalities and its seamier underpinnings. Both Charlotte and Ricky are eccentric, and some aspects of the novel's characterization are a bit implausible (although a brief contextual explanation is given, as a working-class husband of the period Charlotte's husband appears much too tolerant of his wife's lesbian love). Yet it is clear that if Ricky had escaped victimization during the war, she and Charlotte would have reunited as a couple. Through the unfolding of Charlotte and Ricky's story, along with the brief but vivid sketches of other clandestine woman-to-woman loves that momentarily become public in Ricky's nightclub on "Girl's Night In," the representation of lesbian existence as a matter of course in the African American community is certified. Muhanji also renders a totally complementary woman couple; the previous bond Charlotte and Ricky shared is painted as a perfect romantic and sexual union, despite Ricky's ultimate decision to go to Europe. Consequently, neither woman is capable of achieving emotional fulfillment until their reunion. Again, as seen in the works discussed earlier, the emotional affirmation and commitment bring about personal transformation. In this instance, Charlotte's husband, Solomon, always aware that his wife's feelings for him were deficient, observes for the first time in their long marriage "that his wife was capable of deep feeling" (157). This deep feeling extends to her woman lover only, although she and Solomon do achieve a tacit respect for each other as he resigns himself to the realization and the identity of his wife's true love.

Cherry Muhanji's novel gives the greatest affirmation of the "transformative power" of woman-identified love through its immediate and overwhelming effect on the two women. Charlotte's emotional and psychological anxieties are given glimpses throughout the novel; at one point, she is described as walking through the three-story house "tugging at her throat." Her emotional release, which emerges as a type of freedom, ensues after Charlotte sees Ricky's permanently deformed feet (a result of torture in WWII) and hears Ricky proclaim her unfailing love. Thus, their renewed commitment becomes both a healing force and a repair for Charlotte's damaged personality and for Ricky's emotional void.

This transformative aspect of woman-to-woman love is portrayed most realistically and developed most fully through the varied life trials of Ouida Staples and Zella Bridgeforth in Helen Elaine Lee's *The Serpent's Gift*. Unlike the works discussed so far, Lee's novel spans three quarters of this century. With the beginnings of the woman-to-woman relationship given full detail, the later detail is told in retrospect, after Zella's death forty-seven years later. As part of an ensemble of characters, the couple's interaction with the other family members, together and individually, becomes the focus. The novel's considered introspection into the workings of woman-centered love and coupling compels its inclusion in this discussion, even though Ouida may be said to be one of three central characters rather than the protagonist. Like the previous narratives, the woman couple in *The Serpent's Gift* confounds stereotypical roles for Black lesbians. Outward appearance conveys the couple as the typical butch-femme match, with Zella as pants- and fedora-wearing "soft butch," and Ouida as dress wearing, curly haired, femme partner. Yet unlike stereotypical portraits of the masculine-identified lesbian as provider/controller, Zella's characterization is a fluid portrait of nurturer, protector, lover, sister, and counselor. At various moments in their relationship, she becomes all of these for her life-partner Ouida. Zella's nurturing role surfaces particularly during the health crisis Ouida faces after a botched abortion; earlier, she even offers to take the child as her own to prevent Ouida from undergoing the illegal and dangerous procedure. And Ouida's feminine womanliness never hinders her quiet defiance of traditional lifestyle for attractive, "light skinned," Negro women within her community. In the calm course of her everyday life, Ouida divorces, stays single, acquires a job, and has two male lovers when she and Zella meet in 1926. She develops a sense of independence and selfhood as Ouida understands "for the first time in her life, that she owns the choice" (Lee 174).

Setting up their own household and living as a couple at the time is also a defiance of tradition. Neither woman rules the household in their comfortable domestic partnership; both have traditional women's occupations. Zella becomes a teacher after initiating study during Ouida's lengthy convalescence; Ouida works from home as a dressmaker/designer (the abortion damage causes her to walk with a cane). Jeanine Delombard's statement rings true for this couple: "[B]utch-femme is not about aping traditional notions of masculinity and femininity any more than it is about mimicking heterosexuality" (29). Ouida's and Zella's interpersonal connectedness and woman-centered consciousness defy their stereotypical outward appearance.

Through her development of the Black woman-couple in *The Serpent's Gift,* Helen Lee's characters also reveal another aspect of lesbian life, that of the required space for existence and the need for community. Poet Cheryl Clarke found that understanding the apposition of community ideologies provided not only a way to develop her lesbian identity consciousness, but also a guide to the type of community she needed to exist: "I realized that the major contradictions between Blackness and lesbianism were the sexist and heterosexist postures of the Afro-American (bourgeois) community. Witnessing a political Black lesbian community in the flesh was indispensable to this reconciliation of identities/cultures and saved me from wasting years in the closet of false consciousness" (216). Though Ouida and Zella do not have the option of "coming out" in the contemporary sense, they make their home away from their hometown of Black Oak in a place "where they wouldn't be weighted down with so many silences" (Lee 229). Their hometown's reactions follow the logic Evelynn Hammonds explains: "[I]f we accept the existence of the 'politics of silence' as an historical legacy shared by all black women, then certain expressions of black female sexuality will be rendered as dangerous, for individuals and for the collectivity" (137). Lesbianism for the Black community connotes sexuality, specifically unbridled female sexuality. Moving to another town allows the couple to form their own community of friends and couple rituals, but it does not remove them from the "sexist and heterosexist postures" cited by Clarke.

A clear example is Ouida's discomfort with the narrow gaze of the attendees at Zella's funeral. Ouida observes that she and Zella "had been consigned to narrowed space.... For others, these were the spaces where she and Zella had lived, squeezed and folded in by the theories that explained her fall" (351). "For those without understanding of woman-identified love, Ouida is a fallen woman because she has abandoned the sanctity of heterosexual love" (Kemp 4).

Among the narratives discussed here, only Lee's novel recounts detail of a Black woman-couple living together (Birtha's short story does give some glimpses in flashbacks). *The Serpent's Gift* ends in the sixties, whereas the other narratives portray African American society of the eighties and nineties. As stated in my earlier discussion of this novel, "Helen Elaine Lee's successful romantic couple contributes new space to the character worlds created by African American women. Through her progressive development of the lesbian couple as singular but representative women within their community and age, Lee continues the tradition of African American women writers whose written discourse evolves and reveals the complexity of the interrelationship of race, gender, and class stratification. Ouida and Zella's love is not exactly an entirely new literary creation. However, the fact that Lee allows this 'new love' to live and thrive for more than half a century makes it 'new' for Black Women's Literature" (13). It should be noted also that Lee's narrative undertaking and her writing display more complexity than most in this study; she offers an array of characters who are layered, approachable, and most often likable. The characterizations of Ouida Staples and Zella Bridgeforth are notable contributions to the body of woman-loving woman characterizations by African American women.

In her profound wisdom, Audre Lorde stated, "Black women have always bonded together in support of each other, however uneasily and in the face of whatever other allegiances which militated against that bonding" (*Sister Outsider* 49). The women characterized in the preceding works bonded because of their love for one another and because of their difference from traditional heterosexual couples. This act of forming a same-sex romantic and sexual relationship confers an "other" or outsider status from the larger society. Cherrie Moraga aptly explains this in her autobiographical essay: "Lesbianism as a sexual act can never be construed as reproductive sex. It is not work. It is purely about pleasure and intimacy. How this refutes, spits in the face of, the notion of sex as rape, sex as duty! In stepping outside the confines of the institution of heterosexuality, I was *choosing* sex freely. *The lesbian as institutionalized outcast*" (Moraga 125).

These narratives of Black women couples offer the affirmative perspective or the vanquishing of the status of "institutionalized outcast"; the central characters all progress to an awareness of personal empowerment. Through the lessons gathered from resolution of conflicts in emotional commitment, role identification, and physical separation, the authors pose the evolution of lesbian-identified consciousness and the development of sincere romantic love as the mainstays for an acceptable self-image and a healthy mental life. By and large, these characterizations of working-class African American women display the worldview developed from their consciousness as members of families and communities formed within the African American cultural heritage and also steeped in heterosexual ritual. Therefore, as each narrative discloses, forming the affirmative love relationship becomes one essential link to personhood and a touchstone to a community that may view the woman suspectedly (as with Myrtle and Jinx) or reject her outright (as Cat's relatives do). Ann Allen Shockley, Becky Birtha, Julie Blackwomon, Donna Allegra, Cherry Muhanji, and Helen Elaine Lee present women characters who enhance their knowledge as women and who enhance their understanding of their lesbian selves. This is the common bond in these very different lesbian stories—the bonding with each other. That bonding necessitates personal and emotional growth outside the realm of "difference," which actually helps the women overcome feelings of "difference" and ultimately becomes an act of survival.

Notes

1. Though published now by small and/or alternative presses, Audre Lorde's *Zami* and Ann Allen Shockley's *Say Jesus and Come to Me* were originally published by major presses.

2. Naiad Press has carried *Say Jesus and Come to Me* since 1987. Naiad publishes the largest selection of lesbian romance fiction in the United States; only a few of these works are authored by African American women.

3. Barbara Christian notes the reluctance of Black women intellectuals to

use the term [feminist] in their titles even in the late eighties. "But What Do We Think We're Doing Anyway: The State of Black Feminist Criticism" in Cheryl Wall, *Changing Our Words: Essays on Criticism, Theory and Writing by Black Women* (New Brunswick: Rutgers University Press, 1989), 69. Also see "When Black Students Reject Feminism," bell hooks, *The Chronicle of Higher Education,* July 13, 1994.

Works Cited

Allegra, Donna. "Carrot Juice." *Woman in the Window: Tales of Desire, Passion and Love.* Ed. Susan Pratt. Sarasota, Fla.: Starpress, 1993. 17–29.

Clarke, Cheryl. "Living the Texts *Out:* Lesbians and the Uses of Black Women's Traditions." *Theorizing Black Feminisms: The Visionary Pragmatism of Black Women.* Ed. Stanlie James and Abena Busia. New York: Routledge, 1993. 214–27.

Birtha, Becky. "In the Life." *Lovers' Choice.* Seattle: Seal Press, 1987. 139–52.

Blackwomon, Julie. "The Long Way Home." *Voyages Out 2: Lesbian Short Fiction.* Seattle: Seal Press, 1992.

Bogus, SDiane. "The Queen B Figure." *Lesbian Texts and Contexts: Radical Revisions.* Ed. Karla Jay and Joanne Glasgow. New York: New York University Press, 1990. 275–89.

Duncker, Patricia. *Sisters and Strangers: An Introduction to Contemporary Feminist Fiction.* Cambridge: Basil Blackwell, 1992.

Faderman, Lillian. *Odd Girls and Twilight Lovers: A History of Lesbian Life in Twentieth-Century America.* New York: Columbia University Press, 1991.

Gomez, Jewelle. "A Cultural Legacy Denied and Discovered: Black Lesbians in Fiction by Women." *Home Girls: A Black Feminist Anthology.* Ed. Barbara Smith. New York: Kitchen Table Press, 1983. 110–23.

Hammonds, Evelynn. "Black (W)holes and the Geometry of Black Female Sexuality." *Difference: A Journal of Feminist Cultural Studies* 6.2 and 3 (Summer/Fall 1994): 126–45.

Kemp, Yakini. "(Out)side Women or Lesbian Lady Loves in Helen Elaine Lee's *The Serpent's Gift:* A Character Study." Sixth Annual Women Writers of Color Conference. Salisbury, MD. October 11, 1996.

Lee, Helen Elaine. *The Serpent's Gift.* New York: Atheneum, 1994.

Lorde, Audre. "Scratching the Surface: Some Notes on Barriers to Women and Loving." *Sister Outsider: Essays and Speeches.* Freedom, Cal.: Crossing Press, 1984. 45–52.

Moraga, Cherrie. *Loving in the War Years.* Boston: South End Press, 1983.

Muhanji, Cherry. *Her.* San Francisco: Aunt Lute Books, 1990.

Naylor, Gloria. *The Women of Brewster Place: A Novel in Seven Stories.* New York: Penguin, 1982.

Quilter, Yin. "Setting Relationship Limits." 1990. *Life Notes: Personal Writings by Contemporary Black Women.* Ed. Patricia Bell-Scott. New York: W. W. Norton, 1994. 220–28.

Shange, Ntozake. *Sassafras, Cypress, and Indigo.* New York: St. Martin's Press, 1982.

Shockley, Ann Allen. *Say Jesus and Come to Me.* 1982. Tallahassee: Naiad Press, 1987.

Smith, Barbara. "The Truth That Never Hurts: Black Lesbians in Fiction in the 1980s." *Wild Women in the Whirlwind: Afra American Culture and the Contemporary Literary Renaissance.* Ed. Joanne Braxton and Andree McLaughlin. New Brunswick, N.J.: Rutgers University Press, 1990, 213–45.

Walker, Alice. *The Color Purple.* New York: Harcourt Brace: 1982.

Zimmerman, Bonnie. *The Safe Sea of Women: Lesbian Fiction, 1969–1989.* Boston: Beacon Press, 1990.

6

"Devouring Gods" and "Sacrificial Animals"

The Male-Female Relationship in
Ama Ata Aidoo's *Changes: A Love Story*

WEI-HSIUNG (KITTY) WU

When asked whether focusing on the oppression of African women would "damage or undermine the ultimate struggle for a complete social, economic and political liberation of Africa," Ghana's leading woman writer, Ama Ata Aidoo, stated, "On the contrary, I feel the revolutionizing of our continent hinges on the woman question. It might be the catalyst for development" (James 26). It is this conviction, perhaps, that has propelled Aidoo to speak out, in the bulk of her work, against sexual inequality in African societies. Indeed, her work, from *No Sweetness Here* (1969) to *Anowa* (1970) to *Our Sister Killjoy* (1977), affords an insight into African women's struggle against this inequality in a patriarchal society and invites us to compare African women's experience with that of women the world over.

What informs Aidoo's writing, however, is not feminism as it is defined by Katherine Frank in her article "Women Without Men: The Feminist Novel in Africa," in which Frank observes that "feminism is . . . an individualistic ideology in contrast to the communal nature of African society" (17). For the feminist impulse in much of Aidoo's work has always been balanced with her examination of other forms of social injustice that have plagued her continent, such as the African "brain drain," the abuse of Black authority, and the victimization of the disenfranchised. Viewed in this light, much of Aidoo's work is what Chimalum Nwankwo has aptly described as "feminist literature with a difference" (155). And this difference is at the core of African feminism, which Filomina Chioma Steady has clearly defined and distinguished from other feminist ideologies this way: "African feminism combines racial, sexual, class, and cultural dimensions of oppression to produce a more inclusive brand of feminism through which women are viewed first and foremost as *human*, rather than sexual, beings. It can be defined as that ideology which encompasses freedom from oppression based on the political, economic, social, and cultural manifestations of racial, cultural, sexual, and class biases. It is more inclusive than other forms of feminist ideologies" (4). As such, African feminism is not an individualistic ideology, but one that stresses "parallel autonomy, communalism, and cooperation for the preservation of life" (Steady 8). Further, as Carol Boyce Davies has observed in her summary of the characteristics of African feminism, it "examines African societies for institutions which are of value to women and rejects those which work to their detriment and does not simply import Western women's agendas" (9).

This theory of African feminism provides us with a useful model in which to explore the text and subtext of Aidoo's novel *Changes: A Love Story* (1991). In it, Aidoo examines—with humor, irony, and wit—sexual inequity in marriage in modern Africa from a number of divergent viewpoints, thus distancing her authorial position regarding the issue. And by bringing into sharp focus the dilemma of professional African women in contemporary Ghana, Aidoo in effect draws the reader and the critic into doing what her caveat, which prefaces the novel, ostensibly asks them not to do: read the novel as her "contribution" to the ongoing debate over the issue of sexual inequality in her continent. More specifically, she raises a number of important questions about contemporary African women and marriage within the cultural, historical, and social contexts of a traditionally viricentric society that has nonetheless undergone tremendous social changes. What is the proper education for modern African women? Where should the professional African woman's place be? What is the modern African woman's status in marriage compared with the African man's? Can modern African women find love and fulfillment in marriage without compromising their freedom and independence? What effect does polygamy have on modern African women? And, finally, can modern African men and women ever achieve sexual equality in marriage? The answers to these questions lie in the experience of Esi, the protagonist of *Changes: A Love Story*, as well as that of the other female characters in the novel. More important, the divergence and convergence of their experiences not only foreground the clash between traditional African values and contemporary feminist ideologies, but also point up the central irony in African women's struggle for sexual equality.

Set in contemporary Accra, Ghana, the novel dramatizes the confusion, frustration, and loneliness Esi experiences in her futile search for love and fulfillment on her own terms—futile because her terms are grounded in contemporary Euro-American concepts of sexual equality. As such, they are incompatible with the principles on which her society operates. Ambitious, independent, and intelligent, Esi embodies some of the attributes of a liberated woman who seems to have succeeded in balancing a demanding career with a happy marriage. Her job as a data analyst with the government's statistics bureau enables her to own a car and live in a government-provided bungalow with her husband, Oko, who is soon to head a coeducational school, and their five-year-old daughter. In reality, however, her marriage is strained, and she is unhappy.

The storm that finally ruptures the surface calm of her seemingly enviable marriage is precipitated by a number of pressures. For one thing, Esi is the product of the elite European education for women, one that breeds, among other things, romantic individualism, for this education is detached from the nurturing of home and community. The omniscient narrator's comment, which follows Esi's questions about why her family had sent her away to boarding schools, focuses our attention on the ramifications of such an education: "For surely, taking a ten-year-old child away from her mother, and away from her first language—which is surely one of life's most powerful working tools—for what would turn out to be forever, then transferring her into a boarding school for two years, to a higher boarding school for seven years, from where she was only equipped to go and roam in strange and foreign lands with no hope of ever meaningfully re-entering her mother's world . . . all this was too high a price to pay to achieve the dangerous confusion she was now in and the country now was in" (114). Unmoored from both family and community, Esi had cultivated romantic notions about love and marriage; but when pressured by her mother and grandmother, she had married Oko out of gratitude rather than love, "[g]ratitude that in spite of herself he had persisted in courting her and marrying her" (41). Her mother had complained that a woman of Esi's structure—too tall, too thin, with a flat belly and a flat behind—should not have waited too long if she expected to bear children. And her grandmother, Nana, had admonished her, "'[W]ho told you that feeling grateful to a man is not enough reason to marry him? My lady, the world would die of surprise if every woman openly confessed the true reason why she married a certain man'" (41). To Nana, it was simply unwise for a woman to marry for love. In fact, she had told Esi, "'Love is not safe . . . love is dangerous. It is deceitfully sweet like the wine from a fresh palm tree at dawn. . . . The last man any woman should think of marrying is the man she loves'" (42). Esi's romantic notion that love is a requisite for marriage clearly runs counter to this view, but Nana's view is the one that prevails in her society in which women marry to have children. Esi's role as wife and mother, too, is a main source of pressure, for this role has demanded that she make sacrifices in her career advancement goals. After their daughter's birth, Oko had refused to discuss the possibility of her returning to her job as a statistician with the Department of Urban Statistics in Accra. And she had resorted to working in Kumasi (where they were living at the time), keeping the birth and death register. That she was overqualified for the job had made her "fume and rage daily" (40). Being alienated by her colleagues simply because she has a master's degree in statistics had further compounded her predicament, for "they let her know that she was unwelcome, and a burden they did not know what to do with" (41).

But her problem did not end with this job. Now six years into their marriage, Esi and Oko cannot even talk to each other at ease: "[C]ommunication between them had ground to a halt, each of them virtually afraid of saying anything that might prove to be potentially explosive" (7). At the center of their conflict is the issue of where the woman's place is. Although, as a successful data analyst, Esi is highly respected by her colleagues and those who know the work she does, she is not successful on the home front, for Oko feels neglected: "Two solid years of courtship, six years of marriage. And what had he got out of it? Little. Nothing. No affection. Not even plain warmth. Nothing except one little daughter! Esi had never stated it categorically that she didn't want any more children. But she was on those dreadful birth control things: pills, loops or whatever. She had gone on them soon after the child was born, and no amount of reasoning and pleading had persuaded her to go off them. He wanted other children, at least one more . . . a boy if possible. But even one more girl would have been welcome" (8). Oko's thoughts vividly reveal the dissatisfaction and frustration of a husband in a modern marriage that is at odds with the traditional values of his society. His mother and sister, for example, have warned him about the danger of having an only child; one of his sisters had even suggested that he father additional children in an extramarital relationship.

A product of his society after all, Oko subscribes to the traditional view that a woman's place is in the home. Therefore, he resents the fact that Esi puts her career above her duties as a wife, "leaving the house virtually at dawn; returning home at dusk; often bringing work home" (8), not to mention the business trips Esi has had to take: "Geneva, Addis, Dakar one half of the year; Rome, Lusaka, Lagos the other half" (8). That his friends have been laughing at him only exacerbates his frustration and resentment. He complains to Esi, "'They think I'm not behaving like a man'" (8).

Oko's forcing himself on Esi to assert his manhood may be the natural outcome of his bruised ego, but she is outraged by his behavior, considering it marital rape rather than an expression of his love. More important, the incident brings to a head her latent desire to leave Oko. But for her to follow the dictates of her heart under the circumstances is deemed both unjustifiable and unwise. For one thing, the concept of marital rape is alien to her culture: "The society could not possibly have an indigenous word or phrase for it. Sex is something a husband claims from his wife as his right. Any time. And at his convenience" (12). Therefore, it would be ludicrous for Esi to file for divorce on the grounds that her husband had violated her. Second, to Esi's best friend, Opokuya, it is natural for men to be possessive, and Oko's behavior is merely a reflection of his love. Opokuya explains to Esi, "'[I]f a man loves a woman, he would want to have her around as much as possible'" (44, 45). Third, as Opokuya sees it, "men are not really interested in a woman's independence or her intelligence" (45), and what Esi fails to realize is that "the few who claim they like intelligent and active women are also interested in having such women permanently in their beds and in their kitchens" (45). It is, in other words, perfectly understandable why Oko has behaved the way he has, even though he had initially been attracted to Esi by her "air of independence" (45). Furthermore, it is foolish of Esi to think that she can have her independence by being single again. Opokuya is quick to point out to Esi that societies frown on the unmarried woman and that "they put as much pressure as possible on her" because her single state is deemed "an insult to the glorious manhood of [their] men" (48). To Okopuya, it is equally foolish for Esi to think that she can be single again without being lonely, or that she can have it all—a condition which, as Opokuya reminds Esi, no society on this earth would allow women to have (49).

To Oko and his relatives, too, Esi's behavior is outrageous. It is tantamount to an insurrection and thus is a serious threat to the security of his phallocentric domain. Oko thinks to himself, "[T]o have to fight with your woman's career for her attention is not only new in the history of the world, but completely humiliating" (70). If Oko is baffled by Esi's behavior, his relatives are outraged by it, and they chastise her by calling her "a semi-barren witch" (70), telling her that it is better for Oko to be without her.

Divorcing Oko and, subsequently, falling in love with Ali, a married Muslim businessman from the northern part of Ghana, at first seem to be a dubiously promising solution to Esi's dilemma in that they enable her to bask in Ali's attention and love without being suffocated by his demands on her. Even when she and Ali enter into a polygamous marriage at his insistence to make her "become occupied territory" (91), she is unprepared for anything but happiness. In fact, she even finds polygamy exciting, for she tells Opokuya, "monogamy is so stifling" (98). Little does she know, as Opokuya is aware, that "in the traditional environment in which polygamous marriages flourished, happiness, like most of the good things of this life, was not a two-person enterprise" and that "it was the business of all parties concerned" (98). Oblivious to this vital aspect of polygamy, Esi gloats over her relationship with Ali: "In all, her basic hopes for marrying a man like Ali had been fulfilled. Ali was not on her back every one of every twenty-four hours of every day. In fact, he was hardly ever near her at all. In that sense she was extremely contented. She could concentrate on her job, and even occasionally bring work home" (138). In other words, she seems to have succeeded in having it all.

Her naivete, and the disillusionment in which she finds herself when this relationship fails, poignantly underscore the irony that informs the experience of women like Esi. What contributes to her disillusionment, first of all, is that she is blind to this simple truth: When African men leave their women for other women or "add those new women to their old ones" (101), they seldom do so for the sake of love. Among the various reasons cited by Aba and Ama—apparently speaking for the community at large—are the woman's birth (that is, her family's influence and wealth), level of education, economic power, and social status (102). Nowhere is love mentioned.

In a sense, Esi is no more to Ali than a valuable piece of property or a sexual object. It is her body, after all, in which Ali has a vested interest, for he finds her uninhibited, free from the overwhelming combination of forces that have adversely affected the mind of the modern African woman, such as "traditional shyness and contempt for the biology of women; Islamic suppressive ideas about women; English victorian prudery and French hypocrisy imported by the colonisers" (75). What she thinks they have found in each other, then, is little more than sexual love, which can be recharged when its novelty with one partner diminishes. Esi also forgets that "if a man can have two wives . . . he can have three wives . . . four wives . . . and on and on" (156). In a polygamous marriage, one of the cardinal rules, as her mother and grandmother had reminded her, is "never to show jealousy" (116). Yet, although they had warned her that "if she broke the rules, then her new marriage would be like a fire that had been lighted inside her" (116), she is heartbroken when she realizes that Ali is romantically involved with his new secretary. All the gifts that he has ever lavished on her have suddenly become meaningless, for they cannot fill the void left by the absence of his love.

Knowing what her materialistic relatives would say if she sought an annulment of this marriage, Esi can only live in desolation and loneliness, teaching herself not to expect Ali at all and not to wonder where he is when he is not with her. Disenchanted by his way of loving and unwilling to accept the status quo, Esi is nevertheless hopeful that her ideal love is still attainable: "So what fashion of loving was she ever going to consider adequate? She comforted herself that maybe her bone-blood-flesh self, not her unseen soul, would get answers to some of the big questions she was asking of life. Yes, maybe, 'one day, one day' as the Highlife singer had sung in an unusually warm and not-so-dark night" (166). Since this romantic vision of love and fulfillment in a marriage is drastically at variance with her society's terms for male-female relationships, her continued search is doomed to be more of the same: an exercise in futility.

Esi's experience attests to the fact that, given the cultural and social realities in Africa, the development of a self beyond one's communal traditions is not a viable enterprise. But if Esi seems foolishly naive, she is not altogether beyond redemption. There is, after all, dignity in her refusal to condone Ali's abuse of his male privileges. There is dignity, too, in her decision to spurn Opokuya's husband's sexual advances during her loneliest and most desolate hours. As she ponders over the incident, she concludes, "There are things you don't do to a friend. Opokuya was not just a friend. She was a sister, almost her other self" (164). The support that Esi and Opokuya have provided each other is, in fact, what sustains them in their experience of living in a male-dominated world.

That sexual inequality is entrenched in the African consciousness and that it is nearly impossible to change this status quo manifest themselves in the attitudes or experiences of other female characters in the novel as well. Only their acceptance of the status quo sets them apart from Esi. A repository of communal myths and history, Nana is clearly resigned to this inequality, and nowhere is her attitude more evident than in this litany with which she counsels Esi: "My lady Silk, remember a man always gained in stature through any way he chose to associate with a woman. And that included adultery. Especially adultery. Esi, a woman has always been diminished in her association with a man. A good woman was she who quickened the pace of her own destruction. To refuse, as a woman, to be destroyed, was a crime that society spotted very quickly and punished swiftly and severely" (110). This perception of the woman's sacrificial role is made even more vivid to Esi when Nana refers to the wedding ceremony "as a funeral of the self that could have been" (110) and when she adds a cosmic dimension to this perspective: "'Men were the first gods in the universe, and they were devouring gods. The only way they could yield their best—and sometimes their worst too— was if their egos were sacrificed too regularly. The bloodier the sacrifice, the better'" (110).

Ali's own mother, Fatimatu, was just such a sacrificial animal. She was only fifteen years old when she bled to death upon giving birth to Ali. This, as the narrator tells us, is the act of the devouring god: "Like most men everywhere and from time immemorial—who have been able to pay for the luxury—Ali's father preferred his women young and tender. They had to be virgins, of course. And he had acquired one such woman for a wife in each of his eight favourite stops on his trade routes" (23). Men like Ali's father not only perpetrate this sacrificial "ritual" but also perpetuate it in one form or another.

Opokuya, more levelheaded than Esi, certainly understands the insidious ways in which this "ritual" has found itself into male-female relationships. Resigned to the fact that men's egos have to be sacrificed to, she believes that for a marriage to work, the woman has to be a fool (49). Compromising her independence of will for the sake of her marriage is a case in point. A practical nurse and a mother of four children, Opokuya needs transportation of her own; yet her husband, Kubi, refuses to let her use his car. Even when he goes on a business trip, he insists that the car stand on its spot the entire day until he returns. To sacrifice to his ego, Opokuya plays the fool, for, as the omniscient narrator's comment suggests, few would express sympathy for her resentment of Kubi's unreasonable attitude about the car: "As far as [her female colleagues] were concerned, it was Opokuya who was unreasonable or mad. Clearly, she didn't know anything. She should listen to the stories of women who paid for cars which their husbands then took over completely. In some cases, whisking their girlfriends around town in them" (18). Given this prevailing attitude toward what is reasonable, Opokuya can only submit to Kubi's will and secretly envy Esi's freedom of movement until Esi sells her old car to Opokuya. Like Opokuya, Ali's first wife, Fusena, is no less a loser in the battle of the sexes. When Ali asks Esi to marry him, he takes for granted that there is no need to consult Fusena. And when the elders honor Ali's request to marry Esi despite Fusena's complaint, all she can do is share the older women's shock and resignation concerning the matter. The narrator tells us, "So an understanding that had never existed between them was now born. It was a man's world. You only survived if you know how to live in it as a woman. What shocked the older women, though, was obviously how little had changed for their daughters—school and all" (107). The fact that Fusena was Ali's classmate at a teacher's training college in Ghana apparently does not make any difference at all. Once married, she has suffered a loss of status and become aware of how precarious her relationship to Ali really is: "She had allowed Ali to talk her out of teaching. . . . And now the monster she had secretly feared since London had arrived. Her husband had brought into their marriage a woman who had more education than she did" (100). Despite her jealousy and lame protest, to remain married to Ali, Fusena resorts to accepting the status quo.

And herein lies the central irony of the woman's question: African women may have gained equal access to higher education and attained greater economic power than they had in the past, but sexual inequality remains essentially unchanged. To this issue, Aidoo provides no solution, but through Nana, Aidoo has sounded this call for a fundamental change of attitude in male-female relationships: "Life on this earth need not always be some humans being gods and others being sacrificial animals. Indeed that can be changed. But it would take so much. No, not time. There has always been enough time for anything anyone ever really wanted to do. What it would take is a lot of thinking and a great deal of doing. But one wonders whether we are prepared to tire our minds and our bodies that much. Are we human beings even prepared to try?" (111). The vision that undergirds this proposition for change is clearly African feminist in its humanistic thrust. The ideal world Nana envisions is one in which men and women treat each other as equal human beings, and the proposed change can be effected without bloodshed.

How African men and women respond to Nana's question perhaps will ultimately determine whether any positive change can be achieved. In the meantime, with this novel Aidoo has obliquely sent a fivefold message to her readers: (1) It is naive for African women to think that they can succeed in balancing a happy marriage with a challenging career without compromising their freedom and independence; (2) Society should not dictate that a woman must marry; (3) African men are still accorded more privileges in marriage than are African women; (4) While African men are largely responsible for this inequality, African women themselves—either by acquiescing to the status quo or by perpetuating the language and attitudes of patriarchy—have contributed to its continued existence; and (5) As long as polygamy is sanctioned and practiced by African societies, women will continue to be victimized by its excesses.

Of Aidoo's vision and significant writings, Alice Walker has remarked, "It has reaffirmed my faith in the power of the written word to reach, to teach, to empower and encourage" (Gilbert and Gubar 2348). What Aidoo has written in this novel may not be overtly as empowering as, say, Mariama Bâ's novel *So Long a Letter,* but her message certainly aims to elicit soul-searching on the part of African men and women. One can only hope that it will reach and teach those for whom it is intended.

Works Cited

Aidoo, Ama Ata. *Changes: A Love Story.* London: Women's Press, 1991.

Davies, Carole Boyce. "Feminist Consciousness and African Literary Criticism." *Ngambika: Studies of Women in African Literature.* Ed. Carole Boyce Davies and Anne Adams Graves. Trenton, N.J.: Africa World Press, 1986. 1–23.

Frank, Katherine. "Women Without Men: The Feminist Novel in Africa." *Women in African Literature Today.* Ed. Eldred Jones, Eustace Palmer, and Marjorie Jones. Trenton, N.J.: Africa World Press, 1987. 14–34.

Gilbert, Sandra M., and Susan Gubar, eds. *The Norton Anthology of Literature by Women.* New York: W. W. Norton, 1985.

James, Adeola, ed. *In Their Own Voices: African Women Writers Talk.* Portsmouth, N.H.: Heinemann, 1990.

Nwankwo, Chimalum. "The Feminist Impulse and Social Realism in Ama Ata Aidoo's *No Sweetness Here* and *Our Sister Killjoy.*" *Ngambika: Studies of Women in African Literature.* Ed. Carole Boyce Davies and Anne Adams Graves. 151–59.

Steady, Filomina Chioma. "African Feminism: A Worldwide Perspective." *Women in Africa and the African Diaspora.* Eds. Rosalyn Terborg-Penn, Sharon Harley, and Andrea Benton Rushing. Washington, D.C.: Howard University Press, 1986. 3–24.

7

Snapshots of Childhood Life
in Jamaica Kincaid's Fiction

BRENDA F. BERRIAN

Increasingly, books by English-speaking Caribbean women writers concerned with the female protagonist's recollection of childhood memories and her fight for self-independence within the context of close family relationships have been showing up in bookstores in North America, England, and the Caribbean. One writer—and one who has captured the admiration of well-established writers like Andrew Salkey, Derek Walcott, and Anne Tyler—is Jamaica Kincaid of Antigua. In 1983, Kincaid, then a staff writer for the *New Yorker* magazine, published a collection of ten unusual short stories under the title of *At the Bottom of the River,* seven of which had previously appeared in *The New Yorker.* Two years later, Kincaid's first novel, *Annie John* (1985), one of the three finalists for the 1985 international Ritz Paris Hemingway Award, appeared and became the first novel published by an Antiguan woman.

Upon reading *At the Bottom of the River,* one realizes that the terminology "short stories" needs to be replaced with words like prose poems or poetic vignettes. Kincaid serves up slices of life that are surrealistic images or abstract snapshots of introspective dreamlike cogitations. Demonstrating an uncommon descriptive style of writing, each of the ten stories is like an individual snapshot frozen in place and left to be inspected as a detailed record of a pleasant or an unpleasant moment. Kincaid's ability to pull one into her world of haunting beauty as well as painful legacies of colonialism into photographs from one book to another provides the structure of this paper. Also, Kincaid's preoccupation with the female rite of passage cast against the imposed sociopolitical barriers that inhibit a Caribbean female from being a first-class citizen is explored. Although the female narrator in *At the Bottom of the River* is never identified by name, some concerns and themes are repeated in the character of Annie in *Annie John*. As a result, the two will be referred to as Annie or the narrator/Annie throughout this essay.

Snapshot #1: The Mother

Within the life story of a Caribbean female, the convergence of gender and class in the passage from childhood has its own configuration. Therefore, the portrait of the mother needs to be examined first, for she is essential to her daughter's journey toward self-definition. The mother's major roles are those of a nurturer and a safe refuge and, as Gloria Joseph contends, "To a baby a mother is 'tree of life'; to a mother the infant is a prime responsibility" (76). This strong bond is well illustrated in Kincaid's two books. For example, in "My Mother" from *At the Bottom of the River* there is an outpouring of mutual love, and in "At the Bottom of the River," the eponymous final short story, the narrator/Annie admits: "I see myself as I was as a child. How much I was loved and how much I loved . . . How much I loved myself and how much I was loved by my mother."[1]

This mutual love in *Annie John* is packed symbolically into the mother's trunk, which was transported from Dominica to Antigua. Since Annie's birth, her belongings have been placed in the trunk from which the mother periodically removes an item and proceeds to relate a story connected to it to the daughter. These storytelling sessions are important for they reaffirm Annie's individual and collective family identities. Also, the process of retelling Annie's life becomes an unfolding of the mother's past, which reinforces the close bonding between the two. As Annie remarks, "No small part of my life was so unimportant that she hadn't made a note of it, and now she would tell it to me over and over again."[2]

One of the luxuries of being an only child is that Annie spends most of her time in the exclusive company of her mother, rather than with both parents. However, a disadvantage is that neither parent has close friends or extended family members with whom the daughter can interact, and the father is placed along the periphery. In addition, the mother's relatives reside in Dominica; the paternal grandparents are deceased; and the father is thirty-five years older than the mother. This major age difference, along with carryovers from the father's former liaisons with other women before the parents' marriage, prompts the mother to hide the daughter to avoid an obeah spell. This act of protection—keeping the daughter in the home as much as possible—both isolates and situates them into a temporary kumbla.[3] This action also explains why it is to the mother's bosom that the child presses her face to breathe in strength, wisdom, femininity, and a value system.

Oddly enough, although the mother does not hesitate to talk about Annie's coming of age, she provides an edited version of her own story about why she fled Dominica to come to Antigua. Her story is mainly told by the daughter. Few passages exist in which the mother actually articulates her thoughts. When she does speak, it is to initiate a separation when Annie reaches age twelve. Having become accustomed to wearing clothes made out of the same fabric as her mother's, Annie unexpectedly hears the declaration: "It's time you had your own clothes. You cannot go around the rest of your life looking like little me" (*AJ* 26).

This sudden announcement produces an end to the numerous affectionate embraces and the verbal expressions of love and adoration between mother and daughter. It further propels Annie into a confused state of mixed emotions about love and death dominated by betrayal. Previously, her life had been written by her mother when they shared baths, kisses, cooking lessons, and walks along the ocean. Now, this intense intimacy is being removed and the child is being asked to write her own life without a gradual transition. As a consequence, Annie regards her mother's announcement with trepidation. She fears her mother might die and leave her alone: "My mother and I each grew two faces: one for my father and the rest of the world, and one for us when we found ourselves alone with each other" (*AJ* 87).

Hence, the mother's decision precipitates a series of tantrums and an emotional warfare between her and Annie, which only increases the mother's disfavor. Finally, a resentful Annie rebels against this unwanted change by lying and stealing money from the mother's purse. The message is if you (Mother) do not give me any love, then I will take something of value from you (your money), because I (Annie) deserve it. This defiant behavior is an indirect way of demanding the mother's attention, because Annie wants back her anchor. The unprepared child, on the verge of puberty, is not ready to differentiate herself from her mother.

Snapshot #2: the Rebellious Child

What is traumatic for Annie is that she thinks that she has no identity without her mother. Her harmonious world of doubleness revolved solely around her mother and now it has to be replaced. Lacking strong self-esteem, the twelve-year-old Annie wonders how she can survive on her own. Her fragile self-confidence is shaken to its foundation, because her former beloved mother no longer provides a constant flow of advice, gives no positive reinforcement, and switches from compliments to complaints. On the other hand, Annie's thefts and lies inflict pain on her mother, escalating the tensions and hostilities between them. Incorrectly seeing herself as removed from the pedestal of a well-loved child, Annie feels saddled with the unbearable burden of defining herself so soon.

Although the mother defied her own father's authority and departed his house, she contradicts this decision by trying to mold her child into a proper lady by requiring her to exhibit good manners, attend a Christian church, and obtain a British colonial education. In her desire to raise a daughter to move from a working-class status to a bourgeois one, the mother embraces Victorian double standards that control a woman's body and social conduct. First, she registers a reluctant child for piano lessons, to which the child responds with eating the teacher's plums without permission. Second, the child is required to take courses in etiquette, which result in farting exercises. Not pleased with Annie's inappropriate behavior, the mother delivers a litany of "do's" and "don'ts" in "The Girl," which all begin to stifle Annie's movements, style of dressing, comportment, and eating habits. In retaliation, the daughter tries to break free, as Kincaid had to do in her own life: "I was brought up to be full of good manners and good speech. Where the hell I was going to go with it I don't know" (Edwards 88).

Eventually, in *Annie John*, the mother explodes when she happens to observe a fifteen-year-old Annie engaged in a public conversation with some boys. In a heated exchange, Annie's mother overreacts and calls her a slut; Annie, in turn, goes on the defensive because the mother's tone of voice was "as if I [Annie] were not only a stranger but a stranger that she did not wish to know" (*AJ* 102). Without thinking, and overcome with an uncontrollable anger about the mother's agitated state and unfair reaction, Annie replies, "Well, like father like son, like mother like daughter" (*AJ* 102). After a lengthy silence, her mother responds, "Until this moment, in my whole life I knew without a doubt that, without any exception, I loved you best" (*AJ* 103).

This statement brings Annie to a halt, for, like a typical child, until this confrontation she was only concerned with her own desires. Due to the mother's silence toward and emotional movement away from her, Annie never realized that the separation was just as painful for the mother. The error resides in the mother's failure to articulate these concerns to a bewildered Annie, who finds it impossible to make a quick adjustment. The mother's silence doubly contributes to Annie's negative outburst upon seeing her family structure (in which she was the pivotal figure) disintegrate. As the older narrator/Annie remarks later in "At Last": "Children are so quick: quick to laugh, quick to brand, quick to scorn, quick to lay claim to the open space" (*ABR* 17).

According to Tracey Robinson and Jane Victoria Ward in their study of resistance among African-American female adolescents, there is a tendency for the adolescents to resort to short "quick fix" survival strategies as a chosen mode for social and psychological traps (96). Annie definitely follows this pattern with stealing, lies, and a determination to play marbles underneath the parents' home. Her everyday behavior even becomes erratic when she displays evidence of her menstrual cycle to her classmates in a cemetery, indicating a new chapter in her life and the demise of another. Socially, Annie's sexual awakening and memories of verbal assaults upon her personhood become forces that encourage her to flee the small island.

Needless to say, the mother's reactions to her daughter's entrance into puberty are mixed. On the one hand, she encourages Annie to contemplate marriage and motherhood when she reaches adulthood. Yet, on the other hand, the mother finds it extremely difficult to engage in a woman-to-woman talk about sex. The main message that Annie receives is that double standards exist regarding sexual desires outside of marriage for a woman and a man. If a woman should flirt or enter willingly into a premarital affair, she will be called a slut; whereas men, like the father with his former mistresses, do not acquire a corresponding label. Annie's response to all of this is to decide not to marry.

Regarding her education, Annie dislikes the foreign teachers who insist that she should study and accept the theory that Christopher Columbus discovered Antigua. Her response is to deface the textbook underneath Columbus's picture. The dislike can be mistakenly interpreted by her teachers as a dysfunctional cultural adaptation to induced socio-political pressures from outside; and her behavior results in abetting her own subjugation with the mother's constant surveillance and gaze upon her. There is no escape from the colonial classroom within the private home. Annie's disruptive behavior is classified as aggressive and anti-social because she is fighting two battles—a dual separation from both the mother and from Antigua.

In *Annie John* more so than in *At the Bottom of the River,* the child's world can be seen as the Garden of Eden, a place where innocence reigns and the world is in harmony. Like the original inhabitants of the Garden, Annie John is forced out of her enclosed paradise. Unlike Adam and Eve, however, the child has committed no sin. She is just growing older. Her exile is unexpected and, she feels, undeserved. The departure from para-dise causes Annie to turn on her evictors, her mother and the school-teachers. In her mind, she has done no wrong, so she labels her mother a hypocrite who was kind and loving at the beginning but then, for some unknown reason, turns her back on her child just when she is teetering between the past innocence of childhood and the sexual awakening of adolescence.

For the psychologist E. H. Erickson, the dominant crisis of adoles-cence is finding an identity.[4] In the child's world all people are seen as interrelated; existence is defined by the role one plays in relation to an-other person. For Annie, her parents are mother and father; they have no proper names. Annie, herself, is what her mother and father tell her she is—little Miss. Like the house at the bottom of the river in Kincaid's story of that name, the child's world is one without divisions. The family exists as a whole unit; therefore, during the transition from childhood to adolescence, Annie is obligated to answer for who she is, from where she comes, in what she believes, and what she wants to be. During this pe-riod of self-realization Annie's basic drives, combined with her intellec-tual and physical capabilities, are successfully integrated. This merger leads to a stage during which an ambivalent alternation between reluc-tance and a desire to be independent, tied in with the imagery of shad-ows, darkness, and finally lightness, develops in both *Annie John* and *At the Bottom of the River.* Consequently, in spite of the anger and the con-tradictory feelings for her mother and Antigua, Annie John's life parallels that of Kincaid's admission: "My mother wrote my life and told it to me" (O'Conner 6).

Snapshot #3: Friendships

Kincaid describes the difference in the amount of intimacy found in mother/daughter relationships as opposed to child/friend relationships as a function of coming-of-age. A familiar concept is that adolescents shift from their parents and become subjugated to peer influence. This partially occurs in *Annie John* when Annie quickly seeks to replace her mother's love with that of a female peer. Yet, simultaneously, a high degree of parental influence impacts upon Annie's first and second choices of friends, for they are almost duplicates of the mother. In short, the establishment of her own social network is still connected to, and is an offshoot of, contradictory feelings about love and anger directed at the mother.

As a maturing female, Annie is involved in activity and intimate, intense relationships among a small group of friends. The movement from the closed inhabited world of childhood expands with the impending adolescence; it is characterized with a confusion about which direction should be taken. Since no clear-cut directions are provided by the mother—with the exception of those that dictate ladylike behavior—and the father is removed from the conflict, Annie gravitates toward and cultivates friendships with Sonia, Gweneth, and the Red Girl. The three friends appeal to Annie's developing personality in that they either flatter her ego (Sonia), shower her with support (Gweneth), or challenge societal values placed upon Antiguan female children (the Red Girl).

Annie's first friendship is with Sonia, for she is smaller in size, two years younger, and the class dunce. Intrigued with Sonia's status as the dunce, Annie reaches out and steps into the double roles of mother and tormentor. In "My Mother," the narrator/Annie relates, "I had grown big, but my mother was bigger, and that would always be so" (*ABR* 56). With Sonia, she is taller, intellectually superior, and the leader. The fascination with Sonia ends when Annie hears that Sonia's mother has died in childbirth: "She [Sonia] seemed such a shameful thing, a girl whose mother had died and left her alone in the world" (*AJ* 8). This comment confirms that Annie's relationship with her mother is still so intense that she cannot conceive of a permanent loss or be in the company of someone who has to cope with a mother's death.

The second friendship is established with Gweneth "Gwen" Joseph, because she is someone with whom girlish secrets, kisses, treasures, and the exposure of budding breasts to the moonlight can be shared. Nevertheless, whenever the two friends overhear remarks by their classmates, they exclaim and make gestures that are the exact copy of what they have seen their own mothers do. However, Annie's love for Gwen is so overpowering that it almost brings to an end her fear of death. Instead, new dreams about sharing a house with Gwen surrounded with high hedges to keep out the world intrude when Annie says, "I thought how dull was the fresh pressedness of her uniform, the cleanness of her neck, the neatness of her just combed plaits" (*AJ* 66). The two lovebirds begin to drift apart once Annie meets the exciting Red Girl and starts her menstrual cycle. The same pattern with Sonia is repeated, for Annie excels in school and grows taller than Gwen.

The third friendship marks a departure from Sonia and Gwen, who have both embraced the mother's value system, to one of revolt with the choice of the Red Girl. One way of severing the umbilical cord is for Annie to select someone who is totally opposite to Gwen. What is so appealing about the Red Girl is that she avoids the stereotyped roles and leads a daily life that Annie's mother would find to be offensive. For instance, Annie is drawn to the "wild Red Girl with the bare, flat feet, fingernails that hold at least ten anthills of dirt" (*AJ* 57), and an unbelievable smell "as if she has never taken a bath in her whole life" (*AJ* 57). The Red Girl appeals to Annie's mischievous and rebellious nature, and she dares to do the very things (such as climb a tree better than a boy) that the mother labels as taboos. Together, the two girls explore off-limit areas of the island, play marbles, and hold clandestine meetings at the forbidden lighthouse. This hidden friendship from the mother heightens Annie's search for an alternative to dependency upon parental approval.

Through the friendship with the Red Girl, Annie finds someone with whom she can experience a feminine merging, while at the same time deny feelings of merging with her mother. The Red Girl permits Annie to acknowledge openly that she is neither pleased with the mixed messages that she has been receiving from the mother nor the claustrophobic limitations of living in Antigua. For example, one day the two girls observe a cruise ship passing by Antigua occupied with wealthy passengers; they fantasize about sending confusing signals that will cause the ship to crash. This fantasy is a double rejection of the colonial influence of the British upon Antigua and the internalization of imported Victorian rules of etiquette by the mother. Since the ship will sink into the sea, the narrator/Annie in "At the Bottom of the River" can go live with the red-skinned woman in a mud hut near the sea and watch her own skin turn red. What must be noted is that during her ambivalent struggle for psychological and physical separation, Annie fails to see that the Red Girl represents her mother's double extension. Nobody ever gives voice to all of their thoughts, dreams, or beliefs. Annie dares not bring the Red Girl home to be introduced to her parents and never learns her true name. Within the confines of her own privileged social network, Annie does not introduce the Red Girl to Gwen. Instead, she aligns herself with the Red Girl, who represents and actually lives the life of a rebel. She also uses the friendship to construct intrapsychic and social conditions to battle against the negative forces of colonial oppression reinforced by the mother.

Snapshot #4: The Revision

The constant struggle between asserting her opinions and rejecting those of her mother, along with the strain of conducting a secret friendship, begins to impact upon Annie's physical and mental stamina. The inner conflicts combined with societal restraints evolve into a three-and-a-half-month self-imposed illness. Nature intervenes by providing a nonstop rainfall and a deep, dark hole/void in which she withdraws from her journey of initiation from childhood to adolescence. In "What I Have Been Doing Lately" from *At the Bottom of the River,* the narrator/ Annie observes: "[S]o on purpose I fell in. I fell and I fell, over and over, as if I were an old suitcase. On the sides of the deep hole I could see things written, but perhaps it was a foreign language because I couldn't read them. Still I fell, for I don't know how long" (*ABR* 42). While in the dark hole/void, the narrator/Annie of *At the Bottom of the River* is able to control her subconscious inner world and to decide when to emerge into the conscious outer world: "As I fell I began to see that I didn't like the way falling made me feel. Falling made me feel sick and I missed all the people I had loved. I said, I don't want to fall anymore, and I reversed myself. I was standing again on the edge of the deep hole. I looked at the deep hole and I said you can close up now, and it did" (*ABR* 42). No terror is associated with the dark hole, for it is a solace and brings comfort. Also, in the world of darkness and fantasy there is harmony. In "Blackness" the female narrator/Annie asks, "What is my nature, then?

For in isolation I am all purpose and industry and determination and prudence" (*ABR* 4). To answer this question, a special lens to see into "the darkest of darkness" is needed. The fall experienced by the narrator/ Annie into a dark hole at the bottom of the river symbolizes the downward descent of the adolescent girl from innocence, followed by an upward movement to knowledge of the adult woman. In "At the Bottom of the River" the adolescent girl describes her movement into maturity: "And so emerging from my pit . . . I see things in the light of the lamp, all perishable and transient" (*ABR* 82). This retreat into a dark hole enables Annie to return to the protective infant stage of paradise to illuminate her feminine power through the intervention of the obeah. She is involved in an exploratory stage, struggling to make commitments but has not yet found the right ones.

This disappearance into a void of blackness, which leaves Annie voiceless and bedridden, provides Annie with the necessary time to face reality and to develop her own self-identity separate from her mother. Like a badly focused camera that emits a photo without a clear image, Annie has to erase her angry resentful feelings directed at her mother and accept the mother's otherness as well as her own. Initially, Annie only notices, "My happiness was somewhere deep inside of me, and when I closed my eyes I could even see it. It sat somewhere—maybe in my belly, maybe in my heart; I could not exactly tell" (*AJ* 85).

This short-lived happiness turns into an unhappiness that takes the "shape of a small black ball, all wrapped up in cobwebs." Everything that Annie used to care about turns sour and is cloaked in a misty depression, to the point at which she is unable to see her own hand stretched out in front of her. At first, a British-trained doctor is called in to check Annie and finds nothing wrong with her. Then Ma Chess, the maternal grandmother who arrives unannounced from Dominica on a steamer that was not scheduled for Antigua, comes with her knowledge of the obeah. This unexpected visit, combined with the utilization of Ma Jolie's herbs, helps to bring Annie back to the world of reality.

Kincaid admits that "the role obeah plays in my work is the role it played in my life. I suppose it was just there" (Cudjoe 229). This is exactly what occurs in *Annie John*, because one day Ma Chess was there to heal and comfort Annie by sleeping at the foot of her granddaughter's bed. Helen Pyne Timothy insists that Ma Chess lives in the world of African spirits and is an "African healer, bush medicine specialist, and

Caribbean obeah woman, extremely conscious of the presence of good and evil in life and able to ward off evil" (241). As the grandmother figure who is more rooted in the African continuum than in the European one, Ma Chess is the direct lineage to the mother and becomes her substitute when she sleeps with her body curved like a comma around Annie. By duplicating the womblike enclosure in which Annie had grown within her mother before birth, Annie spiritually experiences the double maternal strength of Ma Chess and her mother. This psychic and physical journey into the past and another reality with the foremothers is a return to the present. With the grandmother's and mother's help, the Afrocentric importance and centrality of obeah among Caribbean women is validated.

Annie cannot deny her grandmother's mysterious power and connection with the spirits during her journey toward womanhood. The trip back to her conception and into the traditional past with the "mothers" is both crucial and necessary for her recovery to transcend imposed systemic barriers. The descent into the dark hole ends with the arrival of sunshine when, interestingly enough, the first thing that the cured Annie does is to focus upon four family photographs. A visual recording of familial incidents that have been touched by colonialism, these photographs begin to contract, expand, and perspire until they emit an unbearable odor. Suffering from vertigo and the desire to erase the colonialism that has touched her family (white communion dress, wedding dress and cricket outfit), Annie washes the pictures. During the washing process Annie erases what has distressed the rebellious self to transform herself into an older and wiser person. To explain this ritual, Wendy Dutton comments, "She treats the photographs as human and thereby expresses a desire to experience life to its fullest, to go below the surface, as she does in *At the Bottom of the River*" (407). After all, demonstrating her newly found convictions, Annie does not erase the section of a photo that shows her wearing shoes that had been termed unsuitable by the mother.

By delving beneath the surface in "The Mother," the narrator/Annie recognizes the strength her mother has offered. In connection with a new sense of anticipation she finally accepts that the subject of her mother is a difficult and contradictory one, but they will always be linked together: "What peace came over me then, for I could not see where she left off and I began, or where I left off and she began . . . As we walk through the rooms, we merge and separate, merge and separate; soon we shall enter the final stage of our evolution" (*ABR* 60). In her efforts to revise her life after a three-and-a-half-month illness toward reaching a healthy feminine and sexual perspective, the narrator/Annie pronounces her name: "I claim these things then-mine-and now feel myself grow solid and complete, my name filling up my mouth" (*ABR* 82).

Obviously, Annie's psychic illness causes her to accept her body with its normal functions. Previously, she had not liked her prepubescent awkwardness, but the lengthy and healthy illness has transformed the ugly duckling into a "tall, graceful, and altogether beautiful young woman." In "At the Bottom of the River," the narrator/Annie glorifies in her body's beauty as well: "I stood as if I were a prism, many-sided and transparent, refracting and reflecting light as it reached me, light that never could be destroyed. And how beautiful I became" (*ABR* 80). The old, hated body has become a plus. Fully recovered and a little defiant, Annie walks deliberately with her back curved in an exaggerated stoop to intimidate her schoolmates: "I had made my presence so felt that when I recovered myself my absence was felt too" (*AJ* 129).

Snapshot #5: Carving Her Own Turf

The demarcating line between adolescence and adulthood is revealed in the final chapter of *Annie John*. Here, the eighteen-year-old Annie is cast in the role of the nurturer, for she caters to and tightens her arms around her mother as she walks to the jetty to depart for England. Her friendships with Sonia and Gwen had prepared her for this role when each time she remarked on her height and the fact that she had been the initiator of each relationship. The mother's betrayal is placed into the background, because the role reversal has the mother leaning upon her daughter for comfort and support. This is an unsettling observation for Annie, and the actual walk away from her parents and Antigua is overwhelming. Compared to the shedding of old skin by replacing it with a new one, Annie, at last, is ready to embrace her future alongside the past and the present. By emerging from the pit and uttering her name aloud, which is the same as her mother's, Annie is ready to assert her own power.

In her mental photo album, Kincaid turns to the past in an effort to gain an understanding of the troubled present and the promising future. In and through the narrator/Annie of *At the Bottom of the River* and *Annie*

John, photographs of negating, transcending, and accepting the present are taken. The collision between Annie's evolving self and the Antiguan society's imposed values upon female identity occurs consistently throughout the two books. By resisting the mother's inherited Caribbean and colonial value system of what constitutes a proper lady, Annie has taken a political stance against that which destroys female affirmation and self-determination. The journey through the void is a psychic stratagem to force Annie to appraise her real position in society in connection with her acceptance that her mother no longer cultivates her aspirations. Just as her mother left Antigua, she has to be uprooted and estranged from her family and Antigua in order to follow her destiny.

The two books under discussion are stories of triumphant identity. Both books re-create childhood and the sociopolitical setting of Antigua to understand why the narrator/Annie decides to leave.[5] A restless seeker, Annie learns what it is to be a woman in the context of personal identification with her mother, grandmother, foremothers, and female friends. The narrator/Annie has explored her identity formation by adopting behaviors and making lifestyle choices. Her resistance for liberation has transformed her into a woman who recognizes clearly the pitfalls of the "mother school" society to create her own sickness as a therapy for female empowerment. Finally, the narrator/Annie's awareness of self is a transparently joyful one, a refraction of sunlight, and a reflection of many colors onto the lens of a camera that clicks to take snapshots from childhood to adolescence and womanhood.

Notes

1. Jamaica Kincaid, "At the Bottom of the River," from *At the Bottom of the River,* 73. All further citations use the abbreviation *ABR* where needed for clarity.

2. Jamaica Kincaid, *Annie John,* 22. All further references use the abbreviation *AJ* where needed for clarity.

3. The kumbla is a term coined by the Jamaican writer Erna Brodber in her novel *Jane and Louisa Will Soon Come Home* to designate a protective enclosure for women.

4. E. H. Erickson, *Identity Youth and Crisis.* Various adolescent stages are described in the book.

5. On pages 127 and 128 of *Annie John,* Annie declares her longing to be in a place where nobody knows a thing about her and likes her for that reason. She finds the whole world of Antigua to be an unbearable burden.

Works Cited

Brodber, Erna. *Jane and Louisa Will Soon Come Home*. London: New Beacon, 1981.

Cudjoe, Selwyn. "Jamaica Kincaid and the Modernist Project: An Interview." *Caribbean Women Writers: Essays from the First International Conference.* Wellesley, Mass.: Calaloux, 1990. 215–32.

Dutton, Wendy. "Merge and Separate: Jamaica Kincaid's Fiction." *World Literature Today.* 63 (Summer 1989): 406–10.

Edwards, Audrey. "Jamaica Kincaid Writes of Passage." *Essence* (May 1991): 88.

Erickson, E. H. *Identity:Youth and Crisis.* New York: Norton, 1968.

Joseph, Gloria. "Black Mothers and Daughters: Their Role and Function in American Society." *Common Differences: Conflicts in Black and White Feminist Perspectives.* Ed. Gloria Joseph and Jill Lewis. New York: Anchor, 1981. 75–126.

Kincaid, Jamaica. *Annie John.* New York: Farrar, Straus and Giroux, 1985.

———. *At the Bottom of the River.* New York: Farrar, Straus and Giroux, 1983.

O'Conner, Patricia. "My Mother Wrote My Life." *New York Times Book Review* (7 April 1985): 6.

Robinson, Tracey, and Jane Victoria Ward. "A Belief in Self Far Greater than Anyone's Disbelief: Cultivating Resistance among African American Female Adolescents." *Women and Therapy* 11, 3/4 (1991).

Timothy, Helen Pyne. "Adolescent Rebellion and Gender Relations in *At the Bottom of the River* and *Annie John.*" *Caribbean Women Writers.* Ed. Selwyn Cudjoe. Wellesley, Mass.: Calaloux, 1990. 233–42.

Fire and Ice

The Socioeconomics of Romantic Love in *When Rocks Dance* by Elizabeth Nunez-Harrell

THELMA B. THOMPSON-DELOATCH

Somewhere among the older Jamaican rhymes and quips is, or was, this couplet:

Men are dogs, they are made to roam
Women are cats to stay at home.

To the Caribbean woman writer, the deeper cultural norm that supports such a notion is well known and well examined. It is the basis for Susheila Nasta's observation that "the post-colonial woman writer is not only involved in making herself heard, in changing the architecture of male-centered ideologies and languages. . . . [S]he has also to subvert and demythologize indigenous male writings and traditions which seek to label her" (xv).

Critical exegeses on Caribbean women's writings are replete with examinations of the contrasting issues represented in this literature: past/present/future, oppressor/victim, youth/age, native/foreign. But one focus that marks the emergence of Caribbean women's fiction as significant is the varied responses to the female dilemma and their varied strategies for resistance and survival.

In Elizabeth Nunez-Harrell's novel *When Rocks Dance,* seemingly, a conscious effort is made to include the various oppositional forces that tend to appear in the postcolonial writings. The novel takes its integrity from conflicts whose roots rest in the colonial system; race; and gender, class, politics, religion, culture, history, and geography. Romantic in the classical sense, the novel balances the mythical with the historic and sociological concepts of womanhood and seeks to resolve selected conflicts through very old methods of land tenure now seized by new hands—the black woman's hands.

The ownership of land has been a fundamental manifestation of power in most societies. The land, mother earth, has been the source of economic, social, and political might, as well as a cause for war for eons, and it is Ileana Rodriguez who best captures the concept as it relates to colonial societies. She writes, "In all writings on 'nation,' there is a truth which some locate in the strict terrain of language and words . . . [O]thers, like myself, situate [this truth] in the discussion of land, territory, and land tenure, that is, in the political arena of struggle. . . . Both theories, one linguistic, the other political, fight for the representation of nation. But this 'nation' . . . is a nation in which neither Indians, nor blacks nor women have a space" (4).

Elizabeth Nunez-Harrell and other female Caribbean writers are settling the linguistic notion, but the political fight for recognition and representation is often explored in fictional constructs such as *When Rocks Dance*. In this case, the land supplants the love bond in marriages and unions. Used as a substitute for romantic love and its attendant features, the possession of land fails as a sustaining basis for family life, even if it offers socioeconomic place or space to the characters. In some significant way, by grounding the novel in the land, Nunez-Harrell calls attention to the most enduring recorded problem of humankind, the cause of feuds, disputes, and wars, ancient and modern—land, territory, borders, the economic significance to individuals and nations, and the national "love" relationships based upon resources.

When Rocks Dance is an essentially feminist novel, taking its name from an African proverb that posits that men are like eggs while women are the rocks of society. It asks, also, "when rocks dance, what right have you among them if you are an egg?" (298), suggesting a selective fraternization of the sexes. The plot reveals women who maintain equilibrium, while the male characters suffer emotional disintegration as the complex pressures of Caribbean life become personal. This classical, romantic novel explores "the region's historical conflicts" through romantic love and exposes the eternal cultural resistance to colonial hegemony that exists and persists in most colonized states regardless of the pronouncements of love, church, and government.

The novel opens with the common-law relationship of an old English cocoa planter, Hrothgar, and a young, shrewd Trinidadian woman,

Emilia, who becomes his lover two months after her twelfth birthday and after the death of her mother, the cook. "He promised that if she would bear him a son, old man that he was, he would will his cocoa estate and his house to her upon his death. . . . That promise made her endure long nights of his body pressing roughly into hers. . . . She stayed in Hrothgar's bed to reclaim the land" (*WRD* 12, 13). The image of the oppressor is a vivid one and the idea of the colonist as a material rapist has been well discussed elsewhere in postcolonial nonfiction.

Such situations give rise to critical observations such as that of Rodriguez, who observes that, "tied more to Independence and the Founding Fathers of the land, the modern woman finds that the only exit possible is through money. Capital/dowry provides the vocabulary for discussing the relation of a marriage/nation-state" (xv). The truism of the interrelatedness of socioeconomics and romantic unions is carried out from the beginning of the novel with Emilia's resolve, to the end with Virginia's visit to the landowning Indian.

Founded upon utilitarian principles, Emilia's and Hrothgar's relationship epitomizes the crux of colonialism, exploitation, and greed. It is not surprising that Emilia's eight sons (four pairs of twins) die, or that upon the advice of the Ibo obeah man they are abandoned soon after their birth. The only child Emilia manages to raise is a daughter, Marina, who survives because she is imbued with the spirit of eight men—her dead brothers, given back to the land.

Beyond the fact that twins die because children need love to survive emotionally, Emilia's twin boys are used as currency, "blood money" to purchase the valued cocoa land from the perceived "oppressor." Emilia's aim now is to reclaim from Hrothgar that which he has seized—mother earth and herself, the boys' birth mother. Emilia's daughter—without realizing that her mother's lot was not by choice, as hers is—later reminds Emilia that there is a name for women who exact a price for their sexual services.

Unaware of Emilia's needs, the proud and elated Hrothgar, the aged father of twin sons for the fourth time, held high hopes that these boys would continue his tradition. Hrothgar "called them his cocoa planters. He made them over-seers. . . . Hrothgar penned his will. . . . The boys would be his heirs. They would send the 'Portogee' trader to the devil and make the Negroes till the soil" (18). Knowing from the obeah man, however, that these boys would not live, Emilia leaves them in the forest in an attempt to rid herself of a curse. She seduces Hrothgar with obeah and in the heat of his passion informs him that the twins are "sleeping in the cocoa patch." This knowledge turns the old man's love to hate even as his hope turns to madness and hers to despair, for male heirs are never to be his and the land was never to be hers. Her contract to deliver live sons is as broken as her husband's last hope of having heirs. The nothingness of Hrothgar's later life then manifests itself in hatred and bitterness toward Emilia and the girl child, Marina. What began as nurturing, cooking food, mutual convenience, dreams unfulfilled—"a marriage" based on market principles—becomes a relationship in atrophy, withered, sick, and dead.

To Hrothgar, the females (wife and child) are not factors in the land tenure system. He feels no responsibility for their well-being, nor does the larger society, including the church, which acts as facilitator for the total and cyclical abuse of the female in this novel.

The female Caribbean fiction writer may be at an observation point at which cultural realities overcome any instinct to label the genesis of the devalued female in Caribbean society. Critics such as Carole Boyce Davies and Elaine Savory Fido point to the Caribbean's cultural history as possible fictional fodder. They record, "There were numerous signs of the conditions of women which were depressing: street insult and verbal and physical beatings from men; women with scores of children who were forced to beg the 'children's father' for support at his workplace on pay day before the money was spent; girls of promise getting pregnant and thereafter losing all the brilliance they had previously shown, sinking into a round of baby-making for men who saw sex as recreation and women as conquests; all this crowned by an oral culture which endorsed this behavior" (xiv).

In response to this literary "burden," newer female Caribbean writers are addressing the topic. Pamela Mordecai and Betty Wilson identify a positive response that focuses on the value of ordinary human beings, "the worth of male to female persons and vice versa; the worth of black persons (or other persons of color) to other black persons and to white persons" (*Her True-True Name* xiii). Although from the perspective of the fictional, white, colonial man, the women were chattel for his comforts and of little emotional significance to him, Emilia was not passive in victim status. She valued herself and her child and became proactive to ensure her daughter's economic well-being. What Ileana Rodriguez found to be true in Teresa de la Parra's *Ifigenia* applies to Marina's portrayal: "Without money, the future vanishes, for the absence of money is poverty and poverty means 'complete dependency' and 'humiliation and pain' . . . happiness, freedom and success are synonyms for money" (62). Also, Rodriguez reports, "Body is capital. The poor, declassé, disinherited and dowryless woman must think in terms of the best use of that capital" (65).

This thinking is manifested in Emilia's own life of total dependency and, naturally, forms the frame of reference for her daughter's future. Emilia's daughter, Marina—spirit child, at once European and African, stereotypically materialistic, sensual and mysterious—marries Antonio de Balboa for his land, despite a curse upon him that causes his three previous wives to perish in childbirth. "Marina's mind clung to just one word that she had heard. Land. de Balboa had land. . . . 'How can I meet him?' Emilia sighed, relieved. 'It will be arranged,' she said" (43).

Equally self-centered, Antonio de Balboa, preoccupied with "a will to live, an innate desire to reproduce, a muffled drumming from the world of his African ancestors that told him without logic or understanding that Marina would save him . . . married the woman" (55). Struck silent by Marina's height and arrogance, her golden hair, grey eyes, almost white skin, "breasts projecting forward ready for an argument, [and] a backside high and rigid," Antonio marries Marina not only because of physical attraction, but "because in the sanctum of his brain where his mind was free from the primitive grappling of the intellect, he knew passionately that this woman would save him" (56).

Proceeding from these motivations, the union of Marina and Antonio is plagued with several conflicts: differences in religion, interferences by mothers-in-law, periodic rejection, problems of self-esteem, problems of class differences, difference of opinions on the purpose and value of land and of heritage, and lack of a unified vision. Although Marina does survive the difficult delivery of her twin children and succeeds in breaking the curse on young de Balboa, her relationship with her husband is merely a physical one. The emotional and psychological distance that separates this couple is enough to lead each of them to the harsh introspection and loneliness attendant to unions founded without love. Marina's constant fear that Antonio's mother will sell the fifteen acres of oil-drenched cocoa land pushes her to torment and taunt her husband about his seemingly incestuous relationship with his mother, his restrictive religion, and worse yet, about his motivation for his marriage to her. Marina fails to see the familial similarities; that like her mother and like her husband, she too is confused about romantic love and the benefits that accrue therefrom. Her major motive for marriage was economics; his, social acceptance.

Antonio de Balboa, the product of a loveless marriage, is twice cursed. His father, an excommunicated Portuguese priest, marries his mother, Virginia, the Black adopted daughter of a white English couple. Distressed at the adoptive father's advances to the regal Virginia, Mrs. Smith, the mother, arranges to give to the ex-priest, de Balboa, a handsome dowry of land if he would marry her adopted daughter and, thus, remove the carnal temptation from her husband's presence. On the following one-sided agreement, the union was made and de Balboa tells Virginia his terms: "I'll not sleep with you as man and wife. I won't share your bed. You may do as you please, I will not have her sell you to me like a lump of coal. I'll have no hand in her slave traffic. Your color offends her. I'll give you the land too. It's your right as her daughter" (60).

Yet the reader realizes that Virginia pays a much higher price to enter this marriage than the dowry her "mother" gave. Her new husband could not keep all his promises. Indeed, on the wedding night, "his stoic detachment oozing swiftly out of his soul," he took her in a "frenzy . . . as though he had lost every ounce of his rational self, his Christian morality" (61).

This is the story of Antonio's conception and the only sexual encounter between his parents and practically the only connection. Years later, the embittered Virginia realizes that her son, Antonio, has forgiven his father for the twelve years of silence and rejection. She challenges her son, "Tell me what should I have understood. You talked to him. Tell me . . . tell me, how do you think he intended for us to live? To eat? . . . I managed. I sold chickens, ducks. I taught school. I managed" (68, 69). It is significant that Virginia focuses on the economics of their existence, not on the emotional and physical needs.

Raised in the darkness and discomfort of his parents' loveless marriage and caught, forever, in his attempt to compensate to his mother for his father's shortcomings, Antonio is overwhelmed by the problems in his own relationship. Cerebral and idealistic, he loses focus, loses control of his life, loses touch with his environment, and learns that good intentions cannot sustain a relationship. When he sets sail for Europe it is not as an adventurer, but as a felon, a loser, a deserter—a man who has failed in his most important ventures in life, a man who tried to establish his sons' economic security through desperate reaction rather than rational proaction. He, a father, a son, a husband, once a respected school principal, must "return," as his father could never do, to Europe, where he will be nothing. His twin sons are left to be raised as he and Marina were raised: fatherless, by a mother who will have to "father" them, despite the fact that a birth father is alive.

Antonio leaves the country, however, with an understanding that could come only from personal experience: "He wished he could tell her [his mother] yes, his father was a he-goat, a ram goat, a hypocritical, self-righteous ram-goat, but he could not. Was it because he too understood how the flesh, the human condition, could so mercilessly remind a man that he is a man, not a god who can control his passion. . . . Was it that he understood that his father was a man although a priest? Antonio's long weeks of abstinence, self-denial, his refusal to make love to Marina had taught him that the body could betray the mind and desire what the mind had decided it would not choose" (210).

How did Antonio arrive at this position from where he was at the beginning of his union with Marina, when "the heavens saw the son of that Portuguese religious dissenter . . . make love without restraint or caution as though the very act and the woman he penetrated were all that gave his life meaning?" (121) One answer is found in Edward Kamau Brathwaite's theory of the duality of love. In his musings on developing a Caribbean aesthetic, Brathwaite invented the term "the love axe/l" (186). This concept of love as a central Caribbean driving force, the central emotion that moves life along (self-love included), also embraces the idea that love acts as an axe, a tool that cuts, chops, breaks open, damages, and reveals an inner core, and that may even "draw blood." Romantic love as represented in Nunez-Harrell's novel bears out Brathwaite's musings. At the core of the novel, as well as at the periphery, the plot and subplots, the major and minor characters, are all connected by romantic love (an axel); yet it is romantic love that fails, that goes to a state of atrophy—axed.

In the cases of the three female characters under discussion, the modern feminine perspective is at once dramatized and negated. While the women are left to any means possible for their survival and that of their offspring, they are somewhat unhappily free from restrictive notions of marriage. Davies and Fido observe that the "strength of the [Caribbean] women surely comes from necessity, from being unable to walk away from being left to raise the children" (xv). Mark A. McWatt, also writing of the Caribbean wife and mother, found that "it is a painfully ambiguous role, for it is that towards which the woman generally aspire, and yet, it is the role that most relentlessly traps and diminishes them [*sic*]" (228).

In her critical evaluation of *When Rocks Dance,* Leah Creque-Harris observes that "none of the male-female relationships in this book are romantically fulfilling" (163). What was not mentioned is that neither the male nor the female characters seemed disturbed about the romantic atrophy in their lives. The women, however, constantly contemplate the material hardships. The consistent irony on the romantic love axel of the plot is the successful demonstration that each of the partners in a union has experienced sexual fulfillment with the mate, and in Virginia's case, outside the marriage. It seems, then, that there is deliberate effort to show, first, that sexual fulfillment by itself is not sufficient to sustain a marriage or a union. Second, the developments demonstrate that the romantic attraction was not the grounds for these unions; therefore that rubric can hardly be used to evaluate their success or failure. It is the land and its significance upon which these unions were erected, and as the land went so, too, did the "love." Finally, the novel overtly shows the impossibility for romantic love to thrive in the presence of other overwhelming personal, social, and economic problems. The fictional landscape in the individual lives mirrors the larger political and cultural dilemma of the Caribbean, captured well by Antonio Benitez-Rojo when he sets forth the dilemma:

> I start from the belief that "Caribbeanness" is a system full of noise and opacity . . . a chaotic system beyond the total reach of any specific kind of knowledge or interpretation of the world. To my way of thinking, no perspective of human thought . . . can by itself define the Caribbean's complex sociocultural interplay. We need all of them at the same time. . . . [I]f . . . we study the Caribbean by paying attention only to the impact of Afro-Caribbean beliefs upon its social and political structures, we are only looking at one among many of the area's fundamental aspects. Moreover, if we were to study the Caribbean's cultural history only in terms of the clash of

two discourses that speak in terms of race, or class, or colonialism, or economic development, we would be also studying dynamics that are fundamental to the system. . . . [C]onstruction of these polarized models constitutes a reduction that is characteristic of modernity, but it is a reduction that had persisted with uncommon tenacity in the area's histography and its literature. (255, 256)

When Rocks Dance gives credence to Benitez-Rojo's theory of chaos and helps to provide reasons for a Caribbean dialectic that ignores established paradigms reserved for more homogeneous societies. Furthermore, the chaos theory provides grounds for Merle Hodge's more pointed conclusions expressed in her landmark essay, "The Shadow of the Whip: A Comment on Male-Female Relations in the Caribbean." Hodge posits that as a residue of slavery and continued colonialism, mutual respect was lost between enslaved men and women and their offspring. The man, unable to provide for his family and take leadership in his affairs, was reduced to the single role of impregnating. The children were/are left to be raised by a female, a mother, grandmother, older sister, aunt, or stranger. "Women became mother and father to the race" (115).

In exploring the complications of romantic love, *When Rocks Dance* extends itself to include the Indian. The fictional situation supports the thesis that Indians, too, suffered from the cultural mores relevant to gender and class. They, too—brought to the Caribbean as indentured labor, to work on sugar plantations—suffered dislocation of family and other humiliations.

On the fringes of the novel, the ambitious East Indian character, Ranjit, becomes interested in learning to read. For one year, under the private tutelage of schoolteacher Virginia de Balboa, he learns much and falls in love with her vitality. Like the other love unions in the novel, Ranjit's marriage is also in that dreaded state of catastrophe. The narrator summarizes his condition and his wife's: "Indira, Ranjit's wife, bore the pain of gossip well. Her job was to bear children, something she also did well. She never spoke to her husband on any topic other than food, clothing, and shelter. . . . None of the East Indian women around her thought that their husband's business was any of theirs. The women had their role and the men theirs" (*WRD* 131). Social practice and the inferiority placed upon Indians in that society had bred such misconception "that the possibility of romantic love between Virginia and Ranjit was not ever a consideration. . . . A Negro woman and an Indian man just didn't see each other that way" (*WRD* 131).

Nunez-Harrell breaks the false barrier of interracial love in several directions and, for a brief moment, shows that some of the characters are caught by the "love axe/l." Aware of the atrophy that has set into their lives, they further realize that it is "what they call love" that has died, but not themselves as lovers. Thus, Nunez-Harrell reveals the naked axel of love in atrophy, the naked truth of human beings who are alive yet dead. The narrator provides again a front seat to this scenario, emphasizing at once the emotional neediness and the capacity to find ecstasy that ironically resides in these outwardly "cold" characters. The tension in the plot is heightened by this and other contradictions. Here, the women characters are juxtaposed for emphasis: "Indira didn't count on the longing for something more than a bed partner that festered in her husband's heart. Nor could she know the pain of loneliness that Virginia suffered because she . . . had no bed partner. . . . For one short evening, with her husband wandering on the beach . . . indifferent to his wife's activities, Virginia knew sexual fulfillment. . . . They [Virginia and Ranjit] clung to each other like lost souls adrift on a raging sea. Unbridled passion, emotions pent up in marriages that they both thought had cooled desire, raged through them. . . . [S]he too felt the flow, the burning fire, the sweet indescribable pleasure" (131).

Experiencing cold, empty marriages, each of the characters in this novel is portrayed, at least once, as a person fully equipped and capable of enjoying "love" physically. The novelist goes to great pains to disclose possible underlying reasons for the "loveless" situations that exist. These, besides the focus on economics and land, range from Father de Balboa's rejection of his slavery-supporting church, his renunciation and denunciation of that church, to his son Antonio's confusion about his role in life. While the novel depicts women as primary "sufferers"—an important Caribbean term—there is no doubt that Nunez-Harrell attempts to capture the torment of the men, the husbands, thereby attempting to present the entire picture of pain. The axe of love dictates and mothers are left with the children, who, like Antonio and Marina, endure the pain of both their parents, the pain of a burdened, bitter mother, and an "absent," maybe idealized, father. This experience is indelible and the outcome unsure, although there is a suggestion in the novel that the pattern is cyclical.

Dubem Okafor, writing of West Indian and West African fiction, calls for a change to be effected only by a "death" of the old ways: "The quest for a unity of being, for psychic and cultural identity, for social and moral redemption . . . will avail us nothing, if at the end of the journeys . . . we are made to begin again because we lack love. It seems that West Africa and the West Indies are bound together by the common fate of the absence of love and the frantic quest for it. . . . Hence a second death is necessary for a realization of the promise of fulfillment, for the unification of being, complete psychic and social regeneration . . . divested of all racial and cultural antagonism and polarization" (172).

It seems that Nunez-Harrell has begun to effect that death of which Okafor speaks. By reaffirming and respecting Emilia's African roots and reality, returning the Amerindian to his territory, and returning Antonio to his "father's land" (Europe); by anchoring Marina on land, revitalizing Virginia, and returning her to the farm, the land, and to Ranjit's love; some death/healing is in process. This is not only the psychological unity of the characters' being but also a revitalization of the self brought about by acceptance of the self, love of the self, respect for and by the self and, thus, of others. This rebirth or epiphany achieves what the Caribbean poet/prophet Brathwaite describes as "those who are no longer concerned with colonial despair, with our having 'nothing,' our 'exile' but with a total roots directed (Emilia) redefinition of ourselves: an aesthetic: word act, vision, value system. The results are still tentative . . . the race between achievement and chaos is still very much on. But the gate is there, broken but open" (185). The economic factor is de-emphasized. Reconciliation to "having nothing" may be a more healthy basis for romance.

Elizabeth Nunez-Harrell helps to make a track through Brathwaite's "gate." By focusing on the economics of love, its mutations and connections, she performs an autopsy on the dead relationships, not so much in hopes of reviving the dead, but to assist the living. Even from the dust of the marriages discussed, some love arises. It may be the love of self. Deceptively, the Caribbean, a naturally beautiful yet economically impoverished region beset by lingering problems and human misery, remains a port of call for the "Love Boat"—those who are seeking love, those who have it, lost it, found it, or desire it. Each may join in the "kumina," when rocks dance. Frail "eggs" may shatter, but the weak may—like Ranjit and Antonio—survive and join Virginia, Emilia, and Marina. They may grow strong from the exercise of love. They may find their own steps and rhythm in the dance; they may hear the music through their experiences; and, most important, they will know that there is no score, no stage directions, no ringmaster save themselves. Like the fire and ice of love, the axe and axe/l of love, the dance must end if another is to begin. And each dancer must take his or her own step to and with the partner, regardless of the setting, be it ballroom or backyard bacchanal.

The symbolism inherent in the title of the novel can then be interpreted on yet another level to mean that continuous breaking of eggs will reduce the ability to provide new life. After all, a rock is tough, but it is lifeless. The dance polishes the rocks, smooths them, refines them externally, but leaves them encrusted with lost life elements, old possibilities resting upon sharp-edged broken shells. The ideal outcome is to soften rocks and harden eggshells, to reevaluate the attempt to decode natural love by economic laws.

In his commentary on the background of the West Indian novel, Kenneth Ramchand makes the following prescriptive observation: "Instead of creating characters whose positioning on one side or other of the region's historical conflicts consolidates those conflicts and does violence to the make-up of 'the person,' the West Indian novelist should set out to visualize a fulfillment, a reconciliation in the person and throughout society, of the parts of a heritage of broken cultures. . . . This vision and a conception of wider possibilities and relationships still remains [sic] unfulfilled today in the Caribbean" (10). *When Rocks Dance* takes up Ramchand's old gauntlet through its treatment of romantic love. After exposing conflicting motivations and stormy violence in several relationships founded upon materialism, the novel, through subtle moral decoding, settles some storms and attempts to effect reconciliations. And it does so not so much with mates, but with the self, where both healing and fulfillment begin, as all the characters learn.

Works Cited

Brathwaite, Edward Kamau. "The Love Axe/l: Developing a Caribbean Aesthetic." *Bim* (June 1978): 186.
Benitez-Rojo, Antonio. "The Polyrhythmic Paradigm: The Caribbean and the Postmodern Era." *Race, Discourse, and the Origins of the Americas.* Ed. Vera L. Hyatt and Rex Nettleford. Washington, D.C., and London: Smithsonian Institution Press, 1995. 255–67.

Creque-Harris, Leah. "*When Rocks Dance*: An Evaluation." *Caribbean Women Writers: Essays from the First International Conference*. Ed. Selwyn R. Cudjoe. Wellesley: Calaloux Publications, 1990. 159–63.

Davies, Carole Boyce, and Elaine Savory Fido, eds. *Out of the Kumbla: Caribbean Women and Literature*. Trenton: Africa World Press, 1990.

Hodge, Merle. "The Shadow of the Whip: A Comment On Male-Female Relations in the Caribbean." *Is Massa Day Dead: Black Moods in The Caribbean*. Ed. Orde Combs. Garden City: Anchor Books, 1974. 111–18.

McWatt, Mark A. "Wives and Other Victims." Davies and Fido. 223–35.

Mordecai, Pamela, and Betty Wilson, eds. *Her True-True Name: An Anthology of Women's Writing from the Caribbean*. Portsmouth: Heinemann, 1990.

Nasta, Susheila, ed. *Motherlands: Black Women's Writings from Africa, the Caribbean and South Asia*. New Brunswick: Rutgers University Press, 1992.

Nunez-Harrell, Elizabeth. *When Rocks Dance*. New York: G. P. Putnam's Sons, 1986.

Okafor, Dubem. "The Themes of Disintegration and Regeneration in the West Indian and West African Novel." *Bim* (June 1978): 158–73.

Ramchand, Kenneth. *The West Indian Novel and Its Background*. Exeter, N.H.: Heinemann, 1983.

Rodriguez, Ileana. *House/Garden/Nation: Space, Gender, and Ethnicity in Postcolonial Latin American Literatures by Women*. Translated by Robert Carr and Ileana Rodriguez. Durham and London: Duke University Press, 1994.

PART 3

War on All Fronts

Race, Class, Sex, Age, and Nationality

Whether born in Dakar, Kingston, New York, or London, African ancestry, economic status, and gender govern the crucial aspects of a woman's life such as her educational level, her personal health, and her childbearing. Even in the United States, where class distinctions are sometimes not as apparent, class determines the amount and the extent of health care given to women and their children. This is particularly important, since Black women head the majority of households with children in African American communities, and the greatest percentage of these female-headed families live at or below poverty level. Novelist/sociologist Erna Brodber states in her essay included here that "a tendency toward matrifocality" in family structure also exists throughout the Caribbean. Indeed, female-headed families are a constant in many areas of the diaspora. The interlocking factors of race, class, and gender help to keep these women and their families impoverished. Their lives exist as a challenge against that poverty, a personal war that consumes and sometimes overtakes its real-life sheroes.

The essays in this section illustrate how Africana writers contextualize these socioeconomic factors and develop them from the personal realm to the political sphere through depictions of women's modern reality and their relationships to the broader community and state. As the writers and the critics assert, exploitation of women is political, a rationing of power. It is not incidental, consequently, that the very nature of their writing about women who defy social tradition, criticize imperialism, or succumb to exploitation intimates the political nature of the texts.

The first two essays in the section exhibit the development of the personal to the political in their disclosure of the social practices that have the potential for limiting and even destroying young women's lives. Janice Liddell's essay, "Agents of Pain and Redemption in Sapphire's *Push*," brings the focus of incest and extreme exploitation of an adolescent female to its broader social implications. Through close examination of Sapphire's explicit narrative, with its rare portrait of mother-as-monstrosity, the essay fairly indicts the abusive parents and the public child-welfare system's adherence to values and rituals bound to race, class, and gender, which foster cruel and negligent treatment of poor Black girls like Sapphire's protagonist, Precious.

Examining the defiance of tradition through the quest for romantic love, Yakini Kemp's "Romantic Love and the Individual" looks at the tenuous relationship between the feminist and the romantic vision in Buchi Emecheta's *The Bride Price*, Mariama Bâ's *So Long a Letter*, and Bessie Head's *Maru*. Kemp concludes that for the formally educated African women protagonists in these three novels, romantic love-choice becomes an expected and an actualized right for the individual.

The third and fourth essays in the section cover forceful political works by Ama Ata Aidoo and Merle Collins. More than chronicles of individuals, these works speak to the question of nationalism and the woman writer's political consciousness. Gay Wilentz's "The Politics of Exile: Ama Ata Aidoo's *Our Sister Killjoy*" argues that Aidoo does what few writers have done: "questions certain prescribed theories of exile." By doing so, Aidoo commits an act of defiance and adds the rare voice of the African woman exile to the continuum.

Carolyn Cooper's "'Sense Make Befoh Book': Grenadian Popular Culture and the Rhetoric of Revolution in Merle Collins's *Angel* and the *Colour of Forgetting*" cogently examines folk expressions as political critique and commentary. Cooper cites the wisdom of the women and men who actively participate in the rebellion. Their folk sayings and original songs are sharp political commentary. According to Cooper, Merle Collins's novels become political commentary through their revelation of unique women and their entrenchment in the Grenadian people's culture and politics.

9

Agents of Pain and Redemption in Sapphire's *Push*

JANICE LEE LIDDELL

In 1982 Trudier Harris wrote, "Although artistic freedom guarantees that any writer can draw upon his or her own culture in the creation of literature, that general mainline theory has certain side roads that many black writers in America believe are to be left untraveled. Some subjects, as discovering one's blackness, first experiencing prejudice, growing up black in the U.S. may be common, but others such as lesbianism, incest, or hateful black mothers, are usually left undisturbed. Incest is especially taboo" (495). Harris proceeds to explicate several fictive pieces by African Americans that explore the theme of incest, though tacitly, according to Harris. In fact, Harris's main point is that even in these few works—with the exception of James Baldwin's *Just Above My Head* (1979)—Black writers only subtly "tread the forbidden soil . . . by being indirect and by leaving more unstated than is made explicit" (504). In her examination of Ralph Ellison's *Invisible Man* (1952); Alice Walker's "The Child Who Favored Daughter" in *In Love and Trouble: Stories of Black Women* (1973); *The Bluest Eye* (1970) by Toni Morrison; and Baldwin's 1979 novel, all but Baldwin's work decentralize the issue of incest in favor of other themes that were more politically acceptable for the times in which the works were written. In most of the instances where incest is an issue—including Walker's later novel *The Color Purple* (1982), and to a lesser degree even Maya Angelou's spirited autobiography *I Know Why The Caged Bird Sings* (1969)—the larger context of race and/or gender victimization is made central at the expense of the victimization of the individual girl-child. In effect, the authors, according to Harris—and the works themselves—"confront the subject of incest without really confronting it" (496).

This rather passive confrontation by Black fiction writers is not surprising given the tenor of the times. Julia Hare, renowned African American sociologist, has spoken about the virtual conspiracy of silence that Black sociologists practiced until the 1970s regarding certain social problems and taboos, such as incest and rape of young Black girls (Hare). Sociologists Robert and Lois Pierce, writing in 1987, establish Hare's point when they explain that only "within the last decade, the sexual victimization of children, especially incestuous sex at home, has become a topic of major concern for lay citizens and professionals representing widely divergent fields of practice and research" (68). The reason for such long-term concealment was simply that the issue was "too delicate and thus not deserving of further investigation" (72).

Undoubtedly, a people so marginalized and oppressed because of their physical difference and their history would not want further devaluing because of their proclaimed social "deviancies." Hence, social taboos such as "lesbianism, incest, or hateful black mothers" were, as Harris suggests, left undisturbed in any forum whose access might extend beyond the Black community. Public discussion of these issues even within the Black community was pretty much off limits. However, Baldwin's exposure of virtually all these taboos was exercised primarily because as an expatriate he refused the unstated strictures imposed on him.

Recent younger African American writers, however, have performed a major literary outing. For these writers there are no more sacred cows. Whatever is part and parcel of the Black experience—real or imagined—becomes fodder for the fictive realities as well. Hence, no longer do Black writers "tiptoe through cultural taboos" (Trudier Harris 495) and closeted domains. What emerges in the work of newer writers is a no-holds-barred approach to Black life and its manifestations. The theme of homosexuality, for example, is handled quite explicitly by E. Lynn Harris's *Invisible Life* (1994), *Just As I Am* (1994), and *This Too Shall Pass* (1996). Tina McElroy Ansa has dared to present the hateful Black mother in her *Ugly Ways* (1993), and most recently the young New York novelist, Sapphire, gives graphic attention to the raw and unmitigated violence of incest. Some African American readers have quietly questioned the sociological veracity of Sapphire's familial dynamics in her first novel *Push* (1996); however, that is a debate for some other venue, some other occasion. The focus here is her treatment of the Black community's greatest social taboo—not the unspeakable sexual violence of father against daughter, but the even more deviant, unthinkable sexual violence of mother against daughter.

In this controversially provocative (some would say pornographic) novel, Sapphire looks boldly at all the proclaimed social taboos—lesbianism, hateful Black mothers, and incest. In fact, she centers what is, no doubt, the most extreme case of family sexual and physical violence, and she does so unapologetically. What is more, her brutal tale exposes without sympathy or qualifications all agents of the horrific family situation. This short but gripping novel, told in the urban unlettered vernacular of its tragic protagonist, reveals the physical and psychological holocaust inflicted on one of society's most innocent by those who should protect and nurture her. Born and raised in what must be the most dysfunctional family in literary history, sixteen-year-old Clareece Precious Jones has undergone violence in a variety of forms since she was in diapers.

Raped by her biological father from the age of seven onward, Precious, as she is ironically called, bears two children by this despicable human being. Her mother, an active colluder in this protracted nightmare, fails her daughter in every way, and finally, an uncaring social system repeatedly ignores the agony as this child-turned-too-quickly-woman screams silently for help of any kind. She acts out her pain by disrupting her classroom. She smears feces on her face, urinates on herself, and bites her fingernails to the quick. Still no one notices her agony. Only her chance encounter with a progressive literacy teacher—who also happens to be an uncloseted lesbian—offers any redemption to an otherwise hellish existence.

The exposure of such pathology is a daring venture by the young poet-turned-novelist, but even more audacious is her deconstruction of this pathology. By giving voice to the victim herself—a phenomenon virtually unheard of in Black sociological, psychological, or imaginative literature—the root causes of the incest are interrogated and the agency of this violence is spread as far as possible. The de-romanticized Black mother—yes, Black mother as co-conspirator—is the most disturbing revelation of Sapphire's novel.

An objective reading of the work, however, renders Mary L. Johnston, Precious's mother, as equal victim. She is, after all, poor, Black, uneducated, and herself lacking in protective resources. Her relationship with Precious's father, Carl, initiated when she was only a teenager (Carl's age is never given), is an oppressive one. Even Precious casually observes that "Carl come in the night, take food, what money they is, fuck us bofe" (85). Mary Johnston, whose first name ironically suggests mother-ideal, is vulnerable and perhaps incapable of providing the protection and nurturance her daughter needs. After all, she is unable to provide her own self-nurturance. Critic Paula Bennett, in her examination of the mother's part in family incest, concludes: "Far from endowing her daughter with strength, the mother's close identification with her, the fluidity (as it is usually called) of the ego boundaries between them, too often becomes the point through which the mother transfers her own sense of deprivation and helplessness. Where the mother compounds the problem by identifying with the oppressor—that is, where she accepts his version of reality, she also will seek to impose this reality on her daughter. Unable to nurture or protect herself, such a mother cannot nurture or protect her daughter. Nor, equally important, will she encourage her daughter to learn how to nurture or protect herself" (126). A global reading of *Push* certainly invites an interrogation of the mother's own victimization.

But the responsibility that the innocent daughter of Carl and Mary's union ultimately assigns to her devastating situation does not account for, nor even acknowledge, her mother's victimization. Instead, from the perspective of Precious, her mother is just as guilty as her father in creating the girl's brutal existence. "This time I know Mama know. Umm hmm, she know. She bring him to me. I ain' crazy, that stinky hoe give me to him. Probably that what he require to fuck her, some of me" (24). This perspective—the guiding point of view of the novel—is the foundation upon which this critique rests.

Sapphire, through Precious's experience and perspectives, dismantles every semblance of the ever-pervasive "good mother image"—that of the "strong resilient mother who is devoted, self sacrificing, and understanding and whose love is absolute and unconditional" (Collins 116). Not only does Sapphire shatter this idealized perception, but, as well, she challenges the more realistic perspectives of motherhood as described and defined by contemporary Black feminist scholars. Patricia Hill Collins's established and often cited "afrocentric feminist analysis of motherhood," for example, embraces this role as it might appear at any given historical moment in Black America. As Collins asserts, her construct aptly provides flexibility dependent on the severity of the oppression of Black women (and I might add, any particular Black woman) and on their (or her) resources for resistance: "[H]ow Black women define, value, and shape Black motherhood as an institution shows comparable diversity" (Collins 118). Collins's paradigm ostensibly makes room for this diversity. However, Sapphire's version of Black motherhood rends Collins's construct to shreds. Virtually no part of Collins's analysis appears applicable to Mary Johnston as mother figure. What Collins calls an Afrocentric ideology cannot and does not work for this loathsome, self-hating, brutal woman. Particularly, Mary's abject violation of the three most fundamental themes of this motherhood construct exposes Precious to her pathologically painful life.

First of all, Mary Johnston is a self-isolated individual. No "organized, resilient, woman-centered network of blood mothers and othermothers" exists to assist her in her mothering responsibilities (Collins 116). This community, according to Collins, is the first theme in a viable, functioning, Black motherhood construct. Instead, for Mary Johnston, the door to her life remains locked, both figuratively and literally, to any who might proffer such an othermother connection. The small apartment, home to her and her daughter, is also a self-imposed prison. Grown too fat even to fit her bathtub, Mary very rarely ventures outside, and perhaps less often does anyone else enter. The only disclosed exceptions are her mother, Toosie (Precious's grandmother), who only enters for the purpose of "gaming" the welfare system, and the periodic visit by the gullible or apathetic social worker. Precious describes these concurrent visits: "Toosie bring Little Mongo over on days social worker come; game is Little Mongo live here, my mama take care of Little Mongo and me. My mama get check 'n food stamps for me 'n Lil Mongo" (55).

Of course, the potential to contribute more than the exploitation of the welfare system exists in this mother/daughter relationship, but aside from the ruse, Grandmother Toosie fails to assist Mary in raising Precious. That Toosie is the primary caregiver for Mongo might be considered a sharing of child-rearing duties; however, the best interest of neither the "retarded" child nor Precious is the focus for either woman.

The only other prospective "othermother" is neighbor Miz West, whose major attempt to aid Precious is thwarted by the locked door. When Mary discovers her twelve-year-old daughter's pregnancy—on the day of delivery—she reacts with a vicious physical attack to which the concerned neighbor responds. From behind the locked door she attempts communication: "Jesus Mary, you didn't know. I knew, the whole building knew. Are you crazy— . . . Nine-one-one! Nine-one-one! Nine-one-one!" (78)

Miz West is also the only potential othermother that Precious, as child, recognizes. Upon the birth of her own second child, she recalls, "Miz West! Live down the hall from us, stop Mama from kicking me to death when Mongo been born. She like me. I always did go to the store for her since I was little; Precious bring me back a pack of Winston and a bag of pork rinds. Yes Miz West. Keep the change, Precious. One time she tell me You ever wanna talk about anything you could come to me. But I never did . . ." (78).

Even Precious recognizes the potential "othermotherhood" in Miz West, potential cut short by the restrictions placed on both their lives by mother Mary. Had Mary but opened the door, figuratively and literally, perhaps she would have been swarmed by the building's constellation of concerned othermothers; however, her isolation denies both her and her daughter these immeasurable benefits.

The second theme articulated by Collins is also problematic in the isolated world created by Mary Johnston. "Socializing her daughter for survival" is never a goal Mary seeks. Returning to Collins, we find that "African-American mothers place a strong emphasis on protection, either by trying to shield their daughters as long as possible from the penalties attached to their race, class and gender status or by teaching them skills of independence and self-reliance so that they will be able to protect themselves" (126).

Mary Johnston never offers her daughter protection. In fact, in the one counseling session mother and daughter attend after the birth of Precious's second child, Mary is forced to recall to the counselor and her daughter her first awareness of the incest. The extensive account is graphic:

> Carl got my tittie in his mouf. Nuffin wrong wif that, it's natural. But I think thas the day IT start. I don't remember nothin before that. I hot. He sucking my tittie. My eyes closed I know he getting hard I can see wifout my eyes. I love him so much . . . So he on me. Then he reach over to Precious! Start wif his finger between her legs. I say Carl what you doin! He say shut your big ass up! This is good for her. Then he git off me, take off her Pampers and try to stick his thing in Precious. You know what trip me out is it almost go in Precious. I think she some kinda freak baby then. I say stop

Carl stop! I want him on me! I never wanted him to hurt her. I didn't want him to do anything to her. I wanted my man for myself. Sex me up, not my chile. So cain't blame all that shit happen to Precious on me. I love Carl, I love him. He her daddy, but he was my man! (136, 137)

Still in diapers, Precious is denied the mother-protection that should be the right of any child. Mary's only protective instinct is geared toward keeping "her man." Pathologically and pathetically, she sees her infant child as competitor for his sexual attention. This perceived competition continues as Precious grows older. Even after Precious's first baby is born, Mary physically attacks her daughter with a cast-iron skillet and chastises *her* for the illicit incestuous interaction. "Thank you Miz Clair-ece Precious Jones for fucking my husband you nasty little slut . . . Fat cunt bucket slut! Nigger pig bitch. He done quit me. He done left me 'cause of you . . ." (19). Mary further denies her daughter protection by permitting Carl to return to the household. Even after Precious's second child is born, Mary's venom continues to be directed toward her daughter instead of toward the true perpetrator. Precious recalls, "I got new baby boy in my arms 'n she calling me bitch hoe slut say she gonna kill me 'cause I ruin her life. Gonna kill me wif her 'BARE HANDS!' It's like a black wall gonna crash down on me, nothing to do but run. First you steal my husband! Then you get me cut off welfare! She MAD! No time to say nothin! Once I'm outside the door I stop at top of the stairs, look hard at her. She still foaming at mouf, talking about her husband I spoze to steal. I do tell her one thing as I going down the stairs. I say 'Nigger rape me. I not steal shit fat bitch your husband RAPE me RAPE ME!'" (74).

Unfortunately, Mary *never* comes to the realization that her young daughter does. She totally fails to understand her role as protector. In fact, she shares the role of perpetrator: "I feel Mama's hand between my legs, moving up my thigh. Her hand stop, she getting ready to pinch me if I move. I just lay still, keep my eyes close, I can tell Mama's other hand between her legs now 'cause the smell fill room . . . Mama's hand creepy spider, up my legs, in my pussy" (21). While Mary's inability or refusal to fulfill her role as protector foredooms her daughter, her own misuse of the power associated with motherhood exacts a closure on any hope for the developing girl-child while under her tutelage. Collins believes such power is transformative, since Black women's relationships with children and other vulnerable community members are not initiated to dominate or to control. Rather, the purpose is to bring people along to 'up lift the race' so that vulnerable members of the community will be able to attain the self-reliance and independence essential for resistance (132).

Mary Johnston appears to understand clearly that motherhood can be invoked as a symbol of power (Collins 132). However, the power wielded by her is far from transformative. It is, in fact, destructive—violent, downgrading, and self-serving. Also, Mary's closed door policy renders this power nearly omnipotent within her household, where she virtually enslaves Precious. No way exists for this power to be diffused except through her interaction with Carl. How this absolute power so thoroughly dissipates in that relationship might be reviewed objectively as somewhat of a contradiction or perhaps a manifestation of her own victimization. However, bell hooks reminds us "that women can and do participate in politics of domination, as perpetrators as well as victims—that we dominate, that we are dominated. If focus on patriarchal domination masks this reality or becomes the means by which women deflect attention from the real conditions and circumstances of our lives, then women cooperate in suppressing and promoting false consciousness, inhibiting our capacity to assume responsibility for transforming ourselves and society" (20).

Precious does recognize this destructive power and her mother's conscious, active, and sustained subordination to a man who: (1) does not live in the home; (2) is legally married to another woman with whom he has children; (3) offers no support to Mary or to her household; and (4) continuously violates father/daughter boundaries. This recognition signals her mother's active collusion in the child's victimization for the sole purpose of her own emotional and sexual gratification.

By violating these foundational premises of African American motherhood–(1) connecting with a supportive network of other mothers; (2) socializing daughters for survival and self-protection; and (3) invoking the transformative power of the role of mother—Mary Johnston becomes a virtually inconceivable image of Black motherhood. While we all know that monstrous Black mothers exist somewhere in the dark cracks and crevices of our communities (or so we choose to believe), we have been virtually unwilling to unmask them for who they are—believing, perhaps, that to do so might undermine prevailing mythic and nostalgic notions of Black motherhood. Hence, no Black mother has ever been dragged into the full sunshine in all her baseness as Sapphire does Mary, for Sapphire, and ultimately Precious, recognize the empowerment of facing the enemy head on—no matter who *she* is. At no time in African American literary history has a Black mother been accorded such conscious agency over the brutal downfall of her own flesh and blood, especially her only daughter. However, the predictable agency of a father whose sexual deviancy wreaks havoc on his household and his family is more familiar: Cholly in *The Bluest Eye,* Trueblood in Ellison's *Invisible Man,* as well as the surrogate fathers in *The Color Purple* and *I Know Why the Caged Bird Sings.* Still, none of these is as reprehensible as Carl Renwood Jones of Sapphire's novel. He is purposeful and perverted, his abuse savage. Precious describes the encounters with her biological father: "Got to where he jus' come in my room any ole time, not jus' night. He climb on me. Shut up! He slap my ass, you wide as the Mississippi, don't tell me a little bit of dick hurt you heifer. Get usta it, he laff, you *is* usta it" (24).

Of course, Precious correctly recognizes the illegal and immoral invasion perpetrated by her identified father. Nevertheless, the situation requires a bit more exegesis. While the incest is unpardonable, the nature of the Mary/Carl/Precious triad all but guarantees sexual and emotional anarchy. Even in the traditional family construct, "the patriarchal family arrangement generally creates and fosters female dependence and powerlessness through male control over women and children" (Jacobs 506). This control, however, is usually mitigated by socially recognizable and accepted rules, values, and boundaries. But in a carnally focused arrangement such as that of Carl and Mary and later Precious, these ordering principles are only as functional as is the integrity of the dominant partner and the willfulness of the co-participant(s). Carl, as predator, creates the chaos even though it is perpetuated by both adults. Precious, the child, is, of course, an innocent victim. Surprisingly, however, Precious offers a fairly clear understanding of this anarchy. Her Farrakan-referenced comparison of Carl's sexual indiscretions to those of the stereotypical white master during slavery is on target. In fact, the comparison is reminiscent of Gayle Jones's fictive account of the sexual anarchy in *Corregidora* (1975), wherein a white slave master is biological father to both a mother and her daughter. The slave master, sexually possessing a female lineage of three generations, is an obvious agent to the same pain and pathology as is Carl.

Such victimization by both parents practically assures the psychic, if not physical, death of a child unless some external intervention saves her. However, prior to the birth of her children, no safety net exists for Precious. The social system whose intercession should have exacted punishment on her perpetrating parents after the first pregnancy and prevented the second actually becomes an apathetic agent in the girl's victimization. Hospital nurses view "the mistake" as hers, investigating police are passive, and the welfare office simply withdraws Mary's welfare check after the second birth. No identifiable aid is accorded the innocent girl. Even a sixteen-year-old Precious recognizes the system's abandonment: "I just wan to say when I was twelve, TWELVE, somebody hadda help me it not be like this now" (125).

But, obviously no help ever came her way. Hence, Precious's "now" consists of her role as mother to two children—one retarded—and a death sentence issued by her father. Precious discovers shortly after the birth of her second child that her father has died of AIDS, and she is HIV positive. In this seeming doom, however, some salvation does exist, salvation catalyzed by the chance meeting with and the chance intervention of Ms. Blue Rain, her "for real hope to die if I'm lying name" (43). While Ms. Rain, the sympathetic and politically conscious literacy teacher, opens Precious's mind to her higher potential, Precious's discovery of her own agency ultimately saves her. The realization that she has choices and possesses the ability to act on these choices enables Precious to provide herself with the developmental and survival mechanism that her mother denied her. Essentially, Precious must mother herself.

The "push" of the novel is not only Precious's physical thrust to birth her father-fathered babies or her psychic discharging of the pain of her rape, but most important, Precious's "push" is the launching of her own agency, essentially the birthing of a new and self-conscious Precious. Precious, the victim/object, becomes Precious, the subject, as she initiates and secures her "self-recovery." Precious's network of friends and role models, she weaves for herself; she also becomes an active participant in both an AIDS and Incest Survivors support group. Additionally, Precious invokes the power of a racial past by educating herself to the contributions of such cultural s/heroes as Harriet Tubman, Langston

Hughes, Farrakan, Alice Walker, and others. Precious comes to realize what her mother, unfortunately, never does: "that the self [exists] in relation, [is] dependent for its very being on the lives and experiences of everyone, the self not as signifier of one 'I' but the coming together of many 'I's, the self as embodying collective reality past and present, family and community" (hooks 31).

The "transformational politic" (hooks 19) of Sapphire's work is its highest value. Weak character development, arbitrary shifts in point of view, linguistic inconsistencies, and some structural faults render this first novel artistically problematic. And its extreme deviancy outside any documented sociological data certainly challenges its verisimilitude. Its overwhelming commercial success is, nevertheless, reflected in a first U.S. printing of 150,000 copies and the transfer of foreign rights to at least six overseas markets—a rarity for any first novel. Perhaps, as several African American readers and critics have privately proclaimed, the pathology and quasi-pornography of the work are the strength of its popular success, having stimulated further the perennial curiosity about the sexuality of Africana peoples. Many readers, particularly non–African American readers, will, no doubt, view this novel as validation of particular sexual stereotypes. This is precisely the kind of exposure and response that served as the source of the fears of so many "lay citizens and professionals representing widely divergent fields of practice and research" (Pierce and Pierce 68) and of so many Black writers who have "tiptoed through taboo." Sapphire's ascendancy above these fears, her graphic and forceful confrontation of the subject of incest, and her deconstruction of its agency, however, enable her to create the atmosphere and the mechanisms for real and significant transformation. Precious's self-recovery from domination to liberation is undoubtedly the most relevant transformation. But, as well, Sapphire has gone far in transforming the literary consciousness of African Americans.

Works Cited

Bennett, Paula. "The Mother's Part: Incest and Maternal Deprivation in Woolf and Morrison." Narrating Mothers: Theorizing Maternal Subjectivities. Ed. Brenda Daley and Maureen T. Reddy. Knoxville: University of Tennessee Press, 1999. 125–38.

Collins, Patricia Hill. *Black Feminist Thought: Knowledge, Consciousness and the Politics of Empowerment*. London: Harper Collins Academic, 1990.

Hare, Julia. A Presentation at the Second Annual Black Family Project Conference, Clark Atlanta University, October 29, 1988.

Harris, Trudier. "Tiptoeing Through Taboo: Incest in "The Child Who Favored Daughter." *Modern Fiction Studies* 28.3 (Autumn 1982): 495–505.

hooks, bell. *Talking Back: Thinking Feminist, Thinking Black*. Boston: South End Press, 1989.

Jacobs, Janet Liebman. "Reassessing Mother Blame in Incest." *Signs: Journal of Women in Culture and Society* 14.3 (1990): 500–514.

Pierce, Robert L., and Lois H. Pierce. "Child Sexual Abuse: A Black Perspective." *Violence in the Black Family*. Ed. Robert L. Hampton. Lexington, Mass.: Lexington Books, 1987.

Sapphire. *Push*. New York: Vintage Books, 1996.

10

Romantic Love and the Individual in Novels by Mariama Bâ, Buchi Emecheta, and Bessie Head

YAKINI B. KEMP

Sensitive and adept depictions of life from the woman's perspective have led a number of critics to cite specific "feminist" elements that exist in the writing of Mariama Bâ, Buchi Emecheta, and Bessie Head. The injustices and mental anguish caused African women by the inequity of patriarchal traditions and the challenges of modern society become woman-centered themes in fiction by these writers. Yet intertwined with their portrayals of tragic or triumphant women, alongside the various feminist elements, rest conspicuous romantic elements, such as the preponderance of sentiment, the inclusion of a gallant or mesmerizing male, and the melodramatic conclusion. Most noticeable among these elements is the sincere acceptance and emphasis on romantic love. In fact, the romantic strain is replete enough in certain novels by Bâ, Emecheta, and Head that the author's perspective may be termed a romantic vision. This romantic vision constitutes a part of the author's overall social perspective, since it results from the writer's perceptions of the individual's relationship to the social and economic forces in her society.

Three novels by these writers, who are from distinct regions of the African continent, best exhibit their romantic vision: Mariama Bâ's *So Long a Letter;* Emecheta's *The Bride Price;* and Bessie Head's *Maru.* Depicting social relationships at their most basic level—that is, in the home and in the family—the novels give ample consideration to the social forces that influence the success or failure of male-female emotional relationships. Consequently, elements of social criticism can be found in the novels because each story confronts a social issue directly.

Yet each plot is undergirded by the protagonist's personal quest for love, specifically romantic love. How the romantic vision supports or fetters the "argument," the social criticism of the novel is the central focus of this study. The impact that romantic love has on women characters' lives is also a concern. Finally, an assessment of the relationship between the feminist elements and the romantic elements will be made.

Because of the idealized notion of male-female relationships that romantic love supports, and because of the patriarchal institutions from which it sprang, the concept of romantic love cannot be claimed as a feminist concept: Romantic love neither demands nor inspires equality of the sexes. However, within the modern Muslim society and the traditional Igbo society depicted by Bâ and Emecheta, the fulfillment of the ideal of romantic love requires that their two women characters defy traditional custom by making individual choices of marriage partners—while the devastation of a romantic heartbreak leads Bessie Head's protagonist directly into a marriage that defies custom. Acts of defiance or assertion are not typical behavior for these women protagonists, and at the time of their actions, the women lack conscious feminist motivation. Instead, their actions result from their existence as modern individuals seeking the personal happiness expected from romantic love relationships.

Romantic love as developed and practiced in Western societies is not indigenous to traditional African society. Emmanuel Obiechina traces the sources of the concept and finds that formal literary study, Christian monogamy, and modern media are most significant in bringing the Western romantic tradition to West Africa (34). The individualistic nature of mate selections and the separation from the traditional family selection process has led Obiechina to write, "No two systems can be more divergent in their assumptions and principles as the Western and the African systems on this matter of romantic love and marriage" (33). Nevertheless, African women writers assert that even within traditional societies, romantic sentiment was common among couples (see Flora Nwapa's *Idu, Efuru,* and Grace Ogot's *The Promised Land*).

The women protagonists of the novels within this study are introduced to Western cultural knowledge and the Western concept of romantic love primarily through formal education. Ramatoulaye (*So Long a Letter*) and Margaret (*Maru*) both complete teacher's colleges, and Aku-nna (*The Bride Price*) finishes secondary education. The degree of acceptance of Western ideas and values varies among the women because of their own particular circumstances. For example, Ramatoulaye is a devout Muslim; Aku-nna is a sheltered teenager; Margaret is a member of an ostracized ethnic group. But for each, romantic love is an expected reality.

As stated earlier, each of the novels contains strains of social criticism by confronting a pertinent social issue. In Bâ's *So Long a Letter,* the issue is modern polygamy. Ramatoulaye, the protagonist, is a middle-aged Senegalese wife whose husband abandons his wife and twelve children after he takes his daughter's best friend as second wife. Ramatoulaye never divorces Modou, and after five years of marriage and two sons with the young Binetou, he dies. The novel is a journal that Ramatoulaye keeps in the form of letters during the required period of isolation for Muslim widows, "four months and ten days." She addresses the letters to her friend Aissatou, also a teacher, who shared a similar desertion but chose a different response. Instead of remaining in Dakar in a polygamous situation, Aissatou moved to her own home with her four sons, sought training in an interpreter's school in France, and eventually obtained a position as translator at the Senegalese embassy in the United States. Aissatou shared Ramatoulaye's view of romantic love, but since her lineage was an artisan background, she had to fight class prejudice in her marriage as well.

Ramatoulaye's worldview is shaped by three sometimes conflicting forces: Muslim religious tradition; petit bourgeois class allegiance; and Western education, along with the romantic tradition found in its literature. Although the belief in monogamy is common among the urban middle classes, the fact that Ramatoulaye (and Aissatou) actually expect their husbands to remain completely "faithful" to them, mentally and sexually, indicates the degree to which they have accepted ideas other than those taught by Islam. Ramatoulaye views polygamy as a question of morality; she attacks polygamy as morally wrong, because men take wives only because of physical desire. Accepting monogamy based on romantic love choice as progressive, she considers it to be the only morally correct form of mating. In fact, she states of Modou, "In loving someone else, he burned his past, both morally and materially. He dared to commit such an act of disavowal" (*SLL* 12).

Ramatoulaye views marriage as a partnership in which each member would share equally, respecting "the inevitable and necessary complementarity of man and woman" (*SLL* 88). As a result of Modou's desertion, she learns a new type of self-reliance, because she must attend the duties that he abandoned. Yet her mature vision of male-female relationships remains crowded with idealism. She writes, "To love one another! . . . If each could only melt into the other! If each would only accept the other's successes and failures! If each would only praise the other's qualities instead of listing his faults! . . . If each could penetrate the other's most secret haunts to forestall failure and be a support while tending to the evils that are repressed!" (*SLL* 89). The romanticism of Ramatoulaye's view of love is clear. With such beliefs about love, it is doubtful that she could live within an active polygamous situation.

Yet her sincere attachment to romantic love served as a liberating force in her life in one sense, as it insured her own preference in choice of a mate, a choice that most women of her class apparently did not have. In her youth, Ramatoulaye chose to marry the handsome, but poor college student, Modou Fall, rather than the older, successful doctor, her mother's choice. The same concern for her individual happiness leads her to reject all offers of marriage after Modou's death, since all but that of the same doctor are motivated by greed rather than love. And though there is no man in her life at the conclusion of the novel, she, like Aissatou, avowedly affirms the belief that women need to have the power to choose whom they will love.

Mariama Bâ's focus on the perspective of a middle-class, educated woman toward polygamy has several advantages. Ramatoulaye's class status and education provide her with the facility to evaluate her emotions and her environment through writing. Freed from day-to-day subsistence-level survival, Ramatoulaye does not have to bargain herself or her villa for economic security in marriage. Although her class prejudices appear throughout the novel, Ramatoulaye avows commitment. Her philosophy of education is that of uplift: She sees herself as part of the generation of Africans whose mission is to stamp out ignorance and create the new independent nation. Her attempts to be progressive with her teenage daughters (even when the second oldest becomes pregnant), and her view of women as the moral torchbearers of society, portray her as a virtuous, understanding, and sensitive woman. The characterization is so sensitively drawn that Ramatoulaye's narrow middle-class perspective is almost excused.

The romantic overtones of Ramatoulaye's outlook on love build sympathy for her as a woman victimized by life in polygamy. Some critics have pointed out that her victimization is minimized by her class status and in comparison to that of poorer women in her society (see Giwa, Kemp, Ojo-Ade). Yet the success of the novel as a moving criticism of polygamy is partly due to Ramatoulaye's overtly romantic view of love. When pitted against Ramatoulaye's idealistic vision of love relationships, the realistic picture of middle-aged men marrying young girls out of lust becomes the portrait of lechery that Ramatoulaye and Mariama Bâ intend it to be.

Whereas Mariama Bâ has a direct spokesperson in Ramatoulaye, who is "not indifferent to the irreversible currents of women's liberation that are lashing the world" (*SLL* 88), Buchi Emecheta's character Aku-nna has little consciousness of her life in broader perspective. Aku-nna's story makes a clear criticism of the traditional bride wealth system, while not openly condemning it. Emecheta achieves this by allowing the ending of the novel to capitulate to the same tradition that she spends much of the novel reproving. The story centers on the romance between Aku-nna and Chike, the village schoolteacher. Their love is generally discouraged by the whole Ibuza village because Chike is the descendant of an "osu," a slave. This supposedly tainted heritage means nothing to Aku-nna, who has spent her formative years in Lagos, educated in Christian schools. The family moved to Ibuza after her father died, and Aku-nna's mother became the fourth wife of her uncle. An ambitious man seeking the "obi" title, the uncle follows through with custom by marrying his brother's widow, primarily because Aku-nna's education will bring a high bride price upon her marriage.

As Palmer states, "[*The Bride Price*] is a most moving Romeo- and Juliet-like love story in which two young people who are powerfully in love encounter the strongest possible objections to their union from a society bound by convention and riddled with prejudice" (31). Emecheta virtually stockpiles sentiment for Aku-nna by dwelling on the narrow disregard for the individual found within traditional conventions surrounding marriage and by building sympathy for the young couple through her emphasis on romantic love. In choice of marriage partners, traditional Igbo custom, as described in the novel, ignores premarital romances: "Some girls did eventually marry their sweethearts, but in most cases the boys are either too young to afford the bride price or were not ready for marriage. They usually stood by and watched their first loves married off to men old enough to be their fathers" (*BP* 97).

From a broader social perspective, Obiechina explains the reasoning for the traditional practices:

> Romantic love, whether as an autonomous experience or as a stepping stone to marriage, was played down and subordinated to familial and community interests. Because of the close linking of the fate of individuals to that of the group to which they belonged . . . romantic individualism was curbed by stringent taboos. . . . In a situation of underdevelopment and fragile political and social infra-structure, families and communities depended for stability largely on the balancing of group relationships and the linking of families and segments in marriage alliances. (Obiechina 34)

Emecheta's novel presents the modern bride price as the selling of young women to the highest bidder. Within the novel, patriarchal greed for high bride prices negates the importance of traditional family networking as a basis for marriage. But foremost, it denies romantic love as the true foundation for marriage. Emecheta's harsh criticism of the Igbo bride wealth system and the male authoritarianism regulating it has led certain Nigerian critics to assert that she makes an "argument against Igbo culture" (Ebeogu 87) and that her "western sensibility" and "feminist thrust" make the "attack" "suspect" (Ogunyemi 70). With its emphasis on the plight of an alienated adolescent, misreading the text as an attack on all Igbo tradition is one possible pitfall. However, the fact that Emecheta shows Aku-nna's trying to adapt by practicing for the aja dance with her age group and the positive portrayal of Aku-nna's well-adjusted cousin Ogugua dispel the idea that the author condemns all Igbo customs.

Emecheta creates a feminine stereotype in an African setting for her romantic heroine. Aku-nna is portrayed as a frail, timid, and swooning woman-child who is alienated in Ibuza by her city ways and her formal education. Her naturally frail constitution tends to endear her to the would-be suitors of the village; they admire the weakness, considering her Europeanlike femininity an extension of her educated city ways. Chike, also smitten by Aku-nna's vulnerability, decides that Aku-nna will be his, despite community taboos.

The similarity between the medieval knight errant of the European romances and Chike's brave rescue of Aku-nna from her kidnapper and would-be husband cannot be overlooked. A tall, handsome young man who has had many love affairs in Ibuza (even though marriage with the women would be forbidden), Chike is the perfect romantic lover. He is one of the few types of men generally characterized in Emecheta's novels. Critics cite Emecheta's tendency to make men either loving fathers who die off rather quickly, or more commonly, boorish and mean husbands. The other type, characterized by Chike, is the "gallant knight who comes to the lady's rescue," a type some find "too romantic to be true" (Acholonu).

The sources for Chike and Aku-nna's romantic views are blatantly apparent during their first romantic encounter. Chike kisses Aku-nna "the way Europeans did in films," and she allows it because "she had read in old copies of *True Romances* that kissing was meant to do something to a girl" (*BP* 98). Even her language is that of the romance novel: Fearing that community taboo will never allow them to marry, Aku-nna tells Chike, "There is no other person for me in this world, Chike. I don't even know anyone else. . . . You are the only person I know who I am not afraid of" (*BP* 98). Chike responds, "You will always be mine." As a result of Western media influences, the couple adopts Western romantic behavior and beliefs. Their education, Chike's "osu" lineage, and Aku-nna's urban background make them both somewhat alienated from Ibuza youth culture; consequently, consciousness of themselves as "individuals" comes more readily.

That individualistic consciousness, which pervades the life and literature of the West, recedes from Aku-nna's mother, Ma Blackie. Although Ma Blackie has some formal education and practiced Christianity before her return to Ibuza, upon her marriage to Okonkwo and subsequent pregnancy, she returns, almost completely, to the traditional ways. The one exception is that she continues to send her daughter to school; Aku-nna is but one of three girls in the school. The appeal of romantic love is absent from Ma Blackie's life. In gratitude and excitement over her first pregnancy after thirteen years, Aku-nna's mother is willing to sacrifice her daughter's happiness for a bride price.

Through the contrast of mother and daughter, Emecheta gives an insight into some of the changes in worldview that modern society wrought. Whereas the daughter holds the individualistic values by seeking happiness through her personal choice of a mate, the mother up-holds the traditional values by gaining fulfillment from her capability as childbearer. Faced with obstacles to personal fulfillment from family and community, Aku-nna gradually gains some minimal insight into her position as a woman in Ibuza. At fifteen, just barely a woman, Aku-nna never deliberately sets out to defy convention. Nonetheless, the trap of tradition pitted against her solid allegiance to love causes her rebellion. After a brief period of happy married life with Chike, Aku-nna dies, ostensibly due to complications of childbirth. Yet Emecheta ends the story by warning of the traditional superstition, "If a girl wished to live long and see her children's children, she must accept the husband cho-sen for her by her people, and the bride price must be paid. If the bride price was not paid, she would never survive the birth of her first child" (*BP* 168). Nevertheless, the case for romantic love choice has been made so thoroughly that Emecheta's capitulation to tradition seems negli-gible.

Bessie Head's novel *Maru* capitulates to another type of tradition with its conclusion, the popular romance tradition. As with *The Bride Price*, *Maru* deals with a young couple's braving community prejudice, the woman being the outcast this time. Margaret Cadmore is a member of the Masarwa, an oppressed ethnic group in Botswana. Her marriage to a young heir to the local chiefdom at the conclusion of the novel is both romantic and contrived; some have labeled it "fairytale" (Abrahams 42). And yet, the fanciful conclusion succeeds because it conforms with Head's overall romantic vision as depicted in the novel. Much of the novel describes attitudes toward and treatment of the exploited and oppressed Masarwa people. In fact, Bessie Head intended that "the love story [in *Maru*] should be regarded as subservient to the work that the book is doing" (Head "In Australia" 6). With a straightforward intent of creating social criticism, Head cushions her critique with a complex romantic overview that draws on Tswana myth and oral tradition (John-son).

In comparison to *So long a Letter* and *The Bride Price*, the theme of romantic love appears muted in *Maru*. This is because the most promi-nent themes "relate to the renunciation of power and political ambition and to the conflict between the individual's personal inclinations and the claims of his society on him." (Johnson 5). As in the discussions of the earlier novels, the central characters in *Maru* own an observable individualism. In fact, Bessie Head's characters may be the most "individual" of all the characters in the novels mentioned thus far. One reason for this is the peculiar situation of the central characters of *Maru*.

The story revolves around the life of a young schoolteacher, Margaret Cadmore, and one of the men who loves her, Maru, the heir-apparent to paramount chiefdom of the village of Dilepe. An orphan from Masarwa and white parentage, Margaret is raised from infancy by a British missionary, the senior Margaret Cadmore. Margaret is given an ample education by the missionary, an education labeled "universal" in the novel because "[t]here was nothing on earth that was not human, sensible and beautiful that had not been fearlessly thrown into the pupil, from Plato to W. B. Yeats" (*M* 20). And Margaret's personality is equally "universal," according to the novel: "It was hardly African or anything but something new and universal, a type of personality that would be unable to fit into a definition of something as narrow as tribe or race or nation" (*M* 16). From these descriptions it is clear that Head's romantic vision rests upon her idea of universal—those ideas that would liberate human beings from the subjective and constricting consciousness that governs social relations between people and nationalities.

Yet a problem arises from the narrow definition of universal knowledge because of its Eurocentric focus ("Plato to W. B. Yeats"). Read literally, the statement makes Western bourgeois cultural knowledge the supreme knowledge in the world. African writers and critics alike have stated the case against usage of the term "universal" for Eurocentric knowledge and culture. Nonetheless, the description of Margaret's personality and education also broadens the case for her individualism.

Margaret's individualism is due to a number of factors, including her Western education. After her British guardian goes back to England without her and she takes her first teaching assignment in the village of Dilepe, she remains an alienated person. The bigoted villagers shy from her, since, as she has been taught, she tells people outright that she is "Masarwa" and not "Coloured," as they believe. Her one friend is Maru's sister, Dikeledi, also a teacher in the village school. The elder Margaret Cadmore gives Margaret education, security, and a mission (she tells her to help uplift her people), but she does not give Margaret genuine maternal love. For the British Margaret, raising the Masarwa child was an experiment to prove her thesis: "[E]nvironment everything; heredity nothing" (*M* 15). Consequently, Margaret has never experienced any genuine form of human love. Perhaps this is why Margaret falls in love with Moleka, second in line to Maru's chiefdom, the first man who is kind to her in Dilepe. Furthermore, in keeping with Head's overall romantic vision, the reader must believe that Margaret's "love at first sight" is a profound and true affection that Moleka reciprocates.

Bessie Head adds another dimension to Margaret's personality by giving her an artistic disposition. Given art supplies by Dikeledi, supplies secretly bought by Maru, Margaret goes on a two-week painting binge. She creates no less than twenty-five dreamlike paintings before exhaustion overcomes her. This sudden exhibition of talent demonstrates that Margaret has the same profundity and capability in creative endeavors that she has for love. Thus, the unique, alienated Margaret holds the necessary criteria for a romantic heroine.

In Bessie Head's novel *A Question of Power,* her protagonist Elizabeth discovers that "the Gods" are actually "ordinary" people "who had consciously concentrated on spiritual earnings" (31). In contrast, "the Gods" in *Maru* are Head's quartet of great souls: Maru, Moleka, Dikeledi, and Margaret. Maru, who has the mystical power to influence the others' thoughts, is the unquestioned leader of the group. His manipulative and suggestive power lurks behind all significant action in Margaret's life in Dilepe. He is the "god-like man" who "intervenes" often in Head's fiction (Gardner 11). Having "a personality too original to survive in an unorganized world" (*M* 49), Maru is more than adequate for the cast of romantic hero.

Like Chike in *The Bride Price,* Maru rescues Margaret by elopement. At the time, Margaret is incapacitated by the news that Dikeledi, who also loves Moleka, will soon marry him (an arrangement plotted and maneuvered by Maru). Maru convinces Margaret that they are complementary souls, explaining that they "dreamed the same dreams" and that he "knew she would love him in the end" (*M* 124). Thus, he saves her from the antagonism she would face as Moleka's wife. As Andrew Peek explains, "Moleka is abrupt, impatient, will make no allowance for the slow removal of prejudice which must be sloughed 'bit-by-bit,' and would have exposed Margaret to the full corrosive impact of a hostile village. Maru is quick to recognize that discrimination is countered and overcome gradually" (127). As Margaret realizes that Maru was "some kind of strange, sweet music you could hear over and over again" (*M* 124), Head's romantic vision completes the novel.

The fairytale/folktale quality of Maru and Margaret's marriage has the sentimental element of romance, as stated earlier. However, it serves a more serious purpose of clinching the political scheme of the novel. The defection of the paramount chief with a Masarwa chief will help to inspire and to add pride to the downtrodden Masarwa. The symbolic marriage denotes "the wind of change" (*M* 126) that will eventually lead the Masarwa to liberation. Therefore, *Maru* is essentially a novel with a central political theme, discussing a political problem from the perspective of male-female interpersonal relationships, which explains the secondary romantic theme. Bessie Head's overall perspective within the novel, like the romantic vision portrayed there, is truly idealistic. As one critic muses, "In spite of the novel's clear intentions and its moments of brilliant idiosyncrasy, however, I find myself left wondering how one can solve racial prejudice by running away; there is the sense of an enduring problem resolved through fantasy only" (Peek 129). Nonetheless, the romantic fantasy does help achieve Head's stated intention to write a novel "that would be beautiful, like a fairytale, about an ugly subject, racism" (Bruner 40; Head "Social and Political" 23).

As the discussions of *So Long a Letter, The Bride Price,* and *Maru* demonstrate, romantic themes, characters, and viewpoints abound and are used by the novelists to support their criticism of specific social issues. But how well do these romantic elements blend with the feminist elements of the works? All three novels point out realistic conditions of African women's lives as they pursue love, life, and work. Mariama Bâ and Buchi Emecheta elucidate woman-centered themes, such as the problems encountered with polygamy, motherhood, and marriage conventions, topics that definitely lend themselves to feminist examination. And whereas Head addresses less overtly feminist themes in *Maru,* the tough individualism of her women make them iconoclasts in their rural society, which in itself may be cited as feminist. Although obvious woman-centered themes are present, these works and other works by the same authors do not "import Western women's [feminist] agendas" (Davies 9).

Nevertheless, the romantic themes and feminist elements form a tenuous partnership. As shown, the protagonists assert their rights as individuals in the choice of marriage partners, yet never is there the contention that the women seek equality with men. The stereotypical male-dominated relationships are not rejected if the man is a benevolent partner. The married lives of both Emecheta's and Head's protagonists exemplify this tendency. After marriage Aku-nna is completely dependent on Chike for her emotional support and development. She remains ecstatically happy during her short married life, even though her fragile health and anxiety over the unpaid bride price increase the dependency on Chike during her pregnancy. Similarly, Margaret's mental state fluctuates with the moods of her temperamental, jealous, but loving Maru, who has complete control over her existence. He can decide to "surrender his wife to Moleka because he had decided that Moleka's love was greater than his own" (*M* 10). Or he "could turn the world to ashes" (*M* 10) by temporarily rejecting her. Margaret lives in wedded bliss under the shadow of Maru's manipulative power, even though part of her heart loves Moleka still. As Bazin aptly states, "Both Head and Emecheta reveal through their fiction a longing for a strong, stable man who will save and protect them" (7).

Needless to say, Ramatoulaye's religious devotion mandates a variety of gender-related restrictions. Yet of the three women characters studied, she is the most aware of her woman's life in broader perspective. Her somewhat broadened perspective does not change her basic acceptance of male-dominated relationships, however. She rejects all suitors whom she does not love, while awaiting that one man who will complete her life. The problem of her teenage daughter's pregnancy is resolved when the university student boyfriend steps in and effectively takes over. Ramatoulaye is happy and satisfied that he will take charge of her daughter's life. Also, Ramatoulaye places the greater burden of virtue on the backs of women, a common view in patriarchal societies. But perhaps more limiting to Ramatoulaye as a feminist is her class outlook. Looking staunchly through middle-class eyes, Ramatoulaye, who has the education, the voice, and the contacts to help organize women, cites the problems but does not take action. The need for public playgrounds so that children like her small son might avoid auto accidents, and the need for laws that would allow pregnant teens to continue their education, are two such problems. Ramatoulaye writes that "each woman makes of her life what she wishes"; her romantic outlook tells her to "go out in search" of "happiness" (*SLL* 89) instead of seeking activities that would benefit women in her community.

Buchi Emecheta stated about her novel *The Bride Price:* "It was romantic. I put in all the romance my life lacked" (Emecheta "Nigerian Writer" 118). Similarly, when asked about the emphasis on "love" in her novel, Mariama Bâ replied, "We are almost ashamed to find love and sentiment.... We have more reason than heart. I believe that what made my book so successful was that it put sentiment, emotion, back into its place" (Harrell-Bond 210). Adding to these Bessie Head's intent to write a novel that would be "so beautiful" and "so magical" ("Social and Political" 23), it becomes clear that the writer's romantic vision actually restricts the feminist elements.

As pointed out earlier, the romantic vision that emerges in these novels is part of the writer's overall social perspective. Whereas each writer achieves a degree of success in utilizing her fiction as creative art and as social criticism, the idealism found in their romantic vision subverts some of the plea for change in fundamental social structures that help perpetuate the social ills they cite. Thus, Bessie Head's novel states the case for freedom of the Masarwa while minimally rejecting the elitist and patriarchal social relations that continue to suppress her Masarwa protagonist. And Bâ wished dissolution of polygamous marriage while ignoring class privilege as equally exploitive of women. Even Emecheta, labeled by one critic "a firebrand upholding the feminist faith" (Ogunyemi 65), posits no need for such changes.

Author Lauretta Ngcobo states that "African women writers reveal more accurately the condition of women than any historical facts can presume to do because they monitor their own changing hearts and minds. For too long women have been constricted into living a lie, for they were not expected to admit to deeper personal needs such as love or fears or jealousies.... These writers admit, on behalf of African women, to a deep need for love and gentle care, not only before marriage, but throughout their married lives" (64). The overt romantic vision found within the portrayals of the women of *So Long a Letter, The Bride Price,* and *Maru* asserts that for these women, educated African women, romantic love is also necessary. As demonstrated in the novels, the romantic vision garners sympathy for the characters, which clearly accentuates elements of social criticism within the narratives. Furthermore, while the romantic vision restricts the degree of challenge that the characters (and the writers) pose to the overall social order, the presence of conspicuously placed romantic sentiment enhances characterization and bolsters the argument for individual choice. Guided by their quest for individual choices in love and life, the women characters affirm their belief that romantic love has foremost place in their emotional outlook.

Works Cited

Abrahams, Cecil. "The Context of Bessie Head's Fiction." *ACLALS Bulletin* 7.4 (1986): 37–44.

Acholonu, Catherine. "Buchi Emecheta." Nigeria, Aluan Ikoku College of Education, Owerri, 1985.

Bâ, Mariama. *So Long a Letter.* Trans. Modupe' Bode' Thomas. London: Heinemann, 1980.

Bazin, Nancy Toppin. "Feminist Perspectives in African Fiction: Bessie Head and Buchi Emecheta." African Literature Association Conference, University of Maryland, April 12–15, 1985. 21pp.

Bruner, Charlotte. "Shock and Loss" Tributes to Bessie Head. *ALA Bulletin* 12.2 (1986): 39–41.

Davies, Carole Boyce. Introduction. *Ngambika: Studies of Women in African Literature.* Ed. Carole Boyce Davies and Anne Adams Graves. Trenton: Africa World Press, 1986. 1–23.

Ebeogu, Afam. "Enter the Iconoclast: Buchi Emecheta and the Igbo Culture." *Commonwealth: Essays and Studies* 7.2 (1985): 83–94.

Emecheta, Buchi. "A Nigerian Writer Living in London." *Kunippi* 4.1 (1982): 114–23.

———. *The Bride Price.* London: Alison and Busby, 1977.

Gardner, Susan. Introduction. *Bessie Head: A Bibliography.* Susan Gardner and Patricia Scott. Grahamstown, South Africa: NELM Bibliographic Series Number One, 1986.

Giwa, Audee Tanimu. "*So Long a Letter:* A Feminism That Is Not." *Kuka* (1985–1986): 26–35.

Harrell-Bond, Barbara, "Mariama Bâ," Interview. *African Book Publishing Record* 6 (1980): 209–14.

Head, Bessie. *Maru.* London: Heinemann, 1972.

———. *A Question of Power.* London: Heinemann, 1974.

———. "Bessie Head in Australia." Interview. *New Literature Review* 14 (n.d.): 5–13.

———. "Social and Political Pressures That Shape Literature in Southern Africa." *World Literature Written in English* 18.1 (1979): 21–26.

Johnson, Joyce. "Bessie Head and the Oral Tradition: The Structure of *Maru.*" *WASAFIRI* 3 (1985): 5–8.

Kemp, Yakini. "'From Knowledge Gained Since': Women and Social Transition in Selected Novels by African Women Writers." Ph.D. diss., Atlanta University, 1986.

Ngcobo, Lauretta "Four African Women Writers." *South African Outlook* 114 (1984): 64–69.

Obiechina, Emanuel. "Romantic Love: Its Sources for West Africa." *An African Popular Literature: A Study of Onitsha Market Pamphlets.* Cambridge: Cambridge University Press, 1973.

Ogunyemi, Chikwenye. "Buchi Emecheta: The Shaping of a Self," *Komparatistische Hefte* 8 (1983): 54–77.

Ojo-Ade, Femi. "Still a Victim? Mariama Bâ's *Une Si Longue Lettre.*" *African Literature Today.* Vol. 12. Ed. Eldred Jones. New York: Africana Publishing, 1982.

Palmer, Eustace. "A Powerful Voice in African Fiction: Introducing the Novels of Buchi Emecheta," *New Literature Review* 11 (n.d.): 21–33.

Peek, Andrew. "Bessie Head and the African Novel." *The Given Condition: Essays in Post-Colonial Literatures.* Ed. Peter Simpson. Christchurch, New Zealand: South Pacific Association for Commonwealth Literature and Language Studies, 1985. 121–36.

The Politics of Exile

Ama Ata Aidoo's *Our Sister Killjoy*

GAY WILENTZ

The term "politics of exile" calls to mind those sufferers who must leave their homeland for political reasons. But there is another aspect of the politics associated with exile—that of the so-called Third World colonial who seeks the benefits and opportunities in a European country perceived as culturally superior, thus avoiding the sociopolitical situation at home. Ama Ata Aidoo's *Our Sister Killjoy or Reflections from a Black-Eyed Squint* is a relentless attack on the notions of exile as relief from the societal constraints of national development and freedom to live in a suitable cultural environment for creativity. In this work, Aidoo questions certain prescribed theories of exile, including the reasons for exile—particularly among African men. The novel exposes a rarely heard viewpoint in literature in English—that of the African woman exile, Aidoo's protagonist Sissie, as the "eye" of her people, is a sojourner to the "civilized" world of the colonizers. *Our Sister Killjoy,* which reflects Aidoo's own travels abroad, was written partially in the United States; moreover, although it was published in 1979, first editions carry a 1966 copyright, closer to the time in which she was traveling. Although Aidoo experienced the supposed freedom of exile herself, her personalized prose/poem novel illustrates her commitment to rebuild her former colonized home and confront those who have forgotten their duty to their native land.

Most critical reactions to the novel have ranged, predictably, from negative responses to silence and nonrecognition.[1] What has disturbed Aidoo most is not the negative criticism but the "unreception" of the novel—the refusal of many African critics to discuss it at all. In a speech,

"Unwelcome Pals and Decorative Slaves," Aidoo refers to the attitude of her male colleagues toward her involvement in political issues, expressed at a meeting on national development: "[Some professors] shouted that I am not fit to speak on public matters. That I should leave politics and such to those [men] most qualified to handle it" (23). Later in this speech, she comments, "I am convinced that if *Killjoy* or anything like it had been written by a man, as we say in these parts, no one would have been able to sleep a wink these couple of years" (38). Clearly, the fact that Aidoo is a woman has made this novel unacceptable to the predominantly male and/or Eurocentric critical community, but because she overthrows male-oriented theories of exile as well as integrating feminist and Afrocentric perspectives, *Our Sister Killjoy* could hardly have been written by a man. Here I examine Aidoo's challenge to prevailing theories of exile, her questioning of the supposed superiority of European culture for the colonial subject, and her exposé of the politics of exile for African self-exile. Through a combination of prose, poetry, oral voicing, and letter writing, Aidoo's Sissie reports back to her home community what she sees in the land of the colonizers and responds to those exiles who have chosen, as Frantz Fanon says, to stand with the white world (perceived as the "real world") in opposition to their own world, the Black world of the colonized (37).

A discussion of some relevant theories of exile may be of use here. Although I do not explore the distinction between exile and expatriation, I exclude from this discussion those who were forced to leave as banishment (on penalty of prison or possibly death); rather, I focus on those who seek exile for personal and/or cultural reasons. Many of the theories concerning these self-exiles (as I call them) entertain the notion that the exile chooses to escape limitations at home. Whether seeking freedom from the small town in the metropolis or from the colonial province in the colonizer's capital, the exile, particularly the exiled writer, sees himself [and I use this term advisedly] as freed from the constraints at home and opened to a world of cultural expression and diversity (Gurr 13–17). In *Exiles and Emigres,* Terry Eagleton clearly confirms this view in relation to the writers Henry James and Joseph Conrad: "James and Conrad chose England [for] its order, its manners, its settled, varied and traditionalist status. . . . [They] settled in England in flight from a *lack of established order and civilized manners elsewhere*" (14).

For the white American James, as for other colonials, there exists the cultural inferiority of the colony, and they are forced to go into exile "as a means of compensating for that sense of cultural subservience" (Gurr 8). For colonial exile of the nonindustrialized Third World, both the difference of color and the lack of so-called development augment these feelings of cultural inferiority. Caribbean writer George Lamming suggests that for colonial exiles, especially those living in the "country which has colonized [their] history," the exiles' sense of culture is intricately bound with that of the dominant culture's; in fact, for those educated in the colonial language, "their whole introduction to something called culture, all of it, in the form of words, came from outside" (27). Although generally stated, most theories of exile and its political implications are based on male experience and are therefore male-oriented in approach. This male-oriented approach ignores women sojourners like Sissie, who are not fooled by the neocolonial lie but see the land of exile as it is. In giving voice to Sissie's viewpoint, Aidoo not only overturns the assumptions of cultural superiority that the self-exiles bring with them in expatriation; she exposes the sham behind the self-exiles' reason for leaving from a polemically female perspective. The African men Sissie meets fit these theories of colonial exile, but Sissie does not. She is the "squint," who, rather than be isolated from her home, becomes the eye of her community in the land of the exiles.

Sissie's reflections open with a section, "Into a Bad Dream," which prepares us for her shamanistic journey to the land of the colonizers. Before we are even introduced to our squint, Aidoo deconstructs the structure of the novel by opening it with a four-page poem/political statement, an attack on the world into which Sissie will descend:

Yes, my brother
The worst of them
these days supply local
statistics for those population studies and
toy with
genocidal formulations.
That's where the latest crumbs
are being thrown! (7)

In fact, it is hard to call this compilation of poetic anger, political commentary, journal entries, oral voicings, and letter writings a "novel" in the conventional sense; rather, it appears to be a formulation of an African prose poem that reverberates with sounds of the orature in the written language and personal dialogue—illustrating Aidoo's comment that "we don't always have to write for readers, we can write for listeners" (Lautre 24). Furthermore, Aidoo's breakdown of the novelistic structure exemplifies one aspect of exile that Lamming suggests affects most writers from colonized lands: the problem of writing in the colonial language. For the Anglophone African author writing in English, "home is in a different language. It is a double exile, in culture and in the tongue" the author feels compelled to use (Gurr 28). In wrestling with this conflict, Aidoo manages to inject the colonial language with the substance and structure of her own Akan. Linguistically, she challenges the sense of double exile that comes with the colonial experience.

"Our Sister" does not choose exile but is picked as a promising student and is given a scholarship to attend an international work-study program in Germany and to visit her colonial "capital"—London. As in a bad dream, Sissie boards a plane to Germany. In a mixture of prose and poetry, Sissie reports her feelings of being seen as an "exotic" by the people of Germany, her experiences with an unhappy German housewife, and her questions concerning the cultural superiority of Europe and its corresponding cruelty. Then, in journal entry form, she recounts her encounter with the colonial power that changed the history of her Ghanaian home—England. While in London, she faces Ghanaian and other African self-exiles, confronts them for deserting their homelands, and in a final "love letter," she berates a lover who has decided to remain in exile as she returns home.

Aidoo comments that her protagonist Sissie sees everything "through the filter of her memories of Africa" (Vincent 2). Moreover, as "Our Sister," Sissie is rooted in her African communal society and all her responses are oriented toward decolonization and the education of this community. Unlike other exiles who have lost the sense of identity that comes from belonging to a community, Sissie becomes the eyes of her community, reporting on those lost ones who have forgotten maternal, familial, and community ties, and squinting at these men—young and old—who refuse to return home to face national realities and rebuild their countries. It is no mistake that Sissie is female; she is the representative of all the mothers and sisters and daughters who have been left behind on this illusive search for artistic, political, cultural, and perhaps even sexual freedom.

In the above statement on Conrad and James, Terry Eagleton focuses on their belief that culture and order existed only in Western Europe, most specifically in England, and by going there one could be freed from the lack of civilization elsewhere—most often, in the colonies. Sissie overturns these notions of civilization by her scathing attack on Western culture and by what she sees and contemplates in Germany. Critic Anita Kern, in a fairly negative review of *Our Sister Killjoy*, comments that Aidoo "seems to have it out for the west" (57), but clearly Sissie's angry language and shocked thoughts reflect a young woman who has heard of this cultural paradise yet sees something far different. Sissie's first encounter with the Germans on the street reminds me of Frantz Fanon's remembrances of the little boy on a train from Paris who shouted "Look, a Negro" a few times, and then, finally, "Mama, see the Negro! I'm frightened" (111, 112). For Sissie, response to her Blackness is not as extreme, but certainly as disconcerting: "Suddenly, she realized a woman was telling a young girl who must have been her daughter: 'Ja, das Schwartze Mädchen.' ... And it hit her. That all the crowd of people going and coming in all sorts of directions had the colour of pickled pig parts" (12). Visibly, through her own crude description, Sissie is striking back at the Europeans who see her skin as unnatural, and she is later ashamed of her mocking words; but it is also evident that being Black and female makes her an oddity for the Germans, who are fascinated by this showpiece, this "African Miss" (43).

Ironically, the one person who sees Sissie beyond her Blackness is Marija, the unhappy housewife, and through their friendship, Sissie is exposed to what she sees not as cultural superiority, but as an example of the West's societal degeneration—the breakdown of the family. Marija, who befriends Sissie, lives in a cold stone house with her son and a husband who never comes home. And lest we miss the point, both father and son are named "Adolph"—albeit a common German name, it certainly is a loaded one. Sissie feels compassion as well as affection for this lonely, frail woman; yet at the same time, she is suspicious, uncomfortable, and angry at their mutual historicity. In her thought poems, Sissie spills out these feelings:

Who was Marija Sommer?
A daughter of mankind's
   Self-appointed most royal line
   The House of Aryan—

An heiress to some
Legacy that would make you
Bow
Down
Your head in
Shame and
Cry. (48)

This section of the novel, called "The Plums"—a European delicacy not available in Ghana—reflects Sissie's, and perhaps Aidoo's, conflicting feelings for the women of this dominant culture. On the one hand, they are intricately connected to the values and privileges of this society, retaining many of the culture's prejudices toward the "other"—male or female; yet, on the other, they are also victims of this society. For Sissie, her comprehension of the emptiness of this isolated woman's life is exacerbated by Marija's attempt to reach out to her sexually. And, although this section may be problematic for some feminist scholars, it is evident that Aidoo—however sympathetically—sees this attempt at a lesbian relationship as a perversion of woman love and part of the degeneration of European family life: "Sissie thought of home. To the time when she was a child in the village. . . . Oo, to be wrapped up in mother's cloth while it rained. Every time it rained. And where was she now? How did she get there . . . where now a young Aryan housewife kisses a young black woman with such desperation, right in the middle of her own nuptial chamber" (64). Through Sissie's perceptions, we witness this sexual affection arising from the despair of a Western-style, isolated, loveless family life; however, it is also clear that Marija is seen as a fellow sufferer, and her home situation is one that many women deal with, in some way or another, throughout the world. For Sissie sees Marija's weeping not only as personal loneliness but also as part of a larger political discourse—the "collective loss" (67) that women within the context of an aggressive patriarchy must endure. Moreover, as she watches older "Bavarian ladies" in black dresses walking through town, she envisions them as war widows, "The blood of their young men was / Needed to mix the concrete for / Building the walls of / The Third Reich" (36).

If our squint Sissie sees the plight of the German woman sympathetically for the most part, she has very little compassion for German culture as a whole. She sees the notion of Aryan superiority as symptomatic of Europe's mandate to colonize and oppress, and she connects the at-

tempted genocide of the Jews to the murder of oppressed people everywhere. When Marija tells Sissie that she must see Munich, Sissie thinks
in her poetic/polemical voice that Munich is the home of the "Original
Adolph," and then her thoughts jump from images of "freshly widowed
Yiddisher Mamas" to the Rhodesian concentration camplike system of
apartheid after the country's 1965 so-called independence (81). The
workings of Sissie's mind on the colonizer and the colonized filter
through her experiences in this supposed paradise for the exile; her
thoughts strike back while her words remain polite. The division between the polite exchange student and the angry woman inside is revealed in Sissie's meeting with the German-born American professor.
He tells her that the one thing Germans and Africans have in common is
that they have both been oppressed. Amazed, she is unable to respond:
"Yes, so frozen was her mind with this icy brilliance of this master discovery, she could not ask him whether after the German, the Irish and
Africans—indisputably in that order—there are or could have been
some other oppressed people on the earth, like Afro-Americans or
Amerindians or Jews" (92).[2] But she also realizes that "the world is not
filled with folks who shared our sister's black-eyed squint at things" (93).

If our black-eyed squint internally reprimands the colonizers because
of their history of domination, she looks equally askance at the African
self-exiles who have bought the colonial line. In Germany, our sojourner
reacts to the various Europeans she meets and plays off her memories of
home against this alien environment. But it is her trip to England that
conjures up a personal response to colonialism and compels her to issue
a direct attack on her countrymen who have considered it politically
expedient to remain in exile. She comments in the opening of this diary-
like section "From Our Sister Killjoy": "If anyone had told her that she
would want to pass through England because it was her colonial home,
she would have laughed . . . but to London she had gone anyway" (85).
This section, compiled as so many journal entries, is a report to family
and community (those mothers left behind) on the state of the self-
exiles, who have not only forgotten to return to help with the process of
decolonization, but who forget even to answer the letters pleading to
learn of their health and whereabouts.

For the African self-exiles in England, Our Sister really *is* a killjoy. She
confronts the life she sees there, not the one that has been paraded before
the folks back home. For many exiles, "the desire to lose oneself in the

[European] world was understandable: a naive faith that this is the way to escape the feeling of exile" (Dorsinville 63). But Sissie does not become caught up in the exiles' dream; she sees the life they lead with clarity. Her piercing look exposes the lies that have been sent back to the provinces. Her amazement at finding so many Black people in London is painfully accentuated by her acknowledgment of their poverty: "Above all, what hurt Our Sister as she . . . watched her people was how badly dressed they were. They were all poorly clothed. The women were especially pitiful. She saw women who at home would have been dignified matrons as well as young attractive girls. . . . She wondered why they never told the truth of their travels at home" (88, 89). Although Sissie focuses on the women when she looks at the poor people in the street, she centers on the men when she explores the psychological poverty of those who feel there is nothing left for them in the colonial provinces, that life in London is where all "culture" begins.

In *Black Skins, White Masks,* Fanon explains the delusion of cultural superiority that the exile in the colonial "mother country" suffers from: "The colonized is elevated above his jungle status in proportion to his adoption of the mother country's cultural standards. He becomes whiter as he renounces his blackness, his jungle" (18). As mentioned earlier, many of the theories of exile focus on a sort of freedom felt by separating oneself from the constraints of the home country; this feeling of freedom is linked with a distorted sense of importance for the colonial exile. Furthermore, for the Third World exile, as Fanon points out, this freedom also involves a rejection of both racial and cultural identification. Again, although this example may extend to women self-exiles, Fanon appears to be using the term "he" not as gender inclusive, but as a specific aspect of the psychological disturbances of these male self-exiles. Aidoo underscores this point in her discussion of a Ghanaian self-exile, Kunle, who believes that the problems of apartheid will be solved by Western technology. He illustrates his point by citing the fact that a "good Christian," white, South African doctor used the heart of a young Black man for a transplant to keep an old white man alive. When confronted by the confused Sissie and her friend on which hearts were used in earlier attempts at transplants, he answers eagerly, "He must have experimented on the hearts of dogs and cats" (97). Kunle, caught up in his identification with the dominant culture's "advances," has no comprehension of the irony of his own comments.

For Sissie, Kunle not only represents the self-exile who values the colonizers' world more than his own, he also represents the "been-to" who comes home with an exile's consciousness to complain and exploit rather than to help build the nation. His identification with the culture of his exile makes him unable to confront the political realities at home. Although he returns to his native land, as Aimé Césaire calls it, he is not willing to sacrifice and utilize his skills to improve conditions. Instead, "Kunle, like so many of us, wished he had had the courage to be coward enough to stay forever in England. Though life 'home' had its compensations. The aura of having been overseas at all. Belonging to the elite, whatever that is. The sweet pain of getting a fairly big income which can never half support one's own style of living" (107). Kunle's death, his chauffeur-driven car "burnt to its original skeleton," illustrates the wastefulness of the African elite, both materially and spiritually. But Kunle's attitude also clarifies, for Sissie, the reasons that many others are "coward enough" to remain in England.

Some of the early novels of Africans in exile (Peter Abraham's *A Wreath for Udomo* comes to mind) examine the conflicting feelings even the forced exiles faced in terms of their life in England versus what they had to confront at home. For the self-exiles who can return, remaining in Europe represents another political decision: to deny the needs of their homeland and ignore the hardships faced by those left at home. *Our Sister Killjoy* forces us to look not only at what happens to those who are coward enough to remain isolated from their community, but what happens to the mothers and other family members who wait for their return. Perhaps it is because more men have experienced exile—unhampered by children and often chosen by community leaders—that Aidoo focuses on them as examples; but with the exception of Sissie's comments about the poverty of the women's clothes, Aidoo does not critique the role of the African women exiled overseas.

Sissie, although a student-exile herself, is clearly attached to her homeland, especially to the women who are waiting for some word from their errant men. As she remembers these women left behind, Sissie's thought-poems construct the mostly unanswered letters from home asking the sons Kofi, Bragou, Obi, and others when they are coming home. The letters—"for which we died expecting and /Which / Buried us when they came"—underscore the financial and emotional hardship the families face when most of their resources have gone into the training of the

"One Scholar." However, the letters also emphasize the love and confusion of these women who have lost their children to false dreams of the dominant culture's ideology:

> There is nothing bad here
> . . . except our family is
> drowning in debts. . . .
>
> Now,
> It is me,
> Your Own Mother
> speaking.
>
> There is nothing bad here
>
> And I am not complaining
> My Child.
> You also know
> we are proud
> that
> you are Overseas. (104, 105)

The pathos of these letters interspersed with the insensitivity of the exiles themselves illustrates the sociopolitical effects of the exile experience on those at home; moreover, the letters critique those feelings of freedom and notions of cultural superiority for the self-exiles who have forgotten their duty to their emerging nations. In the final section of this prose/poem novel, Aidoo jumps from the snatches of letters cited above to what Chimalum Nwankwo has rightly called a "confrontational" love letter. Sissie writes this letter to her lover, who has decided to remain in exile. Although I am unable to agree that this love letter necessarily suggests "communication between man and woman" as "a way out of this morass," as Nwankwo suggests (158), we can see that Sissie clearly speaks her mind. The irony of this section's title is that Sissie's epistle ends up being more a political statement than a traditional love letter. To her lover and the other African self-exiles, Sissie is the killjoy who refuses to allow them to live in their delusions and forces them to acknowledge the duties they have ignored toward their native land and families.

"A Love Letter" is less angry than the earlier sections of this work;

rather, it is full of remorse for a relationship that cannot last and for a world that has profoundly lost its way. Sissie softens her language in writing to this lover, yet the use of colonial language as her medium exiles her from her deepest speech: "[How can I] give voice to my soul and have her heard? Since so far, I have only been able to use a language that enslaved me, and therefore, the messengers of my mind always come shackled?" (112) Sissie's resistance to the language she writes in mirrors the concerns of many writing in the colonial language—a "language which sought to deny" them.[3] Moreover, the realization that Sissie cannot speak to her lover in anything but the colonial language, distancing her from him, is exacerbated by the fact that he does not see this as a problem. What he considers a problem is that she is too aggressive, too outspoken, "too serious" (112). This love letter is composed of her polemical voicings—possibly rearguing points with this unseen lover. She compels him to address the problems colonial rule has left these countries with and the frightening loss of perspective and lack of leadership at home; at the same time, the letter is full of her wishing that she could stop confronting him, that he would hold her once again. For Sissie, her desire for this man comes in direct opposition to her strength as an African woman, as she states, "They say that any female in my position would have thrown away everything to be with you, and remain with you: first her opinions, and then her own plans. But . . . what did I rather do but daily and loudly criticize you and your friends for wanting to stay forever in alien places. . . . Maybe I regret that I could not shut up and meekly look up to you . . . but no one ever taught me such meekness" (117). In a further incorporation of the dominant culture's values, the self-exiled men demand what Sissie calls "hashed-up Victorian notions" for their women, in spite of the fact that they should understand that African women were not brought up to be like the "dolls of the colonizers" (117). In her other works, Aidoo has concentrated on the strength of the African woman as well as the domination—both male and colonial—over her; in *Killjoy,* she confronts the colonized male's notion of the ideal African woman (all softness and meekness) when these men have forgotten the real African women at home.

In this love letter, Sissie recounts her most direct confrontation with the African self-exiles. Sissie speaks out at an African student union meeting. They spend hours discussing the political situation in the home countries, but they do not see the denial of their services as part of the problem. Tired of the "beautiful radical analyses of the situation at home," Sissie asks these exiles why they just don't hurry back and do something about it (121). She examines each of their reasons for exile and calls them excuses; her greatest distress, however, is directed at a doctor who stays in exile because he feels that his sophisticated medical skills would be wasted in his country. Rather than dealing with the reality that it is in Africa where many doctors are needed, he is proud that he can remain to educate the Europeans to "recognize our worth" (129). This, of course, is what Fanon indicates as the final stage of internal colonization: to isolate oneself from one's own society and identify totally with the colonizer. Only in this world are one's skills valuable; the self-exile "congratulates himself" on the fact that "his race no longer understands him" or appreciates his skills (Fanon 14). To Sissie, this "brilliant" doctor becomes the symbol of everything "distasteful about all the folks who have decided to stay overseas" (126). He and others like him, who consider that their only duty to the country is to send some money home to their mothers, deny a deeper commitment to their family and to the land of their birth; they squander their talents on the colonizers, who would rather see them "run, jump and sing" (129).

In the final line of Sissie's love letter, she recalls what her lover asked her when they met: "I know everyone calls you Sissie, but what is your name?" (131). We, as readers, do not find out her name (or the name of her lover), but as Our Sister, she is the messenger of the people, her kin, in the land of exiles. For Sissie, "the tale is not done being told" and, as the eyes of her community, she will return home to tell this tale to the mothers and other family members (121). Here is where the self-exiles are most nakedly exposed; it is not that they are *coward* enough to stay in exile; they are afraid to go home. Sissie's tale, as a sister, is for the community as a whole but especially for the African mother who, as both the self-exiles and Sissie agree, has suffered. But she cannot be appeased—nor can "Mother Africa"—by a paltry sum; she needs to see her children face-to-face, bringing their skills for national development that she "scrimped and saved and mortgaged her dignity for" back home (123). Sissie ends her letter as her plane starts to descend along the West African coast. She decides not to send it; writing it was all that was necessary—and later telling the tale to those at home: "Besides, she was back in Africa. And that felt like fresh wild honey on the tongue: a mixture of complete sweetness and smoky roughage. Below was home with its unavoidable warm and even after all those years, its uncertainties" (133). Although Sissie's lover does not learn from her experience, those who read her thoughts do. This collective novel of political thought/poems and personal perceptions ends on a positive note: Happy to be back from her shamanistic journey, Sissie is ready to tell her tale, dispel the myth, and go to work for her nation.

In an interview, Nigerian critic Theo Vincent questions Aidoo's use of an African woman as the protagonist of *Killjoy*, one as politically astute as Our Sister. Aidoo responds, "But will this kind of vision be part of any African man's awareness of Europe? . . . What makes you think that our men are more politically aware than our women?" (3) Certainly, in this novel, it is the protagonist's social vision that differs from her male counterparts'; she discerns exactly what the politics of self-exile is. And like her protagonist, Aidoo saw through the false paradise of the exile during her stays in the United States and Europe and, until recently, returned to Ghana to be part of its national development. As an African woman writer, Aidoo questions the freedom of the exile who denies both familial and community ties. Furthermore, she—as well as other African women writers, such as Flora Nwapa, Efua Sutherland, Zulu Sofola, and Aminata Sow Fall—is committed to her homeland, in spite of the "uncertainties" that exist there, because of her ties to the land and its people. Aidoo, and other women writers like her, feel bonded to their larger national communities as they do to their extended families. In *Killjoy*, Aidoo presents an African woman who does not flee the constraints imposed on her by her society, but instead takes the responsibility to be the "eyes" of her community and exposes the world of the self-exiles who have forsaken their familial land.

Notes

1. Critics like Vincent and Kern, cited in this article, discount the importance of this work because of its attack on both the exile and the land of exile; it is unfortunate that there have been few critical studies done on this important work. For a more positive, albeit cursory review, see John Ngara, 65–66.

2. In her first play, *The Dilemma of a Ghost* (1965), and her collection of short stories, *No Sweetness Here* (1970), Aidoo explores the relation of the Afro-American to Africa and Africans. In her second play, *Anowa* (1970), Aidoo examines African complicity in the slave trade.

3. This phrase is taken from the introduction to an unpublished manuscript by the Trinidadian poet, Marlene Nourbese Phillip, *She Tried her Tongue, Her Silence Breaks Slowly* (1988). See also George Lamming, "A Monster, a Child, a Slave," in *The Pleasures of Exile*, 95–117.

Works Cited

Abrahams, Peter. *A Wreath for Udomo.* London: Faber and Faber, 1956.

Aidoo, Ama Ata. *Anowa.* London: Longman, 1970.

———. *The Dilemma of a Ghost.* London: Longman, 1965.

———. *No Sweetness Here.* London: Longman, 1970.

———. *Our Sister Killjoy or Reflections from a Black-Eyed Squint.* Lagos and New York: Nok Publishers, 1977.

———. "Unwelcome Pals and Decorative Slaves." *Medium and Message.* International Conference on African Literature and the English Language, University of Calabar, Nigeria, 1980.

Dorsinville, Max. "Senghor and the Song of Exile." *Exile and Tradition: Studies in African and Caribbean Literature.* Ed. Rowland Smith. New York: Africana, 1976. 62–73.

Eagleton, Terry. *Exiles and Emigres.* New York: Schocken Books, 1970.

Fanon, Frantz. *Black Skins, White Masks.* New York: Grove Press, 1967.

Gurr, Andrew. *Writers in Exile.* Sussex and Atlantic Highlands, N. J.: Harvester/Humanities Press, 1981.

Kern, Anita. "Review of *Our Sister Killjoy.*" *World Literature Written in English* 17.1 (1978): 56–57.

Lamming, George. *The Pleasures of Exile.* London: Allison and Busby, 1984.

Lautre, Maxine. "Interview with Ama Ata Aidoo." *African Writers Talking.* Eds. Dennis Duerden and Cosmos Pieterse. New York: Africana Publishing, 1972.

Ngara, John. "Review of *Our Sister Killjoy.*" *Africa Woman* 12 (1977): 65–66.

Nwankwo, Chimalum. "The Feminist Impulse and Social Realism in Ama Ata Aidoo's *No Sweetness Here* and *Our Sister Killjoy.*" *Ngambika.* Ed. Carole Boyce Davies and Ann Adams Graves. Trenton, N.J.: Africa World Press, 1986.

Vincent, Theo. *Seventeen Black and African Writers on Literature and Life.* Lagos: Cross Continent Press, 1981. 1–8.

12

"Sense Make Befoh Book"

Grenadian Popular Culture and the Rhetoric of Revolution
in Merle Collins's *Angel* and *The Colour of Forgetting*

CAROLYN COOPER

*I tell you, the dogs and the spirits did well know
and you know, that was long before human hearing anything
to make them start bawling. So who know? Perhaps if people
had a habit of listening, some other something*

*Might have come to pass. But then people say what is to is
must is. But look at that, eh! Look how in this tower of
babel, most of us, is only one language we know how to talk.*

*All I know is, looking back at it now, one thing that sure
is that before talk break, before thing turn ole mass
I tell you, the dogs and the spirits did well know*
Merle Collins—"The Signs"

Merle Collins's soul-searching first novel, *Angel,* published four years
after the implosion of the Grenada Revolution, articulates the growth to
political consciousness of its female protagonist, Angel, and simultaneously traces the evolution of radical nationalist politics in the small
island state. Focusing on three generations of women, the novel fore-
grounds issues of color, class, gender, (dis)empowerment, voice, and
identity that illuminate the processes of social change in Grenada that
culminate in the revolution and its disillusioning aftermath. In *The
Colour of Forgetting* Collins continues to question the meaning of the
revolution, particularly for those long-memoried peasant folk who never
quite believe the grandiloquent rhetoric of politicians.

Despite the conventional disclaimer, "[t]his is a work of fiction and
any resemblance to persons living or dead is purely coincidental" (2),

Angel does establish correspondences between events in the narrative and the trajectory of Grenadian political history over the three-decade period it documents. The novel's two major fictional political leaders do resemble "persons living or dead." "Leader" and "Chief" are prototypes, each of a different political stripe, of that recurring figure in Caribbean politics: the charismatic leader. Leader and Chief are not fully realized characters for very good reason. The politics of representation require fictional tact, especially when the writer is dealing with a subject as sensitive as the Grenada Revolution. Collins, poet and novelist, effectively uses the mask of artifice to both protect herself and extend her account beyond the merely factual; it is an archetypal tale she tells. In the words of Doodsie, Angel's mother: "'Is the same story all over. Is vye neg on the ground an bakra beke on top. We always startin, always in the beginning'" (*A* 11).

Within the narrative there are embedded songs, proverbial statements, and poems that give the people's perspective on events. These collective fictions, cunningly presented as operating beyond the domain of the controlling creativity of the individual novelist, suggest yet another level of authentication of Collins's fiction. The truth she articulates is not only her personal vision; the novel affirms a sustained tradition of suffering, struggle, and creativity that is encoded in the oral histories of the Grenadian people who speak their wisdom in ritualized song, story, and proverb. It is in the mouth of Sister Miona Spencer, a grandmother and belated student in the Revolutionary Government's literacy program, that Collins puts a calypsonian poem that documents the rise of the Horizon movement. The benefits of the literacy project are acknowledged, but it is Sister Miona's memory, the collective memory of struggle, that will sustain her performance: "'Sister and brothers, this poem that I will do for you I write jus a few weeks ago when ah siddown and really tink bout wey we is today an wey we comin from! I have it in me pocket here, but de eyes not too good today, you know. I forget de glasses, so I hope I could remember it well. But ah sure ah could remember it'" (*A* 247).

The spirit of Miona's performance is expressed in one of the novel's many proverbs, "Sense make befoh book." Sister Miona does not really need glasses for vision; her oral insights are sufficiently penetrating.

Ay! Well we try it in '51!
We say come pa come

Ting bad for so
Take up we burden
We go help you go!
Pa take up we burden
He take up he purse
And when he purse get so heavy
He throw down we burden
Down on de groun!
De Horizon come up
Pa star go down!
An we watchin de Horizon
Like is really a dream
Becus
hear, non!
Me at me age in school again!
Wey you ever hear dat
In dis country here!
Me granchilren in secondary
Dey not paying a cent!
Ay! Wey you ever hear dat
In dis country here.
So Horizon go on
We neck and neck wid you
Don throw down we burden, non!
We depending on yu
Don throw dow we burden, non!
Ting too sweet for dat! (*A* 247, 248)

The poem is performed at a zonal council meeting, the main burden of which is to deal with reports from the head of the Water Commission and a representative from the Public Works Department on erratic water supply and on the poor conditions of the roads. The public officials of the Revolutionary Government speak a bookish English, politically obtuse: "Now the position is this. In a situation such as the one in which we find ourselves, there are certain variables to be considered . . ." (*A* 249). The speaker is immediately cut off by an impatient listener who forces him to consider the basic variable of comprehensibility: "'Mr. Wellington, ah jus want to say dat what you start to say dey ain make no sense, comrade. We want to break it up! We don want you to wrap up nutting in big word so dat we caan understand. Is information we want, and we want it clear and simple!'" (*A* 249). Here is an excellent example of the way in which primarily oral speakers use metaphorical language to convey abstract ideas: big words can be used to wrap up/ obscure meaning.

A female speaker, similarly refusing to be silenced by her lack of literacy, unapologetically goes straight to the heart of the matter: "'I just want to say that I in the literacy program. Not all of us did go to High School, through no fault o we own. So jus give us de ting straight an simple, like, an ting settle'" (*A* 249). Wellington quickly acknowledges the legitimacy of the criticisms: "'Yes. Yes. I accept that. . . .' We learnin too, you know. But you're right. You have a point there. I'll break it up'" (*A* 249). The leaders of the movement themselves have to learn new ways of speaking the abstract ideology of revolution. There is a fundamental contradiction in the process of transfer of power to the masses. The imported, globalizing language of text-book liberation is often oppressive, if not deliberately alienating. Hubert Devonish argues that "the sections of the Grenadian educated elite which took power in 1979 may have had no choice. As a class, they were created to work by the book. They could not, even if they chose to, play by ear" (36).

Conversely, Sister Miona's intimate poem speaks directly to the people. Intellectual activity is not an alien ideology; it is an everyday function of the Grenadian people's lived reality. "People turned, applauding her as she passed by, shaking her hand. 'You could give me a copy of it, sister?' 'Heavy, sister.' 'Yes. Thank you very much, Sister Miona. Sister and brothers, that is the kind of talent that was there hidin all de time, dat the revolution bringing to light'" (248).

That final self-satisfied comment from the comrade chairman of the evening's meeting seems to claim too much for the revolution. The organizational machinery of the party may have created a forum for the expression of Miona's insight in the form of performance poetry at a public meeting, but the folk wisdom she speaks predates the revolution. Her authority comes from generations of Grenadians who intuitively understand the circumstances of their own lives.

Leader's rise to fortune comes at a time in Grenada when people are tired of having their labor exploited by the big landowners. The novel opens with a theatrical event—the burning of the De Lisle estate—which is eagerly applauded by expectant onlookers. The spirit of carnival prevails. With wicked wit, Maisie, one of the spectators who works on the estate, reduces the grand scale of events to a much more personal level. Responding to the noises of the fire she laughingly asks:

> "All you hear dat? Ah sure is me basket o cocoa an dem dat bowling dey." Her voice cut through the laughter. "You hear de juice? You hear how it squelchin scroom, scroom, scroom?" They laughed. Some sucked their teeth. Turned laughing faces in Maisie's direction. They slapped cutlasses against waterboots as they enjoyed the joke. "Maisie, you could talk too much stupidness!" "No joke non, cocoa. Ah plant you, ah pick you, ah dance in you, but you so damn ungrateful, you don even know you mudder. Dead, you nastiness! You tink ah wounta ketch you?" "Ho-hoy!" "Woy!" "Ah tell you!" "Maisie, you don good, non!" "Ay-Ay!" "Tongue an teeth doesn laugh at good ting, non!" (*A* 2)

That final proverbial statement, affirming the necessity of laughter in difficult circumstances, encapsulates the complex mood of the people: anger and a simultaneous capacity to take bad things and make jokes out of them.

The metaphor also evokes the alienation of the worker from the fruits of labor. Forced to rebel, many of the disaffected join ranks with Leader who promises reforms in the labor market. It is Doodsie, Angel's mother, who intuits Leader's potential for betrayal: "'That man?' Doodsie put the green bananas down on the dresser. 'Watch yourself, you know, Regal. Ah hear you was part o de group dat set fire to dose people plantation. Ah not makin noise. Jus as a sister ah tellin you. Don follow dat man lead too close, you know.' She looked around, found the stained, handleless provision knife and stood leaning against the dresser. Regal said nothing. 'Dat man like a lotta flash. You should o see he weddin in Aruba. Real pappyshow. It was so flashy dey make up a song on it'" (*A* 13). Doodsie knows that the showy surfaces of things are more important to Leader than substance. His flashy clothes, like the obfuscating rhetoric of the politician, cover up his lack of commitment to fundamental social change. He, like his wedding, is a real pappyshow. Further, Doodsie reminds us of how anonymous song is used as an instrument of censure and satire in Caribbean societies. A derisive song taken up in full voice by a whole society becomes an effective substitute for more formal sanctions.

It is also Doodsie who, in a letter to a friend abroad, points to the failure of the electoral system to effect change when the homogeneity of candidates makes voting pointless. The letter format allows Collins to demonstrate on an intimate scale, and in the voice of the people, the significance of events that are occurring in the wider society. Doodsie chides her husband for wanting to be too particular about spelling when he's writing a letter to a friend: "'Advancement! Advancement, Doodsie! Dat have an "e" in it? Two "e" or one? Ah does never remember!' 'Well, advance have an "e." Don mine. Is a letter. Not a exam!'" (*A* 44). The real exam is knowing which political leader to vote for.

Some of the proverbial statements used as headings for the sections of the novel that document Leader's rise to prominence warn that appearances can be deceptive:

Not all skin-teet is good grin!
Not all wag-tail is promise not to bite
Someting in de mortar besides de pestle!
Sometimes you have to take de worse an call it de best.

Indeed, the Grenadian people are forced to take the worst and call it the best. They follow Leader because he is the best option they have at the time. Yet, retribution is swift once the people come to recognize Leader's ideological resemblance to plantation owner Mr. De Lisle. Again, it is Maisie who makes the subversive comparison. Leader's downfall is heralded by irreverent song:

Run Leader Run!
The people's on your way!
Run Leader Run
For a spot in an open ba-a-ay!
You got to drown yourself dey
Hide youself wey
Lewwe pull we country straight!
Run Leader Run. . . . (*A* 210)

Another pointed song invites Leader to experience first-hand the problems that the suffering people have to face:

Leader-o-o-oy-y!
Me bucket have a hole
In de centre!
An i-i-if you tink ah tellin lie!
Push you finger!
Leado-o-oy!
Me rooftop have a hole
In de centre!
An i-i-if you tink ah tellin lie
Spen a night dey! (*A* 211)

Asserting the people's awareness of their collective power, the following song is a clear threat:

We will always let our leaders fall!
When dey treat us de worst of all!
We will always let our leaders fa-a-all!
When they treat us
Like shit an all! (*A* 212, 213)

The carnivalesque mood of the novel's opening when the De Lisle plantation is burned recurs as the people take to the streets en masse to protest Leader's failure to help carry the collective burden. It is the Horizon movement that engineers the overwhelmingly successful public rally that precipitates Leader's downfall: "Singing the song of the carnival bands Leader had banned from the streets the year before, the bands in which people covered themselves completely in black grease and paint, clattered through the streets with can, pans horns, celebrating like their African ancestors had celebrated emancipation, parading the blackness that gave so much fear and making sure it left its mark on anything white. 'Ole Ole O' 'Djab Djab'" (*A* 212).

The self-liberation of the people from Leader's stranglehold is thus contextualized within a long carnivalesque tradition of hierarchy inversion. The diabolical energy of the Djab Djab is the assertion of an emancipatory blackness that seeks to leave its indelible mark on anything white. Dirt thus becomes a sign of power, the antithesis of purity, both literal and ideological.

The Horizon movement will itself become vulnerable to the people's subversive, blackening power. The anti-Horizon songs in the novel indicate that the people are not unanimously committed to purist party politics. The pro-Leader forces assert their right to challenge the policies of the Horizon movement, which seem to come from outer space. The alienness of the movement clearly contrasts with the indigenous traditions of resistance that are annually celebrated in the rites of carnival:

Horizon, Horizon
Go far away ah say!
Lose youself in de ocean boy!
We go murder you today!

Horizon Horizon
Wu! Wu!
Horizon Horizon
Go far away ah say!
Horizon, place
is out dey in space!
We don want you here ah say! (*A* 214)

Conversely, the pro-Horizon forces use communally validated proverbs to affirm the necessity to embrace change:

As long as you have life you could turn you han to someting
You have to make a move to help youself! You caan siddown dey like de livin dead
Well yes, wi! You live an learn!
Man proposes; God disposes
Is not everything everything you could believe but some dream trying to tell you something!
Sometimes we have to drink vinegar an pretend we think is honey!

Several of the proverbs used as chapter headings in the section of the narrative that immediately precedes the coup focus on the children as the hope for change. These proverbs optimistically assert the necessity for radical social transformation, and affirm the possibility of a viable alternative to Leader's dissembling, pappyshow politics:

If wasn for de chilren, eh!
Ah have nutting to leave for you when ah dead. All ah have is in you head so make de best of it!

Ah gives as much as ah could, chile, an den you on you own!
We lookin to you young ones to raise we nose
Open up you head an take in what dey teaching you! But don get
grand grand as do as if you foot caan touch de groun! Dat is wey
you ha to walk!
You of age to see after yourself now! So pull up you socks!
Some potato jus doesn follow de vine
The mud dey take an make you dey, dey throw it away when dey
finish
Me? I always in de middle like a maypole, an both sides pullin!
Never damn de bridge you cross.

The proverbs used in the sections of the narrative that recount the
heyday of the revolution are generally optimistic:

When God caan come, he does send
We doin we own ting!
Everybody putting dey grain o salt!
You tink was a easy lesson?
Pwangad waya pike mwen! [Take care lest the wire pricks me]
Is a sure sign! Enemy in de bush
Someting boilin under de surface!
We runnin neck an neck wid you!

The trauma of the betrayal of the revolution and the opportunistic
United States invasion is effectively recorded in proverb:

Secure allyou fowls! Galin [chicken-hawk] in de area!
Tout moun ca playwai! [everyone is crying]
None ouf us din born big!
When water more dan flour!
The Bush-gram busy
Never say never!
It have more ting is [sic] dis world dan what we know about
Today for policeman, tomorrow for tief
Look how trouble could come right inside people house an meet
dem eh!
In cow-belly crossways!
Don look so see who behind you! Look in front to make sure you
see wey you goin!

You not no egg, girl! You caan break so easy!
We never get more dan we can handle!

A particularly poignant metaphor is that of the invasive, predatory *galin* [chicken-hawk] swooping down on the scattered chickens. Earlier in the novel the image is used allegorically to affirm the need for cohesiveness to counter the collective enemy: "'Youall so stupid!' Doodsie looked around the yard empty of fowls which were hiding in the bushes, up on the steps, under the house. 'If youall would stay tegedder, the chicken-hawk won come down an do nutting! Stupes!' She stamped her foot, distressed, shielded her eyes and looked skywards again. The chicken-hawk had disappeared. Slowly, the fowls began to regroup. 'Stupes!'" (*A* 255). In the spirit of Maisie's perennial capacity to laugh in circumstances of dire distress, the proverb "Today for policeman, tomorrow for tief" philosophically accommodates even the invasion as part of a dialectical process that is ultimately egalitarian (*A* 272). The proverb also intuits how today's global policeman becomes tomorrow's thief, swooping down on lesser nations in acts of extravagant overkill.

In *The Colour of Forgetting* many of the preoccupations of *Angel* recur: land is the contested terrain over which succeeding generations fight to claim their right to self-definition; and the revolution remains an evocative signifier. But Collins uses the fictional names Paz and Eden to locate the later novel only one level from historical fact. Blurring the boundaries between myth and history, *The Colour of Forgetting* remembers through indirect allusion. As in the poem "The Signs," the novelist validates the authority of spirit messengers. Carib, the warner woman, is the primary medium through whom the otherworldly wisdom of the fold is articulated. Her enigmatic prophecy, "[b]lood in the north, blood to come in the south, and the blue crying red in between," is a recurring refrain in the text (*CF* 3).

Carib, both prophet and historian, urges the community to recover the collective history. But young people who have lost the "habit of listening" deride the wisdom of the elders:

The people who were really old and had little interest left in the things of the world didn't usually hear Carib in the market square and other public places, but they would lift their heads and listen from inside their houses when they heard her passing along the street. They would push aside the window curtains a little and ask,

"Who dat, nuh? Is Carib? What she saying there?" And some young person would give a long steupes and answer, "Who know? Talking Stupidness as usual." (*CF* 9)

Distinguishing the wisdom she embodies from the misconceptions that abound in the formal school system, Carib tries to ensure that ancestral knowledge is passed on: "'Sometimes the children who should know most is the ones that know the least. Walk back. Walk back over all the story with him. . . . Is not that he don't know, but his head will get twist with all kind of other things he reading'" (*CF* 13).

That metaphor of remembering as a walking back over familiar territory images Carib's own peregrinations throughout the country. The trope also evokes Collins's narrative method: "Where we start is after the beginning" (*CF* 17). The achronological plot twists and returns and the voice of the omniscient narrator often fuses with Carib's in a stream of mystic consciousness: "If people listen, they will hear the wind telling the story that cause so much confusion. Trouble inside is not new story. Is story that there from time. Nation shall rise against itself" (*CF* 27). The revolution and its dire social consequences rise to the fore in the final quarter of the novel. But the upheaval caused by the Government's land policy to consolidate "uneconomic" small plots of land is contextualized as a new chapter in an old, old story; a familiar tale of self-destructive family feuding: "People believed that those in the government who had different views about this land business had used the market to settle scores. That brother had ordered the killing of brother to ensure support for a land policy that said no buying and selling of five acres and less. 'Blood in the south,' as Carib had shouted, and the whole Caribbean was in tears over this killing and tragedy" (*CF* 198).

The marketplace is a cultural crossroads where many stories meet: "Those markets and those forts in this country, was always big centre for deciding things, with blood a lot of the time" (*CF* 141). Carib, presumed to be "talking stupidness," competes not only with the scribal discourse of official narratives of the state but also with the pragmatic language of the marketplace. An impatient market vendor castigates her thus: "'Lower you noise, Carib, let me hear what me customers want. Two bunch of sive an thyme you say, Lady?'" (*CF* 174). Collins concedes the practical wisdom of that market woman who knows that she must get on with the mundane tasks of everyday survival.

In an essay titled "Grenada—Ten Years and More: Memory and Collective Responsibility," Collins contrasts the freeze-frame recall of those who live outside Grenada with the fluid consciousness of those who live inside and have had to come to terms with the "mixture in the blood of the [his]tory" (*CF* 17):

> For those like me who were in Grenada during that 1983 period and have lived largely outside of Grenada since then, the October 1983 events occupy the consciousness in a manner perhaps to some extent frozen in time and intensity. People who since 1983 have lived in Grenada, who may have been intimately involved in the conflict themselves or who in any event are meeting constantly with those identified as being on both sides of the conflict, have had to work out ways of existing satisfactorily with everyone, including brothers, wives, husbands, friends who may hold different opinions. The socio-political circumstances specific to small states make every public crisis personal and many personal solutions public. ("Grenada" 72)

But even those who live in Grenada have had to walk back over the story in order to go forward. Recurring aphoristic statements in the novel affirm the therapeutic function of reflective talk: "Telling the whole story of the confusion to Willive later, Mamag said, 'But, child, that was not even the end of it. Sometimes tongue only keep on talking because it know if it hush, the thins it refuse to reveal could happen again. So let teeth meet with the talking and cut the thread of wickedness'" (*CF* 69). It is also Mamag who declares that "'every story have a long tail. The plainest story is only a little part of the riddle'" (*CF* 71). And the complications are not easily disentangled.

The Revolutionary Government's grandiose policy of land reform has a sting in its tail. The people with the supposedly "uneconomic" plots revolt: "'Them, they all right, yes. They could sit down there and talk through their ass. What they know about land? If they never had land and get chance to have a acre, they would know about uneconomic. Them? They happy, *wi*. They could afford to talk through they bambam hole'" (*CF* 164). With typical folk irreverence, that pungent metaphor goes to the seat of the problem: The revolutionary rhetoric is flatulent. Commonsense wisdom, not the academic logic of textbook economics, is also evident in the protest letter sent to the Government Land Commission: "If you think a two acres here in Content village uneconomic, then you have somebody in another bigger country thinking the whole of Paz that all-you ruling uneconomic because it so small. Might be true, but is all we have. So you do away with me and my land and they do away with you. So soon, none of us will be there to tell the story" (*CF* 164).

In both *Angel* and *The Colour of Forgetting* Collins affirms the efficacy of the oral tradition—folk tale, family history, proverb, and riddle—as an authoritative knowledge system. Sense make befoh book in truth. But Collins's books, suffused as they are with the native wit of her people, exemplify the potency of story-telling that dramatizes both oral and scribal discourses. The technology of writing in the service of mother wit produces a multivocal text that plays on sound and sense in complex ways: "John Bull was a slave that get killed in the market square in Paz City since the days when the Spanish catholics used to listen to the rage in the place and call it Pax, like a joke. *Pax tecum.* Peace be with you. Pax. With a slap. Take that" (*CF* 17). The slap of the "pax" is anything but peaceful. But folk wisdom valorizes the humor that resides in the most tragic circumstances: "'We blood not weak. If we generation couldn't see the funny side of life, not one person live to tell the story'" (*CF* 35). The telling of story, which Collins does with such eloquence, is the art of communal survival.

Works Cited

Collins, Merle. *Angel.* London: Women's Press, 1987.

———. *The Colour of Forgetting.* London: Virago, 1995.

———. "Grenada—Ten Years and More: Memory and Collective Responsibility." *Caribbean Quarterly* 41.2 (1995): 71–78.

———. "The Signs." *Caribbean Quarterly* 41.2 (1995): vii.

Devonish, Hubert. "Working by the book or Playing by Ear: Language, Literacy and the Grenada Revolution." *Caribbean Quarterly* 41.2 (1995): 24–37.

PART 4

Invention and Convention

Womanist Gazes on Literary and Critical Traditions

In her essay, "The Race for Theory," Barbara Christian avows that "women, at least the women I grew up around, continuously speculated about the nature of life through pithy language that unmasked the power relations of their world. My folk, in other words, have always been a race for theory—though more in the form of hieroglyph, a written figure which is both sensual and abstract, both beautiful and communicative" (844). As Africana scholars (female and male) employ varied forms of contemporary theory with the practice of criticism, the result may be a similar syncretic art. These modern African American critics have wider access to publication as a result of the same sociopolitical currents referenced in the introduction to *Arms Akimbo;* the gatekeepers of published literary criticism in the West until the latter half of this century were males. Whereas organization journals that served the Black, educated populace, journals such as *Crisis* and *Opportunity,* offered sparse literary criticism, only a few nationally circulated academic journals such as *Phylon* (1940–), and *College Language Association Journal* (1957–) were consistently open to Africana women literary critics. And these journals were primarily circulated within Black academe, since few Black professors taught at predominantly white universities in the United States before the 1970s, with Africana women professors being a rarity in Africa and the Caribbean. Yet Africana women scholar-teachers have produced vital critical analyses and have tread into the sometimes troubling waters of critical schools and allegiances. As active scholars, teachers, and lovers of literature, they have chosen decidedly clear and varied analytical bases for their criticism. Consequently, in 1977, Barbara Smith's Black feminist vision emphasized for us the absolute need for Black women to recognize that "Black women writers constitute an identifiable literary tradition" (163), a claim that has been variously supported, disputed, or rejected since its stating.

The essays in this section all exemplify feminist critical perspectives, although not all the critics would label themselves "feminist." Their analytical techniques go beyond the linear structural argument, merging the works with a greater unified phenomena, formal traditions that vary from Erna Brodber's sociological analysis to Zain Muse's "afrofemcentrism." These critics delve into what Mae Henderson cites as the "complexity of these simultaneously homogeneous social and discursive domains out of which black women write and construct themselves" (21). One unifying factor within the body of the essays is that all demonstrate—through somewhat varied critical techniques—the Africana women writers' strong ability to posit change in a narrative form.

While debate regarding the nature of the Black woman's critical perspectives continues, the critics here firmly demonstrate the interconnectedness of the created woman character in her economic, social, and political roles. Through these varied critical gazes, ultimately it becomes clear that Africana women's writing is working women's writing, is political women's writing, is mother-women writing: Whatever tradition disclosed is part of the larger national and sociopolitics of cultural production. This should be marked, because foremost Africana women writers' narratives recount inner workings within the domestic sphere of existence; and therefore, the interconnectedness of those imagined lives with the broader political and economic spheres may be overlooked.

Paula Barnes's "Meditations on Her/Story: Maryse Conde's *I, Tituba, Black Witch of Salem* and the Slave Narrative Tradition" places Maryse Conde's novel firmly into the developing narrative tradition in which African American women reconstruct the life experiences of the woman enslaved. Barnes purposefully demonstrates that *I, Tituba* is a neo-slave narrative; and by giving Tituba a full woman's life, love, and African ancestry, Conde has augmented and invigorated the slave narrative tradition.

Novelist Erna Brodber's contribution, "Guyana's Historical Sociology and the Novels of Beryl Gilroy and Grace Nichols," is starkly sociological and empirical, calling on Brodber's own background as sociologist, Caribbean native, Jamaican, writer, and woman. Whereas this article could very well be included in the "War on All Fronts: Race, Class, Sex, Age, and Nationality" section of *Arms Akimbo,* Brodber's elevation of the geophysical elements of the Guyanese landscape to centralizing forces in the women protagonists' sense of selfhood and of place focus it beyond these categories. Focusing on the women in Gilroy's *Frangipani House* and Nichols's *Whole of the Morning Sky,* Brodber gives us a full study of the transforming family structure and social relationships of the post-colonial country, concluding that as Afro-Caribbean women writers, Gilroy and Nichols present truthful sociological perspectives that further rather than fetter their aesthetic achievement.

Both "'A Girl Marries a Monkey': The Folktale as an Expression of Value and Change in Society" by N. J. Opoku-Agyemang, and "Textual Deviancy and Cultural Syncretism: Romantic Fiction as a Subversive Strain in Black Women's Fiction" by Jane Bryce and Kari Dako, represent feminist examinations of traditional literary genres. Opoku-Agyemang exposes the self-deprecating and sexist bias of a representative African folktale of the "difficult maiden." Bryce and Dako demonstrate that the Africana woman writer's use of a "devalued feminine form," the romantic novel, becomes a "subversive" tool for feminist aesthetic presentation of the Black woman in works by Joan Riley, Olive Senior, Valerie Belgrave, and Ama Ata Aidoo.

In her essay "Revolutionary Brilliance: The Afrofemcentric Aesthetic," Zain Muse, takes the analysis a step further through her affirmative womanist/Africanist analysis of Erna Brodber's *Jane and Louisa Will Soon Come Home* and the text of Julie Dash's film, *Daughters of the Dusk.* Ultimately, Zain Muse's analysis brings *Arms Akimbo* full circle, because as Black woman, critic, and student, her voice resounds with the lessons from her Africana sisters and teachers. This anthology of literary criticism, like the majority of critical anthologies, is the production of teachers—working teachers who accept the responsibility of inspiring a love of the literature and of teaching the foundations for critical analysis. Given the task that lies before us, we are inspired and taught as our younger sisters join in the work of historicizing, clarifying, and vocalizing the narratives of Africana women, thus furthering our own critical tradition.

Works Cited

Christian, Barbara. "The Race for Theory." *Literary Criticism and Theory: The Greeks to the Present.* Ed. Robert Davis and Laurie Finke. New York: Longman, 1989. 843–51.

Henderson, Mae Gwendolyn. "Speaking in Tongues: Dialogics, Dialectics, and the Black Woman Writer's Literary Tradition." *Changing Our Own Words: Essays on Criticism, Theory, and Writing by Black Women.* Ed. Cheryl Wall. New Brunswick: Rutgers University Press, 1989. 16–37.

Smith, Barbara. "Toward a Black Feminist Criticism," 1977. *All The Women Are White, All the Blacks Are Men, But Some of Us Are Brave: Black Women's Studies.* Ed. Gloria Hull, Patricia Bell Scott, and Barbara Smith. Old Westbury, N.Y.: Feminist Press, 1982. 157–75.

13

Meditations on Her/Story

Maryse Conde's *I, Tituba, Black Witch of Salem* and the Slave Narrative Tradition

PAULA C. BARNES

Mary Helen Washington titles her introduction to *Invented Lives: Narratives of Black Women, 1860–1960,* "Meditations on History: The Slave Woman's Voice." Through alluding to William Styron's (in)famous line, "meditation on history," Washington seeks to bring to the forefront the voices of slave women who had been "rendered invisible" not only in Douglass's 1845 *Narrative* but also the slave narratives in general, as women's narratives account for only twelve percent of that tradition (7). While none of the female narratives achieved prominence in their time, the recent burgeoning interest in slave narratives has led to their rediscovery and examination. Toni Morrison, in discussing her impetus for writing *Beloved,* noted the "deliberate omissions," that is, silences in these works (Christian 329). Apparently she was not the only writer to note such, for since 1979, there have been a number of novels for which slavery is the central focus, the majority of these written by women. Deborah McDowell, in answer to the question, "[W]hy the compulsion to repeat the story of slavery in the contemporary African-American novel?" suggests that Black female writers are "re-presenting" the female experience in slavery (McDowell and Rampersad 146). Women novelists, rendering the female slave experience visible *and* voiced, are revising the male canonized view; they are creating meditations on her/story.

In 1992, added to the African American novels addressing the female issue of slavery—Octavia Butler's *Kindred* (1979), Sherley Anne Williams's *Dessa Rose* (1986), Toni Morrison's *Beloved* (1987), and J. California Cooper's *Family* (1991)—was the English translation of Maryse Conde's *Moi, Tituba, Sorcière . . . Noire de Salem, I, Tituba, Black*

Witch of Salem. Conde's work is a significant addition, as it is the first African-Caribbean novel whose primary exploration is the issue of slavery. Moreover, it is presented in the tradition of the slave narrative. By working within yet altering the conventions of the slave narrative, Conde moves the genre forward in significant ways. She refigures the historical Tituba, addresses the American-Caribbean slavery connection, explores male-female slave relationships as well as the role of the female in slave rebellions, and expands the recent female discourse of the slave narrative novels. Conde begins by imitating the structure of the nineteenth-century narratives.

James Olney, in Davis and Gates's *The Slave's Narrative,* describes four documents that frame the slave narrative proper and serve to authenticate it; "an engraved portrait, signed by the narrator; a title page that includes the claim . . . 'written by himself' (or some close variant); a handful of testimonials and/or one or more prefaces or introductions written by a white abolitionist friend of the narrator or by a white amanuensis/editor/author actually responsible for the text, and a poetic epigraph, by preference from William Cowper" (152). Maryse Conde demonstrates her familiarity with these conventions, for all of these requirements are met in one way or another. In *I, Tituba,* the book jacket contains not an engraved, signed portrait but a visual rendering, vague yet suggestive, of the enigmatic Tituba. Following are the title page, a statement by Conde, an epigram by John Harrington, and a foreword by Angela Davis.

Conde immediately manipulates the convention of the title page of the slave narrative. There is not the expected "written by herself," nor the "as told to" reserved for the illiterate slave; rather there is the threefold introduction: "I," "Tituba," "Black Witch of Salem." Taken together, they reveal a narrator who, in the position of subject of her work, claims her identity, and takes her place in history. Through the phrase "Black Witch of Salem," Tituba replaces the three-century-old terse encyclopedic entry by which she has been identified: "Tituba, a slave originating from the West Indies and probably practicing 'hoodoo'" (149). As a result of this narrative, Tituba can no longer be seen, says Jeanne Snitgen, as a minor character in historical documents or plays (60).

Yet first-person narration is the technique of the slave narrative. Thus, Conde's innovation of subverting the option available for the illiterate slave is not on the title page but on the page following. She states, "Tituba and I lived for a year on the closest of terms. During our conversations she told me things she had confided to nobody else." Conde makes it clear that Tituba is the subject of the narrative—"*she* told me" (emphasis added); Conde is merely responsible for the text in the role of amanuensis. Because the voice of the text is Tituba's own, Conde returns to the slave narrative the primacy of orality that has also been attained in Williams's *Dessa Rose*, where Dessa eventually narrates her own tale, and Cooper's *Family*, where Clora narrates from the dead. Yet Conde moves even beyond these works by rescuing Tituba's story from being "at the mercy of literature and writing" of dramatists and historians who, like the whites of the nineteenth century, "did not necessarily understand or sympathize" with the slave's experience, to use the words of Barbara Christian (337). Tituba's amanuensis is Black, Caribbean and woman, and although she does not share Tituba's slave experience, Conde is sympathetic to her plight and is able to do what Tituba could not: "write" her story among those of the witches of Salem.

The next slave narrative convention Conde meets—and revises—is that of the poetic epigraph. Rather than an excerpt from the antislavery poet Cowper, she uses one from the Puritan poet John Harrington: "Death is a porte whereby we pass to joye; Lyfe is a lake that drowneth all in payne." As Ann Scarboro in her afterword notes, this couplet foreshadows Tituba's pain and suffering (215). It also summarizes the perspective of life and death presented in the novel and, in its first line, capsulizes the African concept of the afterlife, where death is not the end but a beginning and, consequently, explains Conde's ability to enter into posthumous communication with Tituba centuries after her earthly existence.

The foreword by Angela Davis is by far the most interesting of Conde's revisionings; it is indeed a "testimonial" to Tituba's life as well as to Conde's reconstruction of that life. Davis's foreword serves to affirm Tituba's humanness as a living, loving, sexual self, "who was as much a part of the Salem witch trials as her codefendants of European descent" (xi). Explaining the novel as "Tituba's revenge," Davis accepts Conde's reconstruction of a fragmented, intentionally ignored history through Tituba's own voice and notes that "as Conde offers to Tituba the possibility of filling the silence and voids with voice and presence, we who are Tituba's cultural kin experience the possibilities of our own history" (xii). Thus, her testimonial is not merely for Tituba's or Conde's stories but for all those who were colonized and whose histories of the horrors of slavery have been understated.

After meeting these pre–slave narrative conventions, Conde's adoption of Onley's master plan of the slave narratives extends beyond the narrative proper. After the text, she includes the final convention, "an appendix or appendices composed of documentary materials" (153). Appended to Tituba's narrative is a historical note, which, according to Scarboro, is "factual . . . in every respect," authenticating "the witch-trial proceedings incorporated within the novel itself" (215). The final item is a glossary, with its translation of terms, which serves to remind the readers that *I, Tituba* is not solely the American experience of the Black witch of Salem, but also a Caribbean, African, and imaginative experience. Each of these appendices authenticates the narratives—Tituba's and Conde's—and rather than appealing to the battle against slavery serves as reminders of its reality in both the United States and the Caribbean.

Conde's adoption of the structure of the nineteenth-century slave narrative is completed in the narrative itself with the incorporation of the tropes of: "[A] first sentence beginning "I was born . . ."; "a sketchy account of parentage, often involving a white father"; and "details of first observed whipping . . . with women very frequently being victims" (Olney 153). As seen with the pre- and post-narrative conventions, Conde consciously imitates, manipulates, and revises these tropes.

Conde employs, as do most slave narratives, the trope of "a first sentence beginning 'I was born . . . ,'" yet her novel begins, "Abena, my mother, was raped by an English sailor on the deck of Christ the King . . . while the ship was sailing for Barbados. I was born from this act" (30). Conde, however, immediately reorders the trope; the circumstances surrounding Tituba's birth become more prominent than the birth itself. This reversal refigures the manipulation by which the male places himself at the beginning of the slave narrative and thereby becomes its center. His "I was born," functioning as if he has brought himself into being, can be likened to the biblical "in the beginning." The overall consequence of this for the genre is the privileging of the characteristic, individualistic journey of the male narrator, a rugged individualism that Deborah McDowell notes led to the enshrinement of the male's as the standard slave narrative.

Conde subverts this individualism in two ways. By focusing on the act that initiated the narrator's birth, she places the female experience—the vulnerability of rape—at the center of the narrative, the *consequence* of which is the birth of Tituba. By making Tituba the product of Abena's violation, Conde enters the recent dialogue of African American women writers who are revising the singular nature of the female slave's experience—as sex object. Secondly, her inclusion of the mother in the discussion of Tituba's birth represents the duality (sexual object/breeder), complexity (woman/mother), and communal nature of the female slave experience, and subverts the masculine depiction of one not of "woman born." Finally, Conde is subverting the collapsing of sexuality and maternity that Anne Goldman notes is characteristic of the male slave narratives (318).

Conde also subverts the collapsing of sexuality and maternity through the repetition of the trope. A few pages into the novel, Tituba states, "[W]hen *I was born* four months later, Yao and my mother were in a state of happiness" (5, emphasis mine). In distinguishing between the conception and birth, Conde separates the roles of sexual object and mother. Notable are the two descriptions of Tituba's initiation into life: "[B]orn out" of an act of aggression yet "born into" a state of happiness. This distinction is not only important from the perspective of the woman's role—as woman/mother versus rape victim, but also in terms of the positioning of the child in relation to the mother—as a product of rape versus a being to love. Consequently, Conde adds another level to the complexity of the slave woman's roles that is virtually nonexistent in male narratives.

The next convention important to the slave narrative is that of the account of parentage. Conde, through this convention, allows Tituba the privilege of self-definition and thereby enters the historical discussion surrounding Tituba's race. Chadwick Hansen, in the article titled "The Metamorphosis of Tituba," discusses the "transformation" of Tituba "from Carib Indian, to half Indian, and half Negro to Negro" (3). With the race of Tituba so in question, Snitgen, surmising that Conde makes Tituba of African-European descent to serve as a "figure of Caribbean history" (58), asserts that the native population had disappeared by the time the British arrived in Barbados; thus, the historical Tituba would have been of African-British or pure African parentage (56). Conde entertains both options, as Tituba has two "fathers"—the nameless English sailor and the African, Yao. The first option connects Tituba's story with those of the slave narrators; the majority of them who escaped and published their stories were of mixed parentage.[1]

The last convention that Conde directly imitates is that of the details of the first observed whipping, and in this instance, Conde's techniques are highly reminiscent of *The Narrative of the Life of Frederick Douglass*. Tituba initially relates in passing the experience of other slaves: "[S]everal times I witnessed scenes of brutality and torture. I saw men go home covered in blood, their chests and backs striped in scarlet" (7), utilizing the narrator-as-observer technique characteristic of Douglass, identified as "imaginative distancing" by William Andrews. Yet she, like Douglass, goes into detailed discussion of the mistreatment of a family member. Tituba's first traumatic experience is not that of a whipping, however, but a hanging—her mother's—of which she simply states, "I watched her body swing from the lower branches of a silk-cotton tree" (8). Conde uses understatement as does Douglass, but it is through the singular repetition of "they hanged my mother" that she conveys the action's import. Moreover, Tituba provides her personal response: "When her body swung round and round in the air, I gathered up enough strength to tiptoe away and vomit my heart out" (8). According to Deborah McDowell, Douglass's viewing of his Aunt Hester's beating takes on a voyeuristic stance, and he is not as "detached" as his language suggests ("First Place" 203). Conde's revelation of the female slave's feelings in *I, Tituba* then functions as a more wholesome countertext to Douglass's *Narrative;* she, too, is "participant and witness," but her viewing is not one of libidinal "spectacle."

Before Conde abandons the slave narrative conventions proper, she alters two others—naming and literacy. One of the last observations in the slave narratives is the former slave's taking on a new name—denoting the beginning of a new life. Conde, however, introduces this convention early in her novel. Tituba informs us that it is her African "father," Yao, who names her, not with an African name but one "he probably invented ... to prove that [she] was a daughter of his will and imagination. Daughter of his love" (6). Tituba's actions throughout the work portray the same kind of independence, strong will, and imagination derived from the sense of self that accompanies the African concept of naming. From her rejection of servanthood that Susannah Endicott seeks to impose upon her in Barbados, through her refusal to admit to wrongdoing to save herself in Salem, to her final outcome upon her final return to Barbados, Tituba portrays a strength of character that the power of "nommo" provides. And just as important as the act is the ritual of naming. In a scene that refigures Alex Haley's *Roots*, Yao holds the child by her feet and presents her to the four corners of the earth. One is, therefore, not surprised that Tituba is the feminine version of self-determination that Kunta Kinte displays throughout his American servitude. Conde, as does Haley, and Morrison in *Beloved,* seeks to subvert the African American tradition of naming in the slave narratives with the restoration of the African tradition.

Finally, Conde addresses the all-important convention of literacy. Henry Louis Gates, discussing "the profound importance that the mastery of literacy had for the slave," notes that the slave who learned how to read and write was usually the first to run away (Davis and Gates xxviii). The readers of *I, Tituba* know that Tituba does not write her own narrative; what they do not learn until later on is that Tituba is illiterate and remains so throughout her life. Yet literacy is an issue in the novel raised by Hester Prynne, whom Tituba meets in a New England jail. Hester tells Tituba, "I'd like to write a book, but, alas, women don't write books. Have you read Milton. . . . Oh, I forgot you don't know how to read" (101). Conde, through this brief encounter, underscores the necessity of women's telling their own stories and revises Hester's life as well, by providing a version as different from that recorded in Hawthorne's *Scarlet Letter* as Tituba's version in Miller's *The Crucible*. In response to Tituba's seventeenth-century lament that "there would never be a careful sensitive biography recreating my life and its suffering" (110), Conde produces three centuries later a book—written by a woman—which is as much a tribute to Hester and females in general as it is to Tituba and the twelve percent of the female authors of the slave narratives.

After having invoked the slave narrative genre through a number of its conventions, Conde abandons them when they no longer meet the particulars of Tituba's experience. The young Tituba, living after the death of her parents with Mama Yaya on the periphery of slave society and therefore insulated from slavery, explains why: "[T]he reader may be surprised that at a time when the lash was constantly being used, I managed to enjoy . . . peace and freedom. Our islands have two sides to them. The side of masters' carriages . . . and the other . . . secret side" (156). Living on the "other" side of the island, Tituba is technically not a slave.

She, ironically, "chooses" this way of life by marrying John Indian, for whom she moves to Carlisle Bay. Tituba begins to work for Susannah Endicott, John's owner, and is thus introduced to the life of slavery; however, refusing to succumb to the expected servile behavior, she enters into conflict with Susannah Endicott. Seeking to prevent Susannah from coming between her and John Indian, Tituba strikes her with an illness that eventually leads to Endicott's death but not before she exacts a revenge—selling Tituba and John Indian to Samuel Parris. They leave Barbados and Caribbean slavery only to experience northern American slavery. It is, of course, as a slave in the Parris household that Tituba becomes involved in the Salem Witchcraft Trials, the historical reality that informs the novel. This incident, however, is not *the* central experience of Tituba's life; it is but one of many which shapes her as a person. There is life—and more enslavement—after the witchcraft trials.

Tituba, without John Indian, is resold into slavery to the Jew, Benjamin Cohen d'Azevedo. Their shared misery leads them into each other's arms, and Tituba soon finds herself in "that odd situation of being both mistress and servant" (127). Through Tituba's active involvement with d'Azevedo—she chooses to become his mistress—Conde addresses the issue of female sexuality in conjunction with the notion of "choice." She does this by subverting the seldom-entertained option in the male slave narratives, which is so central to the female tradition, evidenced from its beginning with Linda Brent's preface in *Incidents in the Life of a Slave Girl* and on through to the recent slave narrative novels.[2] Tituba's is not the choice that circumvents choicelessness but is that which is done out of love and compassion. Some slave women, Conde seems to say, had choices regarding their sexuality.

In the same occurrences in which Tituba chooses John Indian and Benjamin d'Azevedo, Conde manipulates an issue central to the slave narratives—freedom. In the first instance, Tituba sacrifices her freedom for John Indian. In the second, when asked early in the relationship what would make her happy, she responds, "my freedom"; yet when d'Azevedo is ready to grant it, she chooses to remain with him (128). Notwithstanding, "d'Azevedo gives Tituba her freedom," observes Scarboro, "because he loves her dearly" (219). As Tituba chooses "enslavement" twice for a man, Mama Yaya's words immediately come to mind: "[M]en do not love . . . they subjugate" (14). Conde, through her word-play questioning "freedom," playfully (?) attacks the depictions of male-female relationships portrayed in the female revisionist texts.[3]

Although Conde acknowledges the mock-epic quality of *I, Tituba* and advises her readers not to take the novel seriously (212), Tituba's choice of enslavement twice cannot be ignored. It is here that Conde moves beyond the subversion of male texts and the revision of female texts to the criticism of feminist views. In affirming Tituba's sexuality and the life-giving aspects of love, Conde supports male-female relationships, a common theme in her works (Scarboro 206, 207).[4] By addressing these issues, Conde significantly expands the female discourse of the slave narratives.

Through the use of the term "freedom," Conde also manipulates the foremost convention of the slave narrative—escape—and again questions the true meaning of the term. Early in the novel it is made clear that Tituba is considered a "witch," and through her connection with Mama Yaya has "powers" that can be used for good or evil. These powers, it is suggested upon her return to Barbados, could have been used to obtain her freedom as evidenced in the question, "[W]hy didn't you turn yourself into a mouse and escape?" (154). Tituba provides no answer; yet upon her return to her homeland, she is no longer naive and has a different sensitivity toward Caribbean slavery. She longs to retreat to her place on the island but reluctantly joins a maroon colony, where she takes a third lover by whom she is impregnated. This time the seed of rebellion, seen in her refusal to be a slave at Susannah Endicott's and her refusal to have John Indian's child at Samuel Parris's, takes hold; the pregnant Tituba encourages a slave rebellion not with Christopher, the leader of the maroons, whom she abandons, but with the young Iphigene, her fourth and final lover. The rebellion is betrayed, and Tituba, along with the others, is hanged; the "fate" she escaped in Boston is now hers, and the "freed" Tituba attains true "freedom." The meaning of the novel's epigraph becomes apparent: Death is merely the "porte" that leads to another life; Tituba reveals in her epilogue, "[M]y real story starts where this one leaves off" (175). Conde, in this discussion of freedom, exposes the multi-layered complexity of freedom and escape in the slave narratives—the freedom of mind versus freedom of body and escape as freedom versus death as freedom.

Conde, in depicting Tituba as Iphigene's co-conspirator, refigures the legendary Nanny of the maroons and explores the issue of the female role in slave rebellions. Interestingly, it is Angela Davis's seminal article, "Reflections on the Black Woman's Role in the Community of Slaves," that introduces this topic. Yet for Davis, as mentioned in her foreword, Tituba's revenge is not her role in the rebellion but the telling of her/story and the placing of herself among the witches of Salem. Nonetheless, an aspect of Tituba's revenge is indeed related to slave women and rebellions. Yielding finally to her "unfulfilled lust for revenge" (144), Tituba represents and (p)refigures all those females whose roles in slave rebellions have yet to be uncovered: Lucy of the Nat Turner insurrection; Sarah, whom John Blassingame calls "the archetype of the rebellious fugitive" (Sinclair); and the unnamed woman after whom Sherley Anne Williams patterns her character, Dessa Rose, to mention a few.

In addressing the female role in the rebellion of slaves, Conde adds a notable dimension to the slave narrative tradition; however, her refiguring of the historical Tituba, rescuing her from a life of obscurity, is probably Conde's greatest contribution to the slave narrative tradition. But there are others. Conde moves the tradition forward by: (1) Providing a Black, female amanuensis; (2) Providing an exploration of a full range of complex female slave roles; and (3) Expanding the concept of female "choice" present in both male and female slave narratives and novels. Furthermore, Conde expands the recent female discourse in the slave narrative novels by bringing a female slave's sexuality to the fore and presenting it as the "most profound aspect" of her experience (Foster quoted in McDowell 201); by challenging the depictions of male/female relationships in the slave narrative novels by women; and by inserting a feminist discourse. In addition, as Scarboro points out, Conde creates the first Francophone-Caribbean novel to link the English Caribbean with the colonial United States (187). In expanding the discussion of slavery beyond one leg of the triangle, she does for the slave narrative novels what Olaudah Equiano in his 1789 *Narrative* did for the slave narratives. Finally, not to be underestimated is her delineation of the Caribbean female slave's experience. In these four major ways, Conde moves the slave narrative tradition forward in her meditation on her/story. The impact of Conde's *I, Tituba, Black Witch of Salem* on the slave narrative tradition will be felt for years to come.

Notes

1. Of the twenty-two narratives that Blyden Jackson discusses in detail in his *A History of Afro-American Literature,* over half of the slave narratives were mulatto. This observation is probably the same for all of the published slave narratives.

2. In fact, it is this notion of "choice" that Douglass ignores in his discussion of Hester's whipping in his *Narrative.* As Sandra Govan notes, "Aunt Hester either loved pain or loved Lloyd's Ned entirely too much. . . . It seems a clear-cut case of . . . a Black woman 'love' object" who suffers because of her lust (36).

3. Motherhood has been the central issue in the female slave narrative novels. With the exception of *Dessa Rose,* the primary concern for the major slave female characters (Alice in *Kindred,* Sethe in *Beloved* and Always in *Family*) is their roles as mothers not as companions/lovers. On the contrary, woman's sexual nature, including the importance of being loved by a man for love's sake, figures prominently in *I, Tituba.* It should also be noted that Tituba remains childless throughout the novel. See Goldman and Hirsch for discussions of mothering as the central issue in the female slave narrative novels.

4. Yet there is in the novel the suggestion of female homosexuality in Tituba's relationship with Hester Prynne, who realizes that she will probably not be able to persuade Tituba to be a feminist (122).

Works Cited

Andrews, William L. *To Tell a Free Story: The First Century of African American Autobiography, 1769–1865.* Chicago: University of Illinois Press, 1986.

Butler, Octavia. *Kindred.* Boston: Beacon Press, 1979.

Christian, Barbara. "'Somebody Forgot to Tell Somebody Something': African American Women's Historical Novels." *Wild Women in the Whirlwind: Afra-American Culture and the Contemporary Literary Renaissance.* Ed. Joanne Braxton and Andree Nicola McLaughlin. New Brunswick: Rutgers University Press, 1990. 326–41.

Conde, Maryse. *I, Tituba, Black Witch of Salem.* Trans. Richard Philcox. Charlottesville: University Press of Virginia, 1992.

Cooper, J. California. *Family.* New York: Doubleday, 1991.

Davis, Angela. "Reflections on the Black Woman's Role in the Community of Slaves." *The Black Scholar* (November–December 1981): 2–15.

Davis, Charles T., and Henry L. Gates, eds. *The Slave's Narrative.* New York: Oxford University Press, 1985.

Douglass, Frederick. *The Narrative of the Life of Frederick Douglass.* New York: Signet, 1968.

Equiano, Olaudah. *The Interesting Narrative of the Life of Olaudah Equiano, or Gusta-*

vus Vassa, the African. Black Writers of America: A Comprehensive Anthology. Ed. Richard Barksdale and Kenneth Kinnamon. New York: Macmillan, 1972. 7–38.

Gates, Henry L. "Introduction: The Language of Slavery." *The Slave's Narrative.* Ed. Charles T. Davis and Henry L. Gates. Oxford: Oxford University Press, 1985.

Goldman, Anne. "'I Made the Ink': Literary Production and Reproduction in *Dessa Rose* and *Beloved.*" *Feminist Studies* 16 (Summer 1990): 313–30.

Govan, Sandra. "Forbidden Fruits and Unholy Lusts: Illicit Sex in Black American Literature." *Erotique Noire/Black Erotica.* Ed. Miriam Decosta Willis, Reginald Martin, and Roseann P. Bell. New York: Doubleday, 1992. 35–43.

Haley, Alex. *Roots.* New York: Doubleday, 1976.

Hansen, Chadwick. "The Metamorphosis of Tituba, Or Why American Intellectuals Can't Tell an Indian Witch from a Negro." *New England Quarterly* 47 (March 1974): 3–12.

Hirsch, Marianne. "Maternal Narratives: 'Cruel Enough to Stop the Blood.'" *Reading Black Reading Feminist.* Ed. Henry L. Gates. New York: Meridian, 1990. 415–30.

Jacobs, Harriet. *Incidents in the Life of a Slave Girl.* Cambridge: Harvard University Press, 1987.

McDowell, Deborah. "In the First Place: Making Frederick Douglass and the Afro-American Narrative Tradition." *Critical Essays on Frederick Douglass.* Ed. William Andrews. Boston: G. K. Hall, 1991. 192–214.

———. "Negotiating Between Tenses: Witnessing Slavery After Freedom—Dessa Rose." *Slavery and Literary Imagination.* Ed. Deborah McDowell and Arnold Rampersad. Baltimore: Johns Hopkins University Press, 1989. 144–63.

Morrison, Toni. *Beloved.* New York: Signet, 1987.

Olney, James. "'I Was Born': Slave Narratives, Their Status as Autobiography and Literature." *The Slave's Narrative.* Ed. Charles T. Davis and Henry L. Gates. Oxford: Oxford University Press, 1985. 148–75.

Scarboro, Ann Armstrong. Afterword. *I, Tituba, Black Witch of Salem.* Maryse Conde. Charlottesville: University Press of Virginia, 1992. 187–225.

Sinclair, Anne. "Studies in Rebellion: Creating the Legend." *Essence* (November 1976): 28, 78.

Snitgen, Jeanne. "History, Identity and the Constitution of the Female Subject: Maryse Conde's *I, Tituba.*" *Black Women's Writing: Crossing the Boundaries.* Ed. Carole Boyce Davies. Matatu Heft 6. 3 Jahrgang 1989: 55–73.

Washington, Mary Helen. "Meditations on History: The Slave Woman's Voice." *Invented Lives: Narratives of Black Women, 1860–1960.* Garden City, N.Y.: Anchor Press, 1987. 3–15.

Williams, Sherley Anne. *Dessa Rose.* New York: William Morrow, 1986.

14

Guyana's Historical Sociology and the Novels of Beryl Gilroy and Grace Nichols

ERNA BRODBER

In *Ride Out the Wilderness,* African American critic Melvin Dixon asserts that "recurring images of place and person in black popular religious culture, but also in Afro-American literary tradition, stake claims to a physical and spiritual home in America" (1). He further contends that "[s]ince major geographical dislocation of blacks from slave trading Africa and through the nineteenth century, issues of home, self, and shelter have loomed paramount in the black imagination" (2). In their efforts to re-root themselves with both an identity and a homespace, African American writers have relied heavily on what Dixon calls "three figures of landscape . . . the wilderness, the underground and the mountaintop" (3).

Just as displaced Africans in America collectively have internalized the fixedness of their immediate physical environment, displaced Africans in the Caribbean have done so similarly. They have found in their own immediate environments socio- and geophysical phenomena that impinge on their consciousness as Caribbean people. In their quest for "self and home," five major phenomena emerge: water, the village space, migration, race, and family structure. Throughout the Caribbean, these five phenomena are preeminent in the definitions of the Caribbean identity and of individual nation identities. Novelists Beryl Gilroy and Grace Nichols make the case in their novels for the importance of these factors to one of those Caribbean nation identities: Guyana.

Guyana's geographical location is close to the equatorial belt and, as such, it is subject to heavy rainfall. The Guyanese soil does not drain easily; the result is a water-logged land. The importance of water as a geophysical phenomenon is magnified when one considers that significant portions of the country are below sea level, thereby increasing the presence of water. Additionally, the country has numerous large rivers, and allied to these geographic conditions is a forested and, therefore, relatively inaccessible hinterland.

One of the sociophysical factors important to the invention of the Guyanese identity is the village space. Reminiscent of the protective and political arrangement left in Africa, villages became likely replacements in post-slavery Guyana, where plantations could no longer serve as primary domiciles and Blacks were the majority. The concomitant sociophysical factor of family structure also contributed to the identification of the country's people. Wherever people exist, family structure exists and serves to impact a people's concept of who and what they are. The Guyanese family structure typifies that seen generally throughout the Caribbean. It has a tendency toward matrifocality with a yearning for the high-statused and European patriarchy.

For the Guyanese, as for nations throughout the Caribbean, the physical existence of diverse races is yet another pressing social phenomenon. Race, in all its permutations—racial separateness and racial conflict/reconciliation—serves to impact the consciousness of the people. In Guyana and most of the Caribbean, the earliest post-Columbian days found white Europeans, Black African, and brown Amerindians as the racial composite. By the mid-nineteenth century East Indians, Chinese, and Portuguese were added to the race mix and colored even more the stamp of Guyana's national identity.

With the exception of the Amerindians, all the other ethnic and racial groups migrated to Guyana after the sixteenth century. Thus, migration in the Caribbean, as in the rest of the New World, has proven to be extremely significant. Forced and volunteer migration to Guyana of millions of peoples from various distinctly different cultures could not but impact the psyche of the nation and serve as yet another socio- (even psycho-) physical factor. In the twentieth century, however, this physical factor takes on a new form—immigration from the country in search of a better life.

The five geo- and sociophysical phenomena mentioned above—water, the village space, race, migration, and a particular kind of family structure—are key elements in Guyana's historical sociology. In both Gilroy and Nichols, intimate involvements with these phenomena occur, providing the reader with poignant insights into the social and psychological development of the Guyanese people.

The Writer and Guyana's Physical Environment

It is not the authorial voice in the novel *Frangipani House* but the note on the back cover of the book that tells us that this novel is set in Guyana. Though Gilroy calls no names, the physical features that she describes in her book add up to the Guyana we see in geography books. There is the cluster of frangipani trees, spreading trees that from time to time shed their colorful, waferlike blossoms. It is a tree renowned in Guyana but also found in other parts of the Caribbean, placing Guyana for the book's readers squarely in the Caribbean. Beryl Gilroy's central character, Mama King, lives in two worlds—the past and the present. Gilroy arranges it so that the present is the public world and the past, Mama King's private world of feelings. It is in this latter world that we see a physical environment that is peculiarly Guyana. And here we meet not just the Guyana that the hand can touch but as well the emotional response to touching that Guyana. So in the interior of Mama King's mind we see her in the interior of Guyana dealing with interior matters—happy yet frightened, searching in this elusive El Dorado for her lover Danny and all the treasure she associates with him both in her past and her present: "I go look for Danny to say I with child. Then I lost meself. Branches trying to grapple me and the sky over me with stars like silver money. Danny! I holler Danny! Then he fine me and lay me back against a tree—and wet me face and lovey-dovey with me and put me to rest" (10).

Again at page fifteen, we are in psychophysical Guyana with Mama King. We get the sense of distance and inaccessibility as we travel with her for five hours in a donkey cart. Gilroy makes the journey worth it: There are precious things at the end. At this journey's end there is the cure of a precious granddaughter. Mama King seems lucky with the Guyanese interior. Others have not been so lucky. They have been seduced and swallowed up and have left behind them negative memories and a negative response to the interior. The matron of *Frangipani House* inherits the tragedy that Guyana's physical landscape can bring. Her Uncle Zeke wanted nothing out of life but a few material things—"small pocketfuls of diamond and a little box of gold" (64). "'But what did poor uncle Zeke get? Nothing. What happen to poor Uncle Zeke? He lose his way in the deep dark bush. . . . His face swell up just like a balloon and his voice, Lord it terrible. And the voice coming out of a big sore mouth. Just like a jumbie voice'" (64).

Miss Ginchi, a more sympathetic character than matron, conspires with Guyana's sociophysical landscape to demolish Danny, her friend's cruel husband, one who sought sexual favors from her and to whom she appears to have been physically attracted. She gets "strong, good man-killing bush rum" (75) from Estaban, an Amerindian—one of that set of native Guyanese who inhabit its interior; she encourages Danny to drink many bottles of it and when he is dead, helps to take him to the Amer-indian's boat and to the oblivion of the interior. "She watched as Esteban sailed away rupturing the shadows thrown by those boats that still waited for their owners to return" (75). Danny, like so many others, had sailed (been sailed) up into Guyana's interior waters, fatally "lost" to life in the flesh.

Guyana's waters are not always for Gilroy the waters of the interior—rivers, mangroves, and other bodies as potentially destructive as the pond in which her grandchild drowns; there is also the sea. "I love the sea water. You can't see where it come from or where it go. It like life and death. It keep going on. High tide is like when things good, neap time, like when they bad" (28). Mama King talks about a love for the sea predicated on its predictability. Generations of evolving strategies for dealing with a sea that was above the level of the land had given Guy-anese a greater sense of control over these waters than they felt they had over the swamps, the rivers, and the falls of the interior. And wasn't the seacoast the cosmopolitan center to which foreign ships came with goodies and from which one could sail or fly to worlds themselves pre-dictable because they were celebrated in books and in the communica-tions of the many Guyanese who have emigrated to find a better life?

Grace Nichols's *Whole of a Morning Sky* uses the autobiographical voice as well as the usual authorial narrative voice, the former coming at us through poetic prose. This latter voice belongs to Gem and offers a prelude to each chapter. In this prelude the reader gets the comments of this pre-teen girl upon the happenings in her environment. Whether we read these affective passages or the more prosaic pieces, we feel Guyana all around. Grace Nichols no more than Gilroy uses the word Guyana. In both cases it is the back cover of the book that tells us that the work is set in this country. Grace Nichols's Gem, however, "through a haze of tears" (31), unequivocally places the book in its geographic setting: She is about to go off to Georgetown, which our pre-knowledge of geography tells us is the capital of Guyana.

In this Guyana, as in that presented in the orthodox geography and history books, water is an active agent. There are allusions to dams, that device by which generations of Guyanese have tried to tame a physical space given to flooding by river and by sea. On the very first page, we meet the backdam. Gem's first prelude tells us about the "ditch covered with floating slimy moss" (2). At the beginning of the narrative Gem lives in Highdam, where "the water, brown, heavy and smooth, was right up in front" (4), where the women fished for shrimp "standing waist deep in water," where "when it rained hard the entire schoolyard became a brown sea with the dingy white school and cottage suspended in the middle" (7). In fact, for the authorial voice in *Whole of a Morning Sky* as well as for the authors of social studies texts on Guyana, "[i]t was the water that gave shape to the land" (9).

Rural Guyana, with its constancy of water, is more treasured in Grace Nichols's *Whole of a Morning Sky* than in Gilroy's *Frangipani House*. The affect in the poetic lines "Standing in sunlight water and watching the dark moving shapes of the fish below/ Standing with your fishing rod at the edge of a dam, waiting for the cork to duck, then jumping like mad after catching a small patwa/ Going to the backdam" (29) is clear. Gilroy's Mama King likes the sea (28), the body of water that is predominant in Georgetown, the capital. Nichols's Gem is frightened of it. "It took the first peel of thunder to send them running home because it felt just as if the whole Atlantic was opening up to swallow them" (39). Gem, now moved to Georgetown, is as aware of water as she was in the rural setting, but this kind frightens her. Whatever the effect then, Guyana's physical features of which water is a crucial aspect impinge on the consciousness of the major characters of the two women writers, born and bred in Guyana.

The Village as a Political Entity

Beryl Gilroy is not inviting readers to see Guyana, the loved space. Her business is more academic: She offers an invitation to explore the aged and the change in their status that the internationalization of Euro-

American values brings. It is a psychological rather than a physical landscape in which she sets her novel. Nevertheless, the reader gets glimpses of the sociophysical landscape, a key aspect of which is, in Guyana, the village. We learn that Nurse Douglas, a "conscientious village girl" (3) and apparently, as such, "glad of the work and status," was on the staff of Frangipani House. This description of her invites us to think of the village as having peculiar attributes that distinguish it from somewhere else, presumably Georgetown, Guyana's major township. This is the notion of the village that the written historical sociology of the area gives us.

Nichols's Gem, in love with rural Guyana, reinforces the written accounts of this space and adds the qualitative. We are in the village with her for the first years of her life. Through Gem, Nichols makes us remember that free Blacks after emancipation bought lands communally and settled into villages that they administered. Her line "Everybody in the village own a piece of backdam" (2) reflects this sociohistorical reality. These communities saw themselves not only as "villages" but as "African villages." Time and with it miscegenation brought a wide range of skin color and could have brought a new perception of Highdam, as Nichols calls this village; yet the racial aspect of Highdam's history continues to be preserved by out-groups, as Nichols's statement, "Highdam itself was looked on as a black community" (4), indicates. The Highdam itself contributes to its perception as peculiarly African and as a tightly knit community, by marrying and mating endogamously; by keeping "queh-queh," an African ceremony, as part of its wedding rites; by communally chastising those motorists passing through whose vehicles hit their livestock; and by overturning "for fun" (5) the mango carts of Indian vendors passing through their villages.

Race

Nichols's description of the village brings us face-to-face with the fact of race in Guyana. The cartmen whose mango carts are toppled over "just for fun," as cited above, are not just cartmen; they are Indian cartmen and for the author, part of the Guyanese population distinguishable by race but also by occupation. They are petty entrepreneurs, both by residence—they live outside of the Black community—and by the colonial administration's perception of their educational orientation—they prize education less than the Blacks do and so have no school; their children have to row to the Highdam school in the rainy season. Nichols's discussion of politics in Highdam also uses the racial categories that we know from the history and sociology of Guyana to be real. We see in *Whole of a Morning Sky* an East Indian reaction and a Black reaction to campaigning in the election year of 1960. We are introduced to the Portuguese party and to the shouts of "Black stooge" when a Black man appears on this platform.

And we see the politics principally from a partisan racial stance. Nichols's Gem has an "African" (15) grandfather and a grandmother with some Amerindian and East Indian genes on her father's side, and her mother has "creamy brown skin" (18). In spite of this mixed racial heritage, we are left with no doubt, however, that Gem has experienced Highdam from a racial perspective, a Black perspective, and that she graduates to Georgetown with a political self that sees race as a category and herself as Black. It is from this perspective that she experiences the conflagration in Georgetown in 1960.

Beryl Gilroy's work is, like Nichols's, aware of Guyana's racial diversity. She portrays East Indians, Portuguese (half) and Amerindians. Esteban the Amerindian, as is historically correct, lives in the interior; the Indian medicine man lives in a village five hours by cart from where the Afro-Guyanese Mama King lives, the fact of the separateness of Indians from Africans being thus underscored; and the (half) Portuguese is presented as the person who controls commercial goods as is also the sociological truth for this racial group in Guyana. But while Nichols fleshes out the sociology qualitatively to give the reader a closer look at Guyanese society in a certain phase of its existence, Gilroy appropriates that sociology to make symbols through which to increase the reader's empathy with her major character. Thus the East Indian (medicine man) is there so that we can see the effort Mama King put into caring for her children's children; the East Indians Sumintra and Pandit Prem are there as beggars for us to see how far from her own culture and station Mama King feels forced to go for solace. The Portuguese appears so that we can appreciate Mama King for choosing dignity over the materials he offers in return for her body, though they would have been greatly helpful to her as a single mother. Apart from these symbolic characters and with the possible exception of Mrs. Gomer, all Gilroy's other characters are Black or colored, the most significant ones being those who are in Mama King's family. The story *Frangipani House* wants to tell is about one racial grouping in Guyana—Blacks—and the development of a new configuration within their family system and how this impinges on their aged. Nichols's *Whole of a Morning Sky* is more interested in Guyana per se, though this author, too, presents a racial perspective so that we are seeing Guyana through the eyes of a Black family and, more particularly, through the excited eyes of a Black girl who has been socialized in a Black village and who has internalized the values of that small society.

Emigration

Both these Guyanese women writers now live outside of Guyana, in England. There has been a tradition established by earlier and usually male Caribbean writers of migrating to Britain, where it is said their craft has a better chance of being developed. This could explain the migration of these writers, but there is another tradition found in the rest of the Caribbean as in Guyana: People of all classes and in Guyana, particularly the Blacks, leave in search of better pay and a higher standard of living. These writers could be part of that tradition, which in Guyana is more honored by Africans than by Indians. But whether they are a part of it or not, these writers are certainly aware of it and of its expansion. This is the circumstance that has brought changes in the family system and produced the lonely matriarch of Gilroy's *Frangipani House*.

The mother in Guyana, as in most of the rest of the Black Caribbean society, moves from being an embarrassed illegitimate young mother, at first fully or partially dependent on her baby's father or on her parents for economic support, to a middle-aged woman who has found a mate and has become the head of the distaff section of a household. By her late forties, she will be the de facto head of the household, either by default—her mate, usually older than her, having died or left her—or through an increase in social and economic resources, which brings her budgetary independence.

The source of this increase is her children's children. Like her, her daughters will have had children outside of the support of union. They will either be in the town or go from the country to the town in search of wage-earning employment and will send their children to her to be cared for. Along with them will come money, so that her household now will virtually be a childcare business; but with the children will come, too, the continuation of a life to which she is accustomed—hard work in the service of a people she loves and whose lives she wants to mold. Grandmother is now matriarch! Her power rests on the physical proximity of her grandchildren.

What happens when they are taken out of her reach? When the wage-earning market, already shifted from the estate nearby to the town, now shifts overseas to North America or England? When their migrant mothers swoop down suddenly and take her grandchildren off across the sea; when their mothers' dependency on her ceases and she gets an allowance from them for doing nothing; when she becomes ill and neither child nor grandchild is around to return the care so that she is sent off to be cared for by an institution? These are problems that arise with emigration. These are the issues that Beryl Gilroy's *Frangipani House* forces us to consider.

Grace Nichols is less preoccupied by the fact of emigration, but her two references to it give us clues as to why some Guyanese leave their country. The clue is in the exchange between Mrs. Steward and Miss DeYoung, two civil servants.

> "This country don't have no future. I glad let me daughter mekhaste and get out of this place."
> "Whey she going?"
> "To 'merica," said Mrs. Steward casually. "She leaving next month. All me family in the States now, you know." (59)

And in the utterance of cousin Lionel, the one-time fringe political leader who says during the racial confrontations of 1960:

> "I done with politics man, man."
> "Is a dirty game. . . . I think is time for me and the family to get out of the place, boy. Canada. We thinking of moving to Canada." (145)

Family Structure

Notice that in the quotation above from *Whole of a Morning Sky*, it is the male/father who announces the forthcoming migration, and that the subject of this statement is "we." Notice, too, that all Mrs. Steward's family have already migrated. Migration—when it does come to the civil servant and the politician—will be of the whole nuclear family—father, mother, and children. At this social level it is an act here in which the father/male is very involved. Compare this with *Frangipani House*, where Cyclette and Token, Mama King's two daughters, go off to America as individuals, by themselves; and though they do get married there and return to their mother's sick bed, they do so without mates. The would-be migrants of the *Whole of a Morning Sky* have a different family constellation, it seems, from those of *Frangipani House*. The would-be migrants of the *Whole of a Morning Sky* are of the father-headed household and those of *Frangipani House* of the mother-centered household. The two styles exist in Guyana, the former being the ideal, immediately possible only to the middle class, and the latter, the form most readily available to the lower class. All the women in *Frangipani House* are like Cyclette and Token, and with the exception of Cindy, as is characteristic of the lower-class Guyanese family, mate-empty. Mama King did marry Danny, but he died shortly after and became a memory. This memory is the strongest of the husband/father presences that we see in *Frangipani House*. Miss Ginchi, Mama King's friend, heads a household in which Carlton, whom she calls her grandson, lives. There is no mention of husband/father in Miss Ginchi's life. Their friend Miss Tilley has many children, but headed a husbandless, fatherless household. Miss Tilley does have a grandson. She is portrayed as having had the power to, and having used this power to, stop him from recognizing his child. There is no mention of a husband/father in Miss Tilley's life.

Frangipani House mirrors the life of the lower-class Guyanese woman. Gilroy makes us see this woman, whether she be in Guyana or in the United States, get her children, lose her mate, and try to find economic support for her headship of her household. She makes us see that this struggle often means migration, and with this the expansion of the family into a transnational unit. This itself brings sudden social power, as the woman is thrown into second motherhood. "They never ask me if I want to be mother and father again. Nobody ever ask me! They just made it so I have to do it" (20). The tragedy for the matriarch poignantly painted by Gilroy lies in the fact that by the time she gets accustomed to this power, to the practice of mothering—a task she knows well—the role and status are swept from her; and like the Frangipani blossoms she is scooped into a heap with others of her kind, an anonymous being, news of whose death is announced to "her children in London" (31).

Gilroy tries to temper the sad picture of the absent male mate, the migrating children, and the faded matriarch by the appending of a character called Chuck, an Afrocentric American male who is the husband of Mama King's granddaughter Cindy. They will migrate as a family of three generations—Mama King, Cindy and her husband, and their two sons. Chuck is in love with Africa and wants to import into his life the primacy of the family as he has seen it there. He even fondly recalls the benefits of polygamy, but Gilroy chooses not to make this an issue in the novel's family dynamics. The only clear solution with which she leaves us is the death of the faded matriarch in the *Frangipani House*. Is this more desirable than "the constipated self-seeking care which large poor families invariably provide?" (2). We are left with this question, too, and no answer to it.

Grace Nichols is interested in describing an event in Guyana's political history. This is the conflagration of 1960. Men dominated the political scene, so we get portraits of the three political leaders, and we enter a civil service in which men hold dominant positions and women are involved in mindless chatter. It is when Nichols takes us into homes that we see the structure of the family. And since she takes us into a wide cross section of homes, we see both the lower-class family, the concern of Gilroy, and the middle-class family. The male absence in the lower class is here in Nichols, as it is in Gilroy and in much of the sociological work on the Black lower-class family in the Caribbean. We see it in Mrs. Payne, whose husband has died, leaving her with several children to rear. We see Mrs. Payne hustling at her black pudding business but apparently using as well a fundraising option used by Miss Tilley in *Frangipani House*— that is, a lover. Here there are Indian women, too, splashing through the water to make a living. We know that Mrs. Lall has no husband and must support herself, but since neither she nor the other Indian women are shown to us with their children, we are allowed no comparison of Indian and African matriarchy in lower-class Guyana. We do get a good view, though, of patriarchy at work in the Black middle-class family.

Nichols's central voice is Gem. Her father is a professional—an elementary school teacher, and as is expected socially of such people, is married and lives with his wife and their issue. Archie, the father, as is also usual, holds the purse strings in the family and is officially the authority here, as he is in the school and in the village in which his school is sited. We see little sustained opposition to Archie's authority in the school and in the district, but his home is a different matter. Grace

Nichols and her female characters effortlessly undermine the patriarch. In the first place, after thirty-eight pages of the book, Nichols takes Archie out of his high social and occupational status and puts the retired headmaster in Georgetown, where he is nervous about the depletion of his resources, and where the real estate in which he has invested a good part of his savings is threatened by the fires of 1960.

Nichols casts the tense patriarch as a background to the lively freedom of his wife, Clara, who giggles fearlessly on any occasion at anything she finds funny; Clara, whom the village loves and later the yard in the city loves; Clara, who lets people into Archie's house whether he approves of them or not; Clara, who resorts to taking credit from the grocery, forcing the patriarch to spend against his will; Clara, who he knows could beat him within an inch of his life, as is clear from the excerpt below, which describes an exchange between Archie and Clara: "[S]o obsessed was he [Archie] by his passion that one morning, couple years after their marriage, he sat at the breakfast table staring at her [Clara]. Staring more than usual, at her face, her neck, her bosom. Then he said in a sudden voice, 'What would you do if I was to hit you eh?' . . . 'Make sure that when you hit me you do a very good job of it,' she said. 'Make sure that you don't leave an ounce of strength in my body. Make sure that I can't get up again, you hear.' Archie knew she meant it" (20).

The patriarch's daughters are no more submissive than his wife. He tried to steer his daughter, Dinah, into the security of the teaching profession, but she rebelled and chose the civil service instead. His pained reaction was merely to keep silent when her name is mentioned. On the one occasion on which he tries to assert his authority over her, she responds with scant respect: "'I don't want that communist chap back here,' Archie said to this daughter, who was inside pulling on a skirt over her shorts. Dinah merely flounced out of the house with Hartley" (128). And even Gem, the first "to loose out his lacings and take off his shoes" (21) on his return from his evening walks while they were in Highdam, was now uncontrollably amused by her father's tight-lipped posture of patriarchism: "Gem, watching her father slowly chewing his food—Archie was always stressing the importance of chewing food—suddenly burst out laughing at the table, sending little bits of wet bread flying" (88). Nor could he really punish her either: "Gem went on laughing, making stifled sounds to stop herself. . . . 'I bet I give you something to laugh about,' cried Archie suddenly, rising from the table, and rushing across to his cupboards to get the wild cane. But Gem was too quick for him, running to the toilet and locking herself in" (88).

The other middle-class Black men fare little better in Grace Nichols's *Whole of a Morning Sky*. Conrad, Gem's hero—"There was nobody else like him. Who else could make white mice disappear down their shirt collar and reappear, peeping out at the cuff of their sleeve?" (75)—is ultimately shown to us as part of an odd family. This was the Conrad who carried a gun, beside whom Archie felt immeasurably safe (67), who knew all about the outside world. Conrad at fifty-plus had not completed the Oedipal phase, as most five-year-old boys had done. He was still tied to his mother's frailty, even sharing a bedroom with her and publicly washing and hanging out her underwear to dry. He would not even share her with a medical doctor. He treated her himself, and without company or assistance dressed her dead body in her favorite dress and put her away in her tomb.

Lionel, the fringe politician, was less odd. If Conrad was a biological male who failed the test of manhood by not being able to comply with the Judeo-Christian dictate to leave one's parents and cleave unto a mate, Lionel, too, fails, in that he put his hand to the plough and looked back. Lionel, either a simpleton or a coward, had entered the political fray with a new party. When the reality of politics hit him in the form of racial violence and international intrigue, he took to confessing: "'I done with politics man, man. . . . Is a dirty game. . . . Now I hearing that they got my name on a hit list. I never done anybody anything in my life. I think is time for me and the family to get out of the place, boy. Canada. We thinking of moving to Canada'" (145).

The middle-class men that Grace Nichols portrays are not heroes. Certainly not to Clara, who, not unreasonably, blames men for the debacle of 1960, since they exercise political power—"'I bet you if men used to bring children into this world, they would have more respect for human life'" (139). These men, however, are not as absent as those in *Frangipani House*, nor would any of the characters have praised the absence of men from the interior of their lives as Miss Tilley did: "No man to mix up things. Man does really mix up things" (21). And neither Gem nor Dinah nor Mrs. Payne's son, Vibert, nor Archie or Clara would have said of their father, as Chuck said of his father: "'My father has no family. . . . Just sons and daughters. Now, they have children but he has no grandchildren. He just goes from place to place like some goddam hobo shouting, 'I've dropped by' and 'I'm taking off later today'" (107).

Conclusion

The critical characterizations of the middle-class men who each exhibit a type of impotence in *Whole of a Morning Sky*, and the forthright view of the negligent male in *Frangipani House*, demonstrate the use of a truthful sense of history, physical place, and class consciousness found in both novels. In particular, the novels aptly present women characters who demonstrate the consciousness of Guyana's sociological configurations through the images of their working lives, marriages, motherhood, and aging. Whether it is Gilroy's aged and reflective Mama King, or Nichols's pre-teen Gem, the writers paint vivid pictures of the integral connections of natural settings and physical environment on the development of the characters' social, political, and personal consciousness of their place in family, community, and country. Elevating the richness of the complicated terrain to the level of symbol—the rural interior, which holds the secrets, joys, and struggles of past and present lives—Beryl Gilroy's and Grace Nichols's stories become more than single stories of Guyanese families. While poetically rendering imagined lives, these novels also serve to document historical, racial, and political identities that emerge as representative in the chronicle of Guyana's (and the Caribbean's) historical sociology.

Bibliography

Dixon, Melvin. *Ride Out the Wilderness: Geography and Identity in Afro-American Literature.* Urbana: University of Illinois Press, 1987.

Gilroy, Beryl. *Frangipani House.* London: Heinemann, 1986.

Moore, Brian L. *Race, Power and Social Segmentation in Colonial Society— Guyana After Slavery, 1838–1891.* London: Gordon and Breach Science Publishers, 1987.

Nichols, Grace. *Whole of a Morning Sky.* London: Virago Press, 1986.

Rodney, Walter. *A History of the Guyanese Working People 1881–1905.* Baltimore: Johns Hopkins University Press, 1981.

Smith, R. E. *British Guyana.* London: Oxford University Press, 1962.

Smith, R. T. *The Negro Family in British Guyana.* New York: Grove Press, 1956.

15

Textual Deviancy and Cultural Syncretism

Romantic Fiction as a Subversive Strain in Africana Women's Writing

JANE BRYCE AND KARI DAKO

Sisi Eko, you no dey shame?
Plenty husband is too much.

If you marry taxi driver
I don't care
If you marry taxi driver
I don't care.

(Popular highlife of the 1960s by the Nigerian musician Bobby Benson)

At the end of Ghanaian writer Ama Ata Aidoo's novel *Changes,* the heroine is left wondering if she will ever "get answers to some of the big questions she was asking of life." Her speculations formulate themselves into the words of a highlife song heard "on an unusually warm and not-so-dark night": "[O]ne day, one day." Highlife, the great popular dance music of West Africa, originated in the 1940s as a hybrid of Western instrumentation and local rhythms. Sung mostly in pidgin, it celebrated the optimism of the independence era and the raised expectations of material prosperity. Aidoo's novel is an ironic commentary on the disillusion that followed the degeneration of the physical fabric of Ghanaian society and the disappointment of those early hopes. The vehicle—the use of which is itself an ironic about-face on what she presents as an earlier, "revolutionary" position, which precluded such frivolity—is that of the romantic novel. This despised "feminine" form is used self-consciously, both to subvert the dominant political and social discourse of Ghana today, and to expose the specific contradictions of gender and its power relationships.

Aidoo is not the only writer whose work falls within the "postcolonial feminist" ambit, to draw attention to the durability and power of the myths generated by romantic fiction. These myths constitute a latent or explicit strain in the work of writers both in Africa and the diaspora— anywhere, in fact, where colonial education imposed its notion of ideal womanhood. This ideal being—essentially, the Pauline Christian one of feminine submission, gentleness, forbearance, suffering, passivity, virginity, and motherhood—has been particularly pernicious to women in contexts of struggle against the combined distortions of racist stereotyping and indigenous male chauvinism.

Writers' responses to it have ranged from radical questioning to strategic reappropriation. In the former category, one thinks of writers like the Jamaican Olive Senior and Joan Riley, a product of Jamaican emigration to Britain. Both these writers demonstrate an awareness of how the stereotype of the (white) romantic heroine functions as a form of class and gender oppression. In Senior's short story "Lily, Lily," a young girl is seduced by a "tall, dark handsome stranger, who appears to her as the fulfillment of the promise held out by her exclusive reading of romantic novels. When he materializes, her fate is preordained. He rides off in a mist after promising to love, honor, cherish her for the rest of their lives" (Senior 125) and is never heard or seen again. Lily, meanwhile, is left "deflowered, trampled, defiled, besmirched, soiled" (126)—and pregnant, the victim of a repressive middle-class morality, which decrees that rather than ruin her reputation she should hand over her baby to her married and infertile sister. Senior, however, breaks the unending cycle of oppression and deception by having the child, the young Lily, run away when her stepfather starts to abuse her, to the older Lily, "Aunt Lily." The older Lily, looking back, regrets that she herself was so hemmed in by the perceived roles available to her—"servile wife, old maid postmistress or slut" (Senior 140)—that she was unable to take such decisive action on her own behalf. As she writes to her sister of the young Lily, "I would never in my wildest dreams have shown such independence of spirit as she is showing" (140), she sees it as grounds for optimism and change. She herself has long since "thrown out the foolish romances, the foolish longings that so inflamed my youth" (139) and plans to leave the island to look for a new life.

The heroine of Joan Riley's *Romance* is similarly ensnared by romantic fantasy. The young Verona's dream that she is the blonde object of a white hero's adoration is not, however, simply a distortion of reality, but expresses her longing for something other, a different reality altogether. Her escapist reading of romantic fiction does not provide her with any more appropriate image onto which to project her own suppressed desire. As Valerie Belgrave says in her romance novel, *Ti Marie:* "For centuries there have been poems, books and letters praising the beauty of women with skins as white as the driven snow, eyes as blue as the cloudless skies, and lips like rosebuds. History has scant record of the equally dazzling beauty of black women, and metaphors and similes come less readily to mind" (46). Riley's use of the romance as a reference point within a starkly realistic narrative is, therefore, ironic, in a way similar to Aidoo's, constituting both an implicit "criticism of a literary genre, and a literary manifesto through negation" (Suarez 306). In this sense it is the exact opposite of the way it is used in Valerie Belgrave's *Ti Marie,* where it is deployed in a partly revisionary attempt to produce a text that *parallels* white romantic fantasy, substituting a beautiful mulatto heroine (who, despite a happy ending, carries overtones of the tragic mulatto convention of earlier fiction) (see Zimra). The setting of the novel— Trinidad, in all its exotic tropical glory—at the end of the eighteenth century, with historical events (the revolution in Haiti and the abolition movement) as background, brings the writer's purpose—to relocate the exotic periphery, and its inhabitants, at the center of the narrative— further into focus. Although exotic locations and period settings are commonplace in romantic fiction, they rarely serve as more than a backdrop to the private drama of the white protagonists. A glance at the covers of the ubiquitous Mills and Boon romance titles reveals how routinely white heroines encounter love in dark places: *Stars over Sarawak* ("the story of two people thrown together in the primitive jungle of Borneo"); *Frail Sanctuary* ("they could not stay on their remote (Pacific) island for ever"); *Jacinta Point* ("Diego Ramirez . . . had more than his fair share of machismo and the masculine superiority of his race"); *Bride of the Rif* ("Sara found herself whisked off into the Rif Mountains of Morocco . . . with such wedding ceremonies as 'the cleaning of the wheat' and being painted with henna"); and *One Brief Sweet Hour* ("Lauren's Caribbean Holiday was meant to be a once-in-a-lifetime thing").

The racial stereotypes that are so conspicuous a feature of such novels are equally central to *Ti Marie.* In her attempt to validate her Black characters and their African culture, Belgrave falls prey to the very stereotypes of color, vitality, passion, and sensuality so familiar in white writers' constructions of the Black as "other": "His senses stirred to the sway and swagger of moving hips and limps so unconsciously alluring—the undeniable animation of the African—as vendors arranged their exotic wares, unfamiliar fruits, strange wild meats and delicacies wrapped in banana leaves" (44). Though this passage is a description of the aristocratic white hero's reactions on first arriving in Port of Spain, Yei, the mysterious half-Indian woman healer, with magical powers and an inscrutable demeanor, expresses something similar when she says, "[L]ive in the white man's way, but the Africans are more like me—more natural" (13). Amerindians are depicted as one more colorful detail in an exotic landscape, as when Barry, the English aristocrat, catches sight of some Amerindians fishing: "[T]o add to the magical effects of the historic river . . . a young boy exclaimed in delight as he caught a small, primitive black fish in his net" (59). The use of a white hero unconsciously perpetuates the orientalist perspective, in which the white man's gaze surveys, describes, and possesses both woman and terrain, in spite of Belgrave's attempt at a utopian reversal.

Enough has perhaps been said to demonstrate that, whatever the divergences in literary response, romantic myths, founded on notions of chaste and desirable white femininity and powerful dominant masculinity, with their barely suppressed subtext of Black sensuality and otherness, are a part of the complex process of the construction of identity in the fiction of Black women writers. It may be that in the diasporan setting, where skin color is still an identifiable factor in the stratification of class and power, the contradictions are such as to elicit extreme reactions—the total rejection of Senior, the wholesale reappropriation of Belgrave. In West Africa, where, in spite of colonialism and missionary education, indigenous tradition is still active and meaningful in people's lives, romantic myths have always been visibly open to question. The Nigerian novelist Flora Nwapa repeatedly explores the contradictions between imported notions of romantic love and Christian monogamy in the context of a contemporary situation marked by the ruthless struggle for survival. Typically, the missionary values of colonial education are seen to be inappropriate. In *One is Enough,* the heroine rejects both the idealization and the offer of marriage itself, with the words, "I don't want to be a wife any more, a mistress yes, with a lover, yes of course, but not a wife. . . . As a wife, I am never free. I am a shadow of myself" (127).

In *Women Are Different,* the boarding school is seen both as the source of alien stereotypes of womanhood and an ideology that seeks to suppress dangerous anti-colonial activism. The 1940s products of Elenenwa Girls' School, groomed to take up leading roles in pre-independent Nigeria, are therefore constructed out of contradiction. They are expected both to forsake the traditional role of women in the polygamous African family—equated by the missionaries with prostitution—and take up middle-class professional positions, and also to fulfill the stereotype of dutiful wife and responsible mother. It is perhaps symptomatic of the difference suggested above that Nwapa's characters invariably come to some sort of pragmatic accommodation with these conflicting expectations and the relentless pressure of a material reality that exposes them as fundamentally irrelevant. When the daughter of one of the older, missionary-educated women in *Women Are Different* leaves her husband and becomes a successful businesswoman by her own efforts, the author comments, "Chinwe had done the right thing. Her generation was doing better than her mother's own . . . telling the men, that there are different ways of living one's life fully and fruitfully. . . . Marriage is not THE only way" (119). This pragmatic, essentially unromantic view is insistently supported by a traditional value system as voiced by the older, not formally educated mothers of Nwapa's heroines, like Amaka's mother in *One is Enough:* "[Y]ou refused to take my advice. You were being a good wife, chastity, faithfulness, my foot. You can go ahead and eat virtue" (32).

Indigenous practice, therefore, constitutes a parallel text to the romantic mythology inscribed by colonial education, through the reading of Marie Corelli and other romantic writers. Yet this parallel text is also contested by contemporary African women who are no longer able to fit themselves within the roles—of fertile motherhood and acknowledgment of male supremacy—which are written for them. What is left? This is precisely what lies behind "the big questions" left unanswered at the end of Aidoo's novel *Changes.*

The author's ambiguous relationship to the romance genre is signaled by the "confession" that precedes the text. In it she "apologizes" for what she calls "an exercise in words—eating," for having once said that she "could never write about lovers in Accra. Because surely in our environment there are more important things to write about?" The self-conscious irony of this statement is highlighted by a consideration of Aidoo's situation in the context of Ghanaian politics and the African

literary scene. For she speaks from an oppositional perspective on both
counts. Educated under Nkrumah, icon of pan-Africanism, Aidoo has
always defined herself as first and foremost a pan-Africanist. Her earlier
novel, *Our Sister Killjoy,* castigated those of her compatriots who left
home and continued to mouth patriotic sentiments while enjoying the
material benefits of the West. After the so-called Rawlings revolution of
1981, Aidoo was appointed to the position of Minister of Education. She
was forced to resign and leave the country because she was deemed too
radical for a revolutionary socialist regime. Word of mouth has it that the
Ghanaian leadership was not ready for an outspoken, irrepressible
woman in its ranks. Aidoo has since lived in Zimbabwe, where she was at
one time chair of the Zimbabwe Women Writer's Group, and has since
returned to live in Ghana. With her activist history, therefore, her deliberate decision to write "a love story" set in Accra already undermines
masculinist presumptions of what constitutes an appropriate field for
revolutionary action. Furthermore, Aidoo is one of the few women
writers to have attained the status of recognition within the "canon" of
African literature. This recognition, though, is limited, in spite of a remarkable versatility of output spanning three decades, and depends to a
paradoxical extent on her adoption by Western critics and readers as an
African feminist—a label she accepts only as part of a wider political
agenda: "I do not see a strict division between being a feminist, being an
African Nationalist and being a Socialist. I don't even see how you can
claim to be an African Nationalist and not be a feminist, whether you are
a man or a woman" (Aidoo interview, 18). However, it is noteworthy that
when it came to finding a publisher for her latest novel, neither Ghana—
where it is set and to whose readership it is, primarily, addressed—nor
Zimbabwe—where she was living when she wrote the novel and where
she was prominent on the literary scene—could provide a publisher capable of taking on so awkward a text. The fact that *Changes* was published by a Western feminist press is not the least of its ironies.

The encasing of a highly subversive message in a devalued "feminine"
form is in itself subversive, and draws attention to the fact that a decade
of revolutionary rhetoric in Ghana has made little difference to the balance of power between the sexes. While it is, as its author says, "a slice
from the life and loves of a somewhat privileged young woman . . . in
Accra" (Aidoo, *Changes,* front matter), it is also a novel of crisis in the
body politic. As Esi, the heroine, herself realizes, her dilemma is symp-

tomatic of the social dynamics of contemporary Ghana. Like Nwapa's women, the product of an elite education, she ponders, "For surely, taking a ten-year-old child away from her mother and away from her first language—which is surely one of life's most powerful working tools . . . from where she was only equipped to go and roam in strange foreign lands with no hope of ever meaningfully re-entering her mother's world. . . . all this was too high a price to pay to achieve the dangerous confusion she was now in and the country now was in" (114). Esi perceives that the state in which she now finds herself, that of "a young Ghanaian woman government statistician divorcee, a mother of one child, getting ready to be a second wife" (115), raises questions to which she, as an individual, cannot provide the answers. "Hopefully a whole people would soon have answers for them" (115) ("one day, one day").

What is the nature of these "questions" and how are they dramatized in the text? Aidoo uses a number of devices, of which a parody of romantic fiction is one. Esi meets Ali, a "self-consciously charming man," on the first page of the novel. She has been delegated, in the absence of the office secretary, to go and check on travel arrangements for herself and her colleagues to a conference in Lusaka. She finds herself hot and bothered from the drive across town in her shaky car, sinking gratefully into "a chair from a group of rather plush and low office furniture" (2) in Ali's air-conditioned office. The encounter is deliberately typical of Mills and Boon, romance tradition from the powerful, exotic male, with kohl around his eyes, the movements of a panther (22), and a hypnotic drawl that almost lulls Esi to sleep, to the "frail" woman with her "asthmatic" car (4) who becomes "aware of something quite new and interesting . . . mak[ing] itself felt in that room that early evening" (3). In the best gothic tradition, peals of thunder announce the arrival of this "new and interesting something" (3).

The scene is thus set for Esi and Ali to fall in love. The next chapter, however, initiates the ironic reversal of the romantic stereotype by contrasting fantasy with the reality of Esi's marriage to Oko. A weeping child overhears her parents quarreling in the bedroom in a morning ritual of antagonism, which is mirrored in the marriage of Esi's best friend, Opokuya, and Kubi, in their wrangling over the car. In Esi's case, it is sex that is used by Oko in an attempt to assert his dominance. In Opokuya's, it is the fact that Kubi owns, controls, and drives the family car, leaving it parked all day at his office, while she copes as best she can with the demands of her hospital job and four children, using hospital vans to get to work. Both these relationships contain a built-in imbalance of power to which Opokuya reluctantly accommodates herself, while envying her friend her freedom of movement (56). Esi, on the other hand, takes the extremely unconventional course of refusing to move with her husband to his new posting, insisting on living alone in her government bungalow in Accra, and surrendering her daughter to her husband's family. In all these respects, Esi is a deviant in terms of Akan culture, and an eccentric in terms of conventional middle-class behavior.

This deviancy is a deliberate rewriting by Aidoo of the text of women's roles in Ghana. The reaction to her husband's demands on her—to demand a divorce—is deviant in that, as her grandmother says, "the best husband you can ever have is he who demands all of you and all of your time. Who is a good man if not the one who eats his wife completely and pushes her down with a good gulp of alcohol?" (109). As far as the elders in the village are concerned, Esi's reasons for divorce are simply too flimsy. Her deviancy extends to her preference for solitude, living alone, keeping a distance between herself and her kin group, having only one child, and allowing that child, in a matrilineal society, to live with the father's family. In Akan terms, Esi is a "bad wife" and a "bad mother," the two primary parameters for measuring the worth of a woman. Ironically, at the same time, Esi is a product of her culture. Her mother and grandmothers made sure she was educated precisely so that she would be able to live a different life from theirs. It is that education that has made Esi unable any longer to be satisfied with the semblance of power and to insist on having it for herself. In the context of the novel, she does this through a rejection of the most sacrosanct of social institutions—marriage—and through her pursuit of personal satisfaction in love. Love, as it is so often in West African women's writing, is a trope for the desire for change: not just for "an other," but for "something other."

Esi seeks an alternative to the restrictions of monogamy, first in a passionate affair with Ali, then in agreeing to become his second wife. Here again she is depicted as deviant. In terms of Akan culture, nakedness is a tabu; yet Esi excites Ali by walking about the house naked. Her body, too, in its thinness and flatness, is far from the Akan ideal of beauty. Her explicit sexuality, her frank addiction to sensual pleasures, is unusual in most African women's writing, where sexuality is generally treated with discreet silence. Furthermore, one of Aidoo's most important subversive devices is her insistence on *naming*. In this novel, there are several instances of this, including that of marital rape. After Oko forces himself on her, Esi's feelings of outrage crystallize around the issue of naming what has happened to her. She imagines the reaction of male academics to a sociological presentation on "The Prevalence of Marital Rape in the Urban African Environment." "Imported feminist ideas," "how would you describe 'marital rape' in Akan . . . Igbo . . . Yoruba . . . Wolof?" (11). In its iconoclastic explicitness, the text itself, like its heroine, is deviant.

When Esi opts for polygamy as a compromise, it is with a clearsighted sense of the irony of her situation. The amazement of the elders of both her own and Ali's family that educated people should want to follow such a custom exposes Ali's hypocrisy right at its roots, whence he claims his validation. Because he loves Fusena, his wife, and because they chose to marry, he is reluctant to go through the socially ordained mechanism of consulting her before taking a second wife. The elders on both sides refuse to allow him to sidestep this essential part of the procedure. Esi too, beyond an ironic "And your wife?" (86), gives no thought to Fusena's feelings about her marriage to Ali, in feminist terms showing a deviant lack of solidarity. She is amused by the Western romanticism of Ali's gesture in giving her a ring—but is herself not immune to it: "'Oh Ali, it is beautiful,' she said in a breathless whisper" (89). The ring, which is not a part of Islamic or indigenous custom, exposes the contradiction of Ali's argument that polygamy is African: "'We have got marriage in Africa, Esi. In Muslim Africa. In non-Muslim Africa. And in our marriages a man has a choice—to have one or more wives" (90). In other words, as Esi's laughter shows, what he is arguing for is the male power to define and name reality as it accords best with his own convenience. The novel, with its multifarious devices of irony, parody, ridicule, and derision, is a repudiation of that power.

Although on one hand, Esi ends up alone and once again dissatisfied, the novel, as Caroline Rooney says of *Our Sister Killjoy*, dictates how it will be read. It imposes, in Aidoo's words, its own "aesthetic imperative," through the oral elements that counterpoint the narrative and offer an ironic commentary on it. Aidoo's technique is very close to the traditional use of "interspersed song" within a narrative. Her open-ended style, with its frequent use of ellipsis and its deliberate imprecision ("'After all,' said somebody to whoever cared to listen" (64); "Opokuya said something to the effect that" (94), constantly invites the reader to fill in the gaps while drawing attention to the external narrator. The text thus consists of both "story" and "chorus," a constant ironic interplay of surface and latent meaning.

This oracular technique is ultimately what makes the text so hard to pin down. Is it, as it claims, a romantic love story, a satire, a parody, or a realistic representation of the condition of life in today's Accra for the middle-class woman? It eludes categorization, insisting on naming itself. In the process, it disguises a radical critique of post-revolution Ghanaian society as the story of an individual woman. Yet everything that happens to her has its resonance on the larger scene, as the following example shows.

The physical degeneration that bespeaks economic collapse is conveyed above all through the iconographic significance of the car in Ghanaian society. As the highlife song in the epigraph shows, cars were once the ultimate symbol of material success. (And so, naturally, women ran after taxi drivers!) In the novel, Esi's car, coughing and spluttering, and Opokuya's terrible frustration at her carlessness, which imposes the only strain on her friendship with Esi, are symptomatic of this shift. Ali's gift of a brand new car to Esi is therefore the grandest gesture of male power available, the bribe with which he buys himself off for his neglect of her. Though she is unable to refuse the car, he is not able to buy her acquiescence. In spite of his lavish gifts, Esi rejects Ali because he cannot provide the one thing she wants most—equality within a relationship. She accepts that "he loved her in his own fashion. What she became certain of was that his fashion of loving had proved quite inadequate for her" (165).

The romantic myth, as elusive as ever, is transformed in this novel into a radical questioning of the power endemic in sexual and social relationships. It points to the fact that change does not come about in one, monolithic, definitive overturning gesture—like revolution, or Esi's divorce. It is a process of minute shifts and subtle emphases, a complex interplay of contradictory elements, constituting *changes*.

Works Cited

Aidoo, Ama Ata. *Changes*. London: Women's Press, 1991.

———. *Our Sister Killjoy*. 1977. London: Longman, 1982.

———. "Ama Ata Aidoo." Interview. Adewale Maja-Pearce. *Index On Censorship* (September 1990): 17–18.

Arbor, Jane. *One Brief Sweet Hour*. London: Mills and Boon, 1983.

Belgrave, Valerie. *Ti Marie*. United Kingdom: Heinemann, 1988.

Graham, Elizabeth. *Jacinta Point*. London: Mills and Boon, 1980.

Hampton, Anne. *Stars over Sarawak*. London: Mills and Boon, 1974.

Hilton, Margery. *Frail Sanctuary*. London: Mills and Boon, 1973.

Nasta, Susheila, ed. *Motherlands: Black Women's Writing from Africa, the Caribbean, and South Asia*. London: Women's Press, 1991.

Nwapa, Flora. *One is Enough*. Nigeria: Tana Press, 1981.

———. *Women Are Different*. Nigeria: Tana Press, 1986.

Riley, Joan. *Romance*. London: Women's Press, 1988.

Rome, Margaret. *Bride of the Rif*. London: Mills and Boon, 1972.

Rooney, Caroline. "'Dangerous Knowledge' and the Poetics of Survival: A Reading of *Our Sister Killjoy* and *A Question of Power*." Nasta. 99–126.

Senior, Olive. "Lily, Lily." *Arrival of the Snake Woman*. London: Longman, 1989. 112–45.

Suarez, Isabel Carrera. "Absent Mother(lands): Joan Riley's Fiction." Nasta. 290–309.

Zimra, Clarise. "Righting the Calabash: Writing History in the Female Francophone Narrative." *Out of the Kumbla*. Ed. Carole Boyce Davies and Elaine Savory Fido. Trenton: Africa World Press, 1990. 143–59.

16

"A Girl Marries a Monkey"

The Folktale as an Expression of Value
and Change in Society

N. J. OPOKU-AGYEMANG

As one of the most active artistic vehicles for the (un)conscious transmission of social values from generation to generation, the folktale has
passed the test of time and still remains a living and integral part of the
diurnal functioning of various people in the world. In his discussion of
the role of the folktale, Dundes argues that it "provides a socially sanctioned outlet for the expression of what cannot be articulated in the
more usual, direct way" (36). Although Dundes overstates the point by
his use of the negative emphatic auxiliary, it is still clear from his argument that the folktale provides a widely accepted and approved forum
through which shared values may be delivered. It is also possible to see
the folktale as a powerful form through which societal values may be
contested, reformed, or overthrown altogether.

This chapter examines the structure of a specific African folktale as it
exists in five primary versions in order to determine how the folktale
deploys received values. The folktale in question is clearly popular with
collectors, but it is most prominent in modern African literature in English in its secondary version in Ama Ata Aidoo's play, *Anowa* (1970).
Aidoo's excellent drama helps to identify the well-known folktale in its
modern context.

The storyline that informs most of the substance of *Anowa* is drawn
from the tale that recounts the story of a young woman who, spurning all
parental choices and other offers of a spouse, makes her own choice and
ends badly. It is a narrative line realizable in an almost infinite number of
ways. As will be shortly illustrated by five summarized versions of the
tale, the names of the dramatist personae change, as do their physical

characteristics and moral strengths; the details of the episodes and incidents also vary. What remains constant in these tales are the basic components of the plot, or what Propp calls "functions" and Dundes designates "*motifeme.*"

In "Why a Girl should marry him to whom she is given in marriage" (Radin 207, 208) the virgin heroine, Kwaboaso, proudly rejected all marriage proposals, and found fault with her would-be suitors, who included a hunter. She found this hunter particularly abhorrent because he had ticks all over his body. It so happened that when she was abducted by "little folks" into the forest, this hunter rescued her from mortal danger. She makes a marriage proposal to the hunter, which he in turn rejects, notwithstanding the intervention by the head of the village. Kwaboaso is thus left unmarried, and the tale ends with a caution: "[W]hen they take you to give you in marriage to anyone, marry him for you do not know whether someday when you are in need, he will not rescue you" (Radin 208).

The version that exists in *An Anthology of African Folklore* edited by Jablow is called "Buje the Slender." This tale shares some common grounds with the previous version, although the specifics differ. Here, the virgin Buje also snubs her suitors who, in her case, include rich men and a chief. This chief was so peeved that he offered a reward for any man who would sexually violate this maiden. The tortoise accomplishes the feat; the humiliated Buje runs into the bush and is metamorphosed into a plant.

Kwasi Gyan's collection of Akan tales includes "Abena et l'oiseau," which tells of a beautiful Abena who, like Kwaboaso and Buje, arrogantly turns down several proposals, including those encouraged by her parents. Abena's reason for immediately accepting, on her own, a marriage proposal from a stranger on horseback is that this marriage will take her far away from home. Her parents respect her choice, although they disapprove of it. Abena leaves her parents' village to make her home in a strange land. What seems a happy marriage in a distant settlement is marred by the appearance of a bird, both in a dream and in physical form, to Abena. The interpretation of the bird's song reveals that Abena has lost all members of her family; but she never got to hear about the deaths, her marriage to a stranger apparently having removed her so far away from home as to make contact with her impossible. Her decision to go back home is kept in check by her neighbors, who remind her that for all she knows the geography of her former village must have changed beyond recognition. Abena thus spends the rest of her life regretting her decision to marry a stranger and to move far away from home.

"A Girl Marries a Monkey" can be found in *African Folktales* (336–43), which R. D. Abraham collected and retold. In this tale the unnamed, beautiful heroine finds fault with her suitors, who included a hunter, as in the story of Kwaboaso. As happened to Abena, this heroine is instantly attracted to a stranger—this time, in a market place. She manages to get this stranger to make a marriage proposal to her and follows him on a journey into the unknown. This attractive stranger turns out to have acquired borrowed human parts, including his teeth and skin. The heroine is not deterred by the slow transformation of this creature into a monkey and ends up living in a tree with this animal. The hunter who earlier on had his proposal spurned rescues her from the unrestrained sexual prowess of the monkey. As in Radin's version, this heroine begs to be married by the hunter, but is left a spinster. The tale ends with a moral: "So ever since that day, when we give our child advice, she should listen closely to what we have to say" (343).

Bernard Dadie's "La jeune fille difficile" (97–110) shares marked similarities with Abraham's tale. In Dadie, the extremely attractive physical characteristics of the heroine supersedes those of the other heroines in the other tales. Cocoh is so beautiful that she stops the sun in its tracks and is also admired by the wind, the seasons, and the parrot. Her beauty provides the lyrics of the cock's crow. Much to the disappointment of her parents, who believe that marriage will "soften" their daughter, Cocoh turns down marriage proposals from chiefs, merchants, and artisans. Her idea of a brave, dignified man worthy of her is the one who will succeed in knocking down, by a single shot of the arrow, a small calabash, which she balances on her head. It was an extraordinarily handsome man who arrives at the village and manages to pass the test. He thus sets off on the journey to his village with his new bride.

As with the young husband in "A Girl Marries a Monkey," this man also gave back his borrowed parts, which in his case included everything except his skull. He takes Cocoh to skull country. She then has occasion to regret her decision to subject men to such an impossible task. She has no way out of her predicament, as she has been handed over to be executed shortly. The old woman who has the task of getting her ready to be sacrificed has a sudden change of mind and arranges with a male messenger to send her back to her parents. Unlike her predecessors, Cocoh has a second chance at the matrimonial life; she marries the first man her mother had proposed and becomes a model wife, humble and obedient.

Obviously, it is a near-impossible task to locate the original among these tales. These summarized tales here demonstrate enough diversity to suggest manipulation of the received version by the narrators. Yet it is possible to classify them as primary versions, because despite the diversity of detail they bear similar literary features: the presence of a single narrator who is external to the elements of plot; the linear shape of the narrative; the emphasis on a single character around whom events of the plot revolve; and, as well, the absence of independent and sustained subplots and of individual authorship.

As folktales, these versions belong to the category of the explanatory tale (Thompson 9) which, like the etiological tale and *pourquoi* story, explains the origins of various phenomena that include mankind and its institutions. The selected tales in this essay affirm the origin of the practice of selecting husbands for brides. They also impose marriage as a social value on women, so that even marriage to a tick-infested spouse is socially preferable to spinsterhood. Whatever the case, the prospective bride must express no opinion in the choice of a husband, as is clearly demonstrated by the use of the passive in the title of the story of Kwaboaso.

In spite of the divergent details, the summarized tales share a structural uniformity. Six morphological elements may be discerned in them. The first element coincides with Propp's initial situation, which here constitutes an expository introduction of the heroines.

Although the physical makeup of Kwaboaso is not evident in the tale, her "asset" as a virgin has a way of setting her apart from others. Built into the concept of virgin is the idea of purity. The adjective "slender" in the title of the tale in Jablow's collection gives evidence of the attractive shape of Buje, while the adjective "flowering" provides a combination of visual and kinesthetic imageries to suggest youth and beauty. The girl who found out she had married a monkey is briefly as "beautiful," but no description equals that which occurs in "La jeune fille difficile." Cocoh's physical makeup is given detailed description, which includes the shade of her hair and the color of her toes. Indeed, her looks made it impossible for the contestants to concentrate on their tasks.

These descriptions are derived from first-sight impressions; they deal with the physical appearance of these women, to the near exclusion of their mental and emotional capabilities. Given the gender of their admirers, one can conclude that there exists an oblique sexist bias to these descriptions; the women are to be of use and service to men. These expository introductions constitute the calm before the storm. All too soon the heroine comes into conflict with society by her refusal to conform to accepted practice. Conflict is the second motifeme of these tables. Society in the tales is made up of adult males and the occasional female, who wield power by virtue of their economic or social standing. In these tales, the role of dominant culture is to ensure that in the question of marriage, the "lady does not protest" at all.

Kwaboaso, like the girl who married a monkey, found fault with her suitors, her complaints resting on the looks of the men. Buje clashes with men of high economic and social standing by rejecting their advances. The only heroines in these tales to have offered reasons that go beyond the physique of the men are Abena and Cocoh. Abena saw marriage as a springboard to expanding her otherwise limited horizon, while Cocoh insisted on bravery and dignity, qualities that are commensurate with her self-worth. In their efforts, both Abena and Cocoh conflict with their mothers as well.

The heroines' uncertain sources of power and pride are attributed solely to their natural endowments. None of them has a power base as solid as those of their suitors, which we have established as socially and economically derived. These women also behave uniformly as prizes that must be won. It is evident from the negative response of Abena's parents to her thirst for knowledge that such yearning for intellectual adventure is regarded as extraneous to the accepted qualities of women.

The physical attraction of these women, which contributes to their pride, creates, eventually, a distance between them and society. Distancing constitutes the third motifeme of the primary versions, and it manifests itself in the central symbol of the journey. Kwaboaso is abducted into the jungle, while the other heroines follow their chosen husbands on journeys into the unknown. The expectations of discovery raised by the journey imagery are given negative connotations.

The distance away from home is depicted in undesirable ways, since calamities befall each heroine. There is the total absence of shared happiness and mutual harmony in all the marriages, except that of Abena, where limited peace with her new family is evidenced. The dangers that the journeys pose include strangulation, isolation, sexual exploitation, and imminent death.

The climax of these tales is realized in the journey because of its attendant confusion and the general feeling of uncertainty and danger created by a sense that the heroines have pushed things as far as they could go. Nothing could be more frightening than a defenseless person in the grips of several hostile people, albeit "little folks," squeezing her unto death; and few experiences could be more humiliating for the proud and beautiful Buje than to be disvirgined by a tortoise, of all creatures. The news of the death of all members of Abena's family sends her into utter confusion, while the transformation—right under the eyes of the unnamed heroine—of a handsome man into a monkey with an insatiable sexual drive is an extreme departure from her ideal companionhood. These women dared to defy the norms of society and paid a heavy toll for it.

Where any form of salvation exists, it takes a male character to rescue the maiden. Rescue is the fourth motifeme of these tales. Hunters save both Kwaboaso and the unnamed heroine from imminent death. Although an old woman initiates the saving process in the tale of Cocoh, she relies on a male character to realize the wish. In the case in which the maiden decides on her own to save herself from her predicament, as with Abena, the voice of society discourages her. Buje is given no chance of going back on her decision to give her suitors a hard time. These tales do not exploit the potential of these heroines to rescue themselves from hardship.

The fifth motifeme, that of interdiction, is characteristic of each of these tales, and it is shown in such forms as regret, spinsterhood, loss of face, abandonment, and complete, negative transformation. Kwaboaso and the unnamed heroine's marriage proposals to the hunters who rescued them are rejected, and they regretfully spend the rest of their lives as spinsters, the implication being that spinsterhood is the appropriate punishment for proud women. Buje's punishment is harsher than that of any of the heroines examined here. Her rejection by society is so complete that she is transformed from a human, not even into an animal form, but much lower down the chain of being, into a plant. Her ostracism from society for guarding her virginity with too much enthusiasm is complete. Abena's unhappiness is made evident by her regret for ever wishing to marry so far away from home. Although Cocoh becomes a "model" wife, there is no indication of happiness for her in that marriage; nothing of the sort was celebrated in the tale. What is certain is that in order to lead any kind of life, she has had to bow to societal demands. These heroines are uniformly punished in the interdiction for violating the rules that govern "normal" marriages.

It is interesting to note that whereas the heroines end up unhappily, the rest of society is restored to its balance; balance is the sixth and last morphological element in these tales. The endings of the summarized tales speak to the equilibrium and the need to maintain the peace. Kwaboaso is left unmarried; Buje is metamorphosed into a plant; Abena is left perpetually in tears; the unnamed heroine is contemptuously rejected by the hunter; and Cocoh's proud wings are clipped: These incidents at the end of the tales appear as logical conclusions. Moreover, it appears as if the heroines got what they deserved. The strong moral statements that close most of these tales vindicate custom and at the same time create a close-endedness to these tales.

Interestingly, in the only similar tale I have discovered where there is a male cental character, Kimanaueze, his fate ends happily. Like the female characters of the other primary versions, Kimanaueze makes a profession out of selecting a bride also (Chatelain 131–41; Radin 73–78). Yet Kimanaueze goes beyond the demands of Cocoh and Abena when he refuses earthly maidens and consciously strives for the hand of the daughter of the Sun and the Moon, who lives in the celestial homestead. With the aid of a sly frog the bride is brought down to earth, and Kimanaueze lives happily ever after with his heavenly bride.

This version would clearly support the thesis that the structures that inhibit the sense of initiative on the part of the heroines are sexist. As these tales indicate, society encourages and sanctions the selection of brides by men, yet it does not grant similar freedom to women. In the version from Chatelain, "Two Men for One Women," the bride's father does the selection, and all's well in the end. This tale tells of a father who gives his daughter's suitors a hard time. He submits them to tests that would eliminate the wife beaters from the contestants. He finally finds his choice, and the daughter is happily settled in marriage. This version is similar in kind to Efua Sutherland's *The Marriage of Anansewa,* in which the heroine's father Ananse plays a role similar to that of the father-in-law in Chatelain's collection. Although Ananse's reasons are strictly economic, Anansewa lives happily ever after.

Notably, the reasons advanced by Abena and Cocoh and indirectly suggested by Buje and Kwaboaso are not radically different from those advanced by the male characters. Yet the women are denied happy endings to their lives. In the tales in which the man either bides his time, as in the case of Kimanaueze, or where the father chooses the groom, as in "Two Men for One Woman," the pattern of the tale conforms to the European Cinderella tale, in which hardship precedes happiness. But in the tales in which the young woman takes on the responsibility of choosing her own mate, the pattern is reversed and the tale moves along in an un-Cinderellalike fashion: What appears as the expression of freedom by the woman always ends with the morphological element of punishment. These patterns once again confirm the male-centered bias that informs the patriarchal system upon which these tales rest.

The suppression of individuality, voice, imagination, and self-expression is a defining quality in the makeup of the central character in these tales, and this is nowhere clearer than in her economic role. Parental prerogative in the choice of a spouse for the woman has embedded in it more than a flagrant exhibition of power. The search is directed and fueled by the economic weight of the prospective groom and the concomitant neutral and weightless economic standing of the woman. The search for a husband is guided by the unstated view that the man must provide for the woman. The buried irony exposes itself when a strongwilled woman must subsume her strengths and initiatives under a watery man so that he will appear economically capable and the sanction arrangement thus upheld.

The economic independence of the woman is not an issue in any of the primary versions. Although Abena experienced a measure of success, her economic power is significantly absent from the details. In Ama Ata Aidoo's play, the eponymous Anowa confirms this societal assumption, albeit with a touch of irony, when she promises her mother that she will help Kofi "make something of himself" and she remains in the background. The point is clear: A woman who walks outside the shadow of her man cannot be rich, no matter her self-achieved wealth.

As is shown by these versions of the tale of the strong-willed woman who found ill by exercising her individuality, the folktale clearly delineates the specific values upon which society rests. When viewed as a social construct, the collective oral tale, the folktale, perhaps, should exhibit the sexism inherent in the society's superstructure. For the clarity and force with which the folktale echoes the social principles, goals, held or accepted standards, as well as taboos enable us to see better the strengths and weaknesses of the society. By so clearly and vigorously defining the unjust and sexist society, the folktale presents itself as a form through which those very ills may be challenged. In this way, the folktale may be seen as a powerful form through which the community itself can grow towards the "just" society, if active progressive discussion evolves.

Works Cited

Abrahams, Roger D. *African Folktales*. New York: Pantheon Books, 1983.

Aidoo, Ama Ata. *Anowa*. London: Longman, 1978.

Chatelain, Heli, ed. *Folktales of Angola*. New York: Houghton-Mifflin, 1984.

Dadie, Bernard B. *Les Contes de Koutou-As-Samala*. Paris: Presence Africaine, 1982.

Dorson, R. M. *African Folklore*. Bloomington and London: Indiana University Press, 1972.

Dundes, Alan. *Interpreting Folklore*. Bloomington: Indiana University Press, 1980.

Gyan, Kwasi. *Contes Akan du Ghana*. Paris: Conseil International de la Langue Francaise, 1983.

Jablow, Alta, ed. *An Anthology of African Folklore*. London: Thames and Hudson, 1962.

Propp, V. *Morphology of the Tale*. Trans. Lawrence Scott. 1964. Austin: University of Texas Press, 1984.

Radin, P., ed. *African Folktales*. New York: Schocken Books 1983.

Sutherland, Efua. *The Marriage of Anansewa*. Accra: Sedco, 1975.

Thompson, Stith. *The Folktale*. Berkeley and Los Angeles: University of California Press, 1977.

17

Revolutionary Brilliance
The Afrofemcentric Aesthetic

ZAIN A. MUSE (OMISOLA ALLEYNE)

There is an aesthetic that is particular and unique to Africana literary and visual artists, an aesthetic grounded in the vibrant ethos of the African American experience. It is an aesthetic simultaneously rich with African antecedents and infused with the subconscious expressions of the worldview of African cultures, and created out of the power and complexity of womanhood. It is an aesthetic that favors fluidity and multiplicity of meaning, that favors cyclical nonlinear structural organization, and speaks (usually literally) in woman's tones from the center. Together these principles of thought, composition, and expression dismantle the imposed supremacy of Western discourse and its implicit phallocentrism. Thus, the works of Erna Brodber and Julie Dash create a metalanguage, a mode of creative communication that expresses the richness of Afro-American women's culture. They transform the language of an oppressive culture and enable it to express the values of a submerged experience. Through this brilliance, Brodber and Dash perform "the most subversive act a people can conceive or carry out short of actual revolution" (Salaam 52). They name themselves in a language that has named them; and this naming is a metalanguage called Afrofemcentrism, distinctly womanist, distinctly African.[1]

In her powerful work *Jane and Louisa Will Soon Come Home*, Erna Brodber vibrantly creates an Afrofemcentric aesthetic. Brodber's poem/song/text is interspersed with layers of texture and rhythm. As other Caribbean writers have done, within the pages of *Jane and Louisa* Brodber ensures that "destructive binaries are impossible to sustain, characters escape fixity . . . the life and death of characters are not absolutes

. . . and [the] text is [never] finally written" (Ashcroft 53). In this way, Brodber destroys the linearity of plot and structure endemic to the Western novel. She rejects absolutes and binarisms in favor of the multiplicity and fluidity of images, words, textures, and sounds.

The main symbol of the nonfixity that informs the text is the image of the kumbla itself. The central motif in the novel, the kumbla carries multiple layers of meaning for the characters throughout the text and becomes myriad expressions of confusion. It is a "parachute . . . a helicopter, a transparent umbrella, a glassy marble, a comic strip space ship . . . and a safe protective capsule" (123).[2] The kumbla exists primarily as *itself*, a calabash gourd enclosure, a neutral that within the novel represents the inclusivity of the thought processes of African cultures. People, places, spiritual power, and events do not have within them innate qualities of good or evil, but rather can be influenced or manipulated to produce malignant and/or creative behavior and/or acts—thus the indeterminacy of the kumbla.[3]

For Nellie, Brodber's central character, a Western-educated sociologist, the kumbla transforms into the exiled space of alienation and negative sexuality. It is simultaneously protective and parasitic, enabling survival while ensuing madness. Nellie manipulates the kumbla to numb her pain and keep her from effectively dealing with the world that leads to her psychosis and fragmentation. Nellie first experiences the kumbla in childhood with her cousins and playmates as she explores a mossy den with overgrowing trees and "oceans of banana leaves" (9). It is dark and cool and buffered from the muted tones of the outside world. A haven and free space of childhood, sustained by ignorance of reality and sheltered from the starkness of the world outside, the sun (Brodber's symbol of the adult world and its concomitant responsibility) is unable to penetrate the warm muddiness of the kumbla. Thus, in Nellie's childhood, even though the kumbla offers a beautiful place for the free wandering of the imagination, it also sows the seeds of dysfunction. Such is the nature of its multiplicity.

Nellie's kumbla is also constructed through her internalization of the complex and insidious caste and class system that pervades her society. Exposed early to the "khaki" assimilation of her family, and by a colonial education system that instills in her a sense of her own "difference," Nellie further retreats into her kumbla by alienating herself from her community. Nellie's great-grandmother, Tia Maria, begins to weave the malignancy of the kumbla out of her white husband's skin (42). Convinced of the superiority of European civilization, Tia completely erases her African culture and instills in her children the belief in the "white helmet" of colonial propriety; Rebecca, Nellie's aunt, and Alexander, Nellie's father, most thoroughly digest the poisonous implications of this lesson. Nellie hears Becca's admonition that "those people" will drag her down (147); and her father, Alexander, feeds her the "pale etchings of principle, invisible gifts of daffodils . . . Hamletian castles and wafer disintegrating on [the] tongue" (30). This classist pretension is subsequently reinforced by Nellie's experiences abroad, where she forsakes rhythm for learning, choosing Plato as the light that will illuminate her people (43). Upon her return, Nellie fosters this attitude through her clinical and detached dealings with her clients and her membership in a psuedo-intellectual liberation group dedicated to meaningless theorizing. Speaking in terms of "them" and "us," Brodber shows Nellie participating in the demeaning Western practice of anthropologizing her own culture.

The most salient aspect of the kumbla that pervades the text is that of its construction as a site of the complex feelings of shame, disgust, and contempt arising from the concept of "negative femininity" that Brodber feels dominates Jamaican culture, the patriarchal repression that causes women to doubt the beauty and validity of their sexuality. Nellie falls victim to this at an early age, as she is ostracized by her male peers immediately after the onset of her first menstrual cycle. She is constantly reminded of her Aunt Becca's "fall" and warned that "woman luck dey a dungle heap [for] fowl to come scratch up," a fact to remember lest she "be weighed in the balance and found wanting" (17). As a result of the strangling and effacing confines of her sexuality, Nellie becomes uncomfortable with sex—and her first experiences shame her into madness and fragmentation. She speaks of the world spinning wildly on its axis as she is overcome with nausea and disgust. She asks herself plaintively, "Is there no way out? No gap in the circle?" (17). As her lover fondles her body in the movie theater, Nellie is torn between her free and colonized selves.[4] On one hand, she wishes to reject the slimy feeling of the boy's phallus; but the side of her trapped by the dictates of feminine propriety prevents her from sending him home. Again, illustrating her victimization, she concludes that she must "vomit and bear it," for therein lies the essence of normalcy (28). These different layers of the kumbla coalesce to engulf. The kumbla is the self-imposed exile of denying the community and the entangling webs of negative sexuality.

Yet the kumbla is also a means of survival, and paradoxically a way to avoid enclosures by systems of domination and oppression. This manifestation of the kumbla is best presented by the folktale involving Anancy, who tells his son, Tucuma, to "go eena kumbla." Camouflaging himself as Anancy's five other children, Tecuma and Anancy trick Dryhead, the man-eating tiger, so that they may escape. Anancy's craft is the "finely woven white silk kumbla designed to protect for generations" (130). Thus, Brodber constructs the kumbla as an indeterminate and neutral container capable of facilitating survival or encouraging destruction. In Nellie's hands, it becomes a dark and lonely cocoon, shutting out the sunlight of personal growth for the stasis of denial. For Anancy it is escape from death.

Another way in which the novel reflects its Afrofemcentrism is in its integration of many different aesthetics. The text alternates between scribal forms and orature and is permeated throughout with a striking musicality that manifests itself in the incorporation of literal symphonic elements and allusions to dance. Thus, through this aesthetic coalescence, Brodber returns to the roots of African culture, where dance, poetry, song, and performance continuously overlap to create a holistic and unified whole. Structurally, the book is organized into a four-part concerto, with each section alluding to a different verse in the popular children's song "Jane and Louisa Will Soon Come Home."[5] In this way, Brodber is in essence making the text a song that slowly unravels along with the many textured threads of the kumbla. By framing the text as song, she is establishing a context for the varied musical notes and tones that fill out and shape the central melody.

As with the kumbla, the novel's musicality is characterized by multiple layers, shades, and textures. On the primary level of musical meaning, Brodber creates an orchestra of words that carry an onomatopoeic lyricism. Words like "jippi-jappa" (25) or "tallawah" (31) ring with percussive, drumlike impact. Brodber also makes reference to the muted *tones* of the sun. The contagious beat of rhythmic words like "janga" and "khus-khus water" that skip throughout the text builds to a literal crescendo in the section "To Waltz With You," in which Nellie's ancestors visit her in a streaming fluid chorus of voice and sound to attempt to reconnect her to her roots. Nellie's gradual reintegration into her community is suggested as she unknowingly begins the concert. Her lyrical and melodic phrase, "Just deep floating sleep, sleep floating deep, Horlicks sleep, floating evenly deep, oohs and ouches," melts into the "choir of warm, lyric sopranos" that are the spirits of her ancestors (78). Once present, the spirits begin to congregate, with "everybody playing the same note" in a "conductor-less orchestra" of voices (79). They also begin to play earthy organic instruments like the kettle drum and bamboo sax, which widen the range of the music. Finally, upon departure, they sing in finale with voices "all blending": "We did our part. Blessings on yours" (81). The spiritual concerto is a success. In place of the dry brittleness of the cracked doll, Nellie is "covered from head to toe with dripping water"—the sign of rebirth (81).

Brodber's use of language also reflects her Afrofemcentrism and her commitment to the cultural and aesthetic principles of her Afro-Jamaican existence. For not only does she deconstruct "destructive binarisms" she also refuses to express herself in the master tongue, instead choosing to claim the rich patois that is a fundamental part of her cultural milieu. To demonstrate these binarisms, Brodber creates wonderfully ambiguous terms like "water table" (11), which simultaneously has free-flowing and rigid connotations. The river in the Anancy tale is both "dark as mud" and like "glistening malarial rainbows of light to give birth to fire flies" (124). Nellie is gripped with "warm fear" (14); there are roses that stink pretty; and one of the characters whizzing by at the church fair is PapaSon—simultaneously wizened by age and marked by immaturity. Yet in addition to Brodber's creation of phrases that contain contradictory layers of meaning, she adamantly rejects the imposed superiority of the "standard" English that was forced upon the first uprooted Africans to grace Jamaican soil. She not only saturates the text with the musicality and richness of her native patois; she also engages in the construction of a narrative voice that uses a patois-derived syntax. Thus, by her injection of patois into the stale austerity of British English, and her subsequent refusal to decode its wonder by way of explanation, Brodber is demanding that the reader enter her culture on her terms. Her choice to leave words unglossed and to intentionally subvert the colonial tongue is truly a political act, characteristic of her entire creative product. For in doing so, Brodber implicitly exposes the inappropriateness of the colonial discourse and confirms its inability to speak adequately to the complexities of the Afro-Jamaican experience. Through

Brodber's ingenious use of language, the colonial tongue, forced upon many, is rendered speechless.

Not only do Brodber's principles of thought reflect her cultural ethos, but so do her principles of composition. Structurally, *Jane and Louisa* is laid out like a colorful quilt, with pieces appliqued upon each other and fragments within fragments coalescing to form an eloquent mosaic. The text wanders easily through past, present, and future without effort. Characters are constantly appearing and disappearing into the fabric. Linearity is shattered and circles abound. In the series of concentric circles, the outermost ring is the kumbla itself. Its rounded contours encompass both Nellie and the reader, as the latter emerges from the dark calabash only at the end of the narrative, when the complete story has been unraveled.[6] Within the circuitry of the kumbla is the children's folk song "Jane and Louisa," which in its cyclical repetitiveness reinforces the concept of the circle, as does the fact that it is usually sung within the context of a ring formation. As in a whirlpool, the novel's circles get smaller and more acute. The first Anancy tale literally revolves around the image of spinning and turning, which is reiterated onomatopoeically through the repetition of the vocalization "ooooooooooh," which both begins and ends the section. Yet a smaller circle is the woman's whisper circle of shame, which ensues upon the entrance into womanhood through menstruation.

Finally, Brodber's evocation of African spiritual antecedents also alludes to her African worldview. Throughout, she conveys the fundamental importance of the ancestors and elders, which she reinforces by making the latter responsible for Nellie's synthesis and healing. The perpetual presence of the ancestors in Nellie's world refers to the African cosmological view that the living always have access to the departed who protect them and watch over them (Mbiti 83). As the physical and spiritual realms cannot be separated, Nellie is assuaged by the love of both the living and the dead. Further, the ring dance and chorus performed by her dearly departed results in the removal of the first layer of Nellie's kumbla, while her grandmother Kitty's "roots life" becomes a tangible model for her approach to her community. In addition to Nellie's own intimate relationship to the dead in her family, Brodber further solidifies the concept of the egungun[7] by referring to the African spiritual belief that the ancestors often choose to appear in their descendants, the latter becoming a vessel through which the spirit of the deceased communicates. Thus, through Brodber's delineation of the inextricable connection to the dead and her theme of ancestor reverence, she reveals her position on the continuum of African cultural and spiritual continuities in the diaspora.

Lastly, the womanist aspect of Brodber's worldview is expressed through the essence of the story itself. *Jane and Louisa*'s theme of a woman attempting to give birth to herself and shatter the confines of an oppressive and stifling cultural definition of womanhood dismantles phallocentric discourse by placing women's concerns and struggles firmly at the center. Through her portrayal of Nellie's psychic fragmentation, Brodber attacks the weighty patriarchy of a society that looks with shame and disgust on women's sexuality; and Nellie's symbolic pregnancy at the end of the text signals the imminent release of the "negative sexuality" that has informed her life.[8] It reflects her decision to define herself and smooth the frayed edges.

In a film of astonishing beauty, Julie Dash expresses perhaps the most overt yet lyrically graceful type of Afrofemcentric aesthetic in her award-winning film *Daughters of the Dust*. Though her most obvious delineation of this ethos lies in her inspiring evocation of core African cultural and spiritual principles, she, like Brodber, weaves a narrative that is deliberately ambiguous and polyvocal and marked by a wonderful nonfixity. Dash's womanist consciousness is expressed most eloquently through her heartstopping portrayal of Nana Peazant, the wise and spiritually enlightened matriarch of the Peazant clan. Nana embodies the power, the gentleness, and the glory of maternal authority, and lovingly guides her children and grandchildren on the path toward a permanent connection with the old souls and the ancestors. Her closest relationships are to her grandchildren, Yellow Mary and Eli, whom she helps to deal with the rape of his wife Eula by facilitating his internal examination of his own sexism. In response to Eli's angry comment, "I don't feel like she [Eula] mine anymore," Nana responds lovingly yet firmly that "You can't give back what you never owned. Eula never belonged to you, she married you" (95).[9]

In addition to Nana's gentle furthering of Eli's already woman-centered perspective (he tells Nana at one point that he believes she is a goddess), Nana's matriarchal strength is alluded to in Dash's many spatial placements of her at the center of the visual composition. When Mr. Snead snaps his photograph of the entire family, it is Nana who commands attention. The richness of her purple dress, itself an allusion to royalty, frames her time-withered body as she sits in the chair (throne) around which her precious children are placed. Dash is clearly making the statement here that Nana Peazant is indeed a queen-mother who fiercely protects her own.

Another way in which a gynocentric theme is delineated in *Daughters* is through the multilayered privileging of the female voice. On a literal level, Dash uses Haagar to express the fundamental and necessary importance of women having the power and space to express themselves into existence. In response to Viola's attempt to silence her and discredit the validity of her claim to the Peazant name, Haagar declares in bitter anger, "I worked hard all my life and ain't got nothing to show for it, and if I can't say what's on my mind, then damn everybody to hell!" (130). The simple and powerful eloquence of this statement hides many levels of meaning. As Zora Neale Hurston wrote of the women whose words filled the night in *Their Eyes Were Watching God,* Haagar is speaking to Black women's historical reliance on the immense power of the word to create a reality that is unique and particular to their experiences, a world in which racism and sexism are kept at bay or reduced to nonentities for the temporary creation of a solace-filled space informed by verbal magic.

Indeed, the idea at the heart of Dash's aesthetic is the privileging of the Black woman's voice. Through the innovative brilliance of her cinematography and filmic language, she also provides a space for the melody of Africana women's songs to be heard. As Toni Cade Bambara elaborates in her introduction to *Daughters of the Dust: The Making of an African American Woman's Film* (which also includes the script), Dash directs the film from the delicate and intimate view of a woman. Her emphasis on shared and communal space in lieu of the hero-dominated frame of Western filmic discourse infuses Black women's multiple experiences into every corner of the viewer's consciousness, as her inspiring images loom from the screen. Dash engages in a "nonlinear, multilayered unfolding" and a "demystified and democratic" treatment of space, where no one is relegated to the traditional confines of the periphery reserved for the native and/or woman "other" (xiii).

But perhaps more importantly, Dash dismantles phallocentric discourse by her creation of indeterminate and deliberately ambiguous women characters, who absolutely escape definition or entrapment within the fixed and suffocating identity enclosures of patriarchal discourse.[10] The opening narration sets the tone for this inexplicable and multiplicitous view of women. Superimposed over a montage of lyrically beautiful visual scenes, an *unnamed* woman speaks of the nonfixity of her existence. In the sweet cadence of the Gullah dialect, the woman says, "I am the first and the last / I am the honored and the scorned / I am the whore and the holy one / I am the wife and the virgin / I am the barren one, and many are my daughters / I am the silence that you cannot understand / I am the utterance of my name" (75, 76). Perhaps this is the lilting voice of the island, perhaps the eternal ethos of femininity; but what is most important is that the expressed definition is not rigid, binary, or an identity that can be contained.

Yellow Mary, especially, and to a lesser extent, Viola, also reflect this internal ambiguity that informs the layers behind the term woman. Yellow Mary, upon the very onset of her arrival, inspires gossip and wonder. Questions are many, suspicions are high; and there is the general intolerance of her status as a prostitute. Yet even the viciousness of Haagar's tongue is not enough to disturb Mary, who largely ignores the loaded inquiries and commentary that are aimed in her direction. To Viola's question, "Lord girl, where have you been all these years, what happened to you?" Mary replies with casual nonchalance, "Pick a story" (108); and later she responds to Haagar's slicing remark that "a woman who knows how to cook is very pretty" with a cool uncompromising stare (112). By and large, Mary is unconcerned with the opinions of others. As she is aware of the oppressive circumstances that led to her "being ruint" she doesn't feel the need to explain the intricate details of her life to those who only desire to see her humbled and shamed. Assured ultimately by an unshakable belief in, and commitment to, herself, she tells Eula how she maintains the sacredness of her precious little box or inner soul when she says, "I don't let nothing in that case or nobody outside of that case tell me who I am or how I should feel about me" (143). Further, when she finally responds to Haagar's venomous insults, it is to declare unapologetically, "I'm Yellow Mary Peazant! And I'm a proud woman, not a hard woman" (154). Mary's inability to be categorized is reflected in other more subtle ways. Owing to her complexity, she contains a variety of different experiences and identities that recede and advance within and without, evading contradiction.

Mary's extensive travels have in a sense infused her with the pieces of each culture she has experienced, creating a colorful and multilayered mosaic. She is fluent in Spanish after a sojourn in Cuba, and speaks knowingly of Canada and Savannah. Her sexuality is equally as textured, as it is slippery and evasive in its avoidance of exact definitions. Though the script acknowledges that Trula and Mary are lovers, the sensual undertones of their relationship are implicit, thus giving the impression that the parameters of their friendship are subject to change and at times often blur. Mary also speaks of her desire for a good man (only to know she could depend on him if she wanted to) and flirts unabashedly with the photographer Mr. Snead. Thus, as with the other facets of her identity, there are multiple expressions of her sexuality, and all coexist without contradiction.

Another expression of Mary's ambiguity is her simultaneous blending of the African past and certain aspects of the Euro-American present. At times seemingly marked by the erasure of cultural assimilation, Mary is in actuality quite capable of proclaiming and savoring the richness of her African past. Though she refers to Eula's revelation that she recently visited with her dead mother as proof of her status as a "real back-water Geechee girl" (120), Mary is clearly favored by Nana Peazant, an indication that she is definitely connected to her roots. Expressing this duality again, Mary embraces the Catholic icon of Saint Christopher and wears his image around her neck, and also lovingly and willingly kisses the *nkisi*-derived "hand" that Nana has tied to the Bible to assure that her children carry her spirit on their journey up north. Finally, though Mary expresses the somewhat Western belief that "A little face powder never hurt [her]" (121), the viewer is left with the implication that it is Mary who will in large part pass on the rich spiritual and cultural legacy instilled in her by Nana Peazant. As the barge is leaving the shore with the majority of the Peazant family aboard, Mary is seen leaning against the old oak tree (roots), her flowing Victorian dress now scrapped for the regal purple tones worn by her grandmother, and her yellow-brown fingers engaged in the age-old African women's art of hair braiding.

Viola is another woman character who defies rigid and confining definition. Though she is in large part constructed as an anthropologist who objectifies, decodes, and studies a foreign culture, she also contains a subconscious belief in the power of African spiritual principles. Viola's anthropological undertones are made quite evident in her very purpose in returning to Dahtaw island. Unlike Yellow Mary, who is coming home to see Nana and reintegrate herself with her community, Viola is accompanied by the photographer Snead, whom Dash says will "take pictures of these very, very primitive people and go back and have a showing of what he's photographed" (38). Further, Viola's occupation as a missionary more firmly establishes her role of collusion with colonial systems of domination that built empires on the belief in the innate inferiority and backwardness of African peoples. Viola expresses these condescending sentiments herself on a number of occasions. Disgusted by Snead's desire to speak to Bilal Muhammed, one of the last survivors of slavery, Viola dismisses him as "a heathen" (130). She patronizes the family matriarch: "Nana was never educated, [that] all she knows are simple things" (129); and in words that no doubt streamed from many a colonizer's mouth, Viola explains to Snead how she sees the day of departure as analogous to "the first steps towards progress, an engraved invitation . . . to the culture, education, and wealth of the mainland" (79).

However, as with Mary, Viola escapes exact definition. Though she participates in Haagar and the Hairbraider's mockery of Nana's bottles, roots, and herbs, she is aware of the principle of elder reverence and refuses to violate it. She says with seriousness, "Haagar Peazant . . . that's an old woman you're laughing at" (128). She declares that "ain't nothing wrong with Nana's tin can" (128) and corrects Snead's irreverence by informing him that the children and the old souls are indeed the "most important members of the family" (136). Yet Viola's multiple layers of self are ultimately expressed through her simultaneous rejection and acceptance of Nana's spiritual ceremony, "A Root Revival of Love." Though her Christian self adamantly rejects this "heathen" practice, the collective unconscious submerged within acknowledges the necessity of maintaining a connection to the ancestors. It is indicative of the ambiguity of women's existence that these two selves are never reconciled. Viola kisses the "hand," but remains somewhat frightened and repulsed. There are no absolutes. Viola, as with all women, will remain between and within boundaries and definitions.

The most obvious aspect of the Afrofemcentric quilt that Dash constructs is the tapestry of images, sounds, and principles that speak to an African-centered spiritual and cultural ethos. Principal characters are loosely based on the models of the Yoruba orishas. Time flows rather than constricts. And throughout Dash affirms the omnipresence of the ancestors, the existence of the living dead, the African belief in the cyclical continuity of life, and ultimately the perpetual presence of the power of the spiritual realm in the land of the living. Of course, the richness of all these African traditions is most firmly embedded in Nana, who at eighty-eight still retains a plethora of beliefs from the Continent. It is she who preserves the sacredness of the bottle tree, its colored containers constant reminders of those that have passed on. She informs Eli of the living's unbreakable responsibility to keep in touch with the dead; and guards the mementos of the past in cloth pouches that contain the spiritual essence of the departed. Her belief in the integral connection between the living and the dead, the spiritual and the physical spheres, is made manifest through her connection to the unborn child who also narrates the film. It is she who asks the child to come and help heal the wounds and pain of Eula and Eli's estranged relationship. As the flowing breeze of the unborn child's spiritual presence stirs the surroundings and blows her hair, Nana affirms her impending arrival with the wispy evocation, "Come, child come!" (99).

In addition to her interjection of the concept of the living dead into the text, Dash also comments on the African belief in the cyclical continuity of life. The narrative begins with the innocent voice of the unborn child, who tells the audience that "My story begins before I was born," when "Nana prayed and the old souls guided me into the New World" (80). Here, Nana's view that the "ancestors and the womb are one" (97) is made clear. The unborn child is merely an extension of the old souls—those who lived and died on the rich soil of the African continent and those who chose to survive slavery—and their presence in the Americas through her is meant to heal festering wounds and continue the endless cycle of life. That the unborn child is rooted in the past and is a reincarnation of those that have passed before her is reiterated through the use of indigo iconography. The smoky blue ribbon that is intertwined in her thick braids, and the similar smudge of azure on her finger, establish the ancientness of her soul, indigo being Dash's symbol of the harshness of slavery—the poisonous dyes of the indigo plant leaving their indelible mark on the calloused hands of those who pounded its leaves (Dash 31). The circle of life continues unbroken. As the film ends, it is the voice of the unborn child that speaks of those members of the Peazant clan who remained behind, "growing older, wiser, and stronger" (164), and thus perpetuating the endless rhythms of the cycle of life.

All of the African spiritual principles that inform *Daughters of the Dust* are reaffirmed through Eli's spiritual rebirth. Shaken by his wife's rape, Eli initially denies the validity of his African spiritual heritage. In anger, he expresses his disillusion at the power of Nana's bottles, " the rice [she] carried in [her] pockets . . . the coins, the roots, and the flowers" (95, 96) to protect him and his family from evil events, saying none of these elements of conjure came in handy while "some stranger was riding" his wife (95). Eli goes on further to ask his grandmother, "Why didn't you protect us . . . ?" and blames the old souls for being too deep in their graves to give a damn (95). Eli throws himself into a kind of forced exile, refusing even to talk to his older cousin, and at the climax of his rage he smashes Nana's sacred bottle tree. Materializing out of the strength of Nana's prayers, the unborn child leads Eli unknowingly into the grave-yard. Recognizing yet fighting the surge within, Eli kneels facedown in the soil in whose depths the vessels of the dearly departed are lodged. The chanting percussion of the African music in the background swells to crescendo and the statuary of the Ibo warrior bobs in the muddy water nearby.

Recalling the aesthetic of Brodber, Dash credits orature with the immense power to heal and facilitate reconciliation. As Eula lyrically narrates the myth surrounding Ibo Landing and Viola whisper-calls the names of the Yoruba orishas, guided by the force of the ancestor spirits, Eli walks *upon* the water and kneels at the wooden image of the African warrior half-submerged in its depths. His transcendence of the physical realm is a necessary step in reclaiming his spiritual self and recalls the miraculous spiritual power of the proud and resilient Ibo nation. As Eli pushes the image away, thus putting peace on his acknowledgment of the vital memories of the past, the transparent spirit of the unborn child is absorbed by Eula, who holds her arms out to welcome its loving presence. Thus, with the blessing of the ancestors and the spirits of those unborn, Eli comes home to the infinite, awe-inspiring spiritual power of his people. As Nana would want, he now has the power to heal himself and to touch his own spirit (96).

Dash's conceptualization of time is also reminiscent of African antecedents. Corresponding to the way in which many African cultures construct epochs, Dash allows *events* (as opposed to syncopated intervals on the clock) to create time, those moments that remain unlived not falling within its boundaries (Mbiti 19). Thus, the present is all there is. The now is omnipresent and more important than a blurry and distant tomorrow (Mbiti 17). Dash visually communicates this concept of time through the fact that the entire movie takes place in one day, thus solidifying the idea that each and every instant of that day of leaving is important. Thus, the timeless, patient preparation of food is equally as important as Nana's spiritual ceremony and the ring dance performed by the children.

Finally, Dash claims her culture by constructing the major characters in her film around the personas of the Yoruba orishas.[11] Nana is modeled upon the cooling presence of Yemonja, the Great Mother and Goddess of the Sea. Trula is a New World Oshun, her symbolic yellow dress an indication of her coquettish and seductive nature. Eli is conceived as Ogun, the god of metalwork, iron, and strength. Eula embodies the beauty and power of Oya-Yansa, who effortlessly blows the winds of change; and the unborn child is Elegba, the youthful counterpart of Eshu, who metaphorically opens the way to the spirit world and to whom appeals are made to overcome indecision. That the characters' functions in the narrative correspond to their orisha origins is clear. Nana is a loving spiritual mother who creates in her children a connection to the power of antiquity. Eula carries within her the future of the Peazants in the person of her unborn child; and she also partakes in a healthy revision of some vital components of the family history. In no way rejecting the validity of the old ways, Eula simultaneously recommends a letting-go of some of the pain of the past. She says, "We carry too many scars. . . . Let's live our lives without living in the fold of old wounds" (157). Eula also urges a revision of womanhood and the myth of the "bad woman," saying that all Black women have been "ruint" and brutalized by the horror of slavery in a white patriarchal society. Finally, as Eula's coming daughter, the unborn child is very much like Elegba in her opening of the way for a future filled with promise.

Thus, the womanist consciousness that informs *Daughters of the Dust,* as well as its embrace of many African cultural and spiritual continuities, makes Dash's piece truly a work created out of an Afrofemcentric aesthetic. She, like Brodber, succeeds in creating a wonderful metalanguage that has the ability to transcend the confines of a repressive colonial culture. Weaving magic out of the richness of their African heritage and the power of their womanhood, Brodber and Dash engage in beautiful and brilliant revolution.

Notes

1. This term came from Freida High-Wasikhongo's article "Afrofemcentric: Twenty Years of Faith Ringgold," Exhibition Catalog, Studio Museum in Harlem.

2. All page numbers without endnote numbers correspond to portions of *Jane and Louisa Will Soon Come Home,* 1980.

3. John S. Mbiti, *African Religions and Philosophy* (London: Heinemann Books, 1990), 202; Henry Drewal, John Pemberton, and Rowland Abiodun, *Yoruba: Nine Centuries of Art and Thought,* 15.

4. This concept was influenced in part by Trinh T. Minh-ha's thesis on the multiple layers of self. It speaks to the constant internal struggle that all oppressed people must carry out between liberated, free, and conscious areas of self and the area that still acquieses to subjugation and erasure.

5. From Ruby Simmonds's presentation on the text in *Africana Women's Fiction,* a Clark Atlanta University graduate seminar taught by Dr. Janice Liddell.

6. Ibid.

7. Yoruba word for ancestors (Drewal, Pemberton, and Abiodun 14).

8. This interpretation is advanced by Carolyn Cooper in her essay "Afro-Jamaican Folk Elements in Brodber's *Jane and Louisa Will Soon Come Home.*"

9. All page numbers without further citation refer to the screenplay found in Julie Dash, Toni Cade Bambara, and bell hooks, *Daughters of the Dust: The Making of an African American Woman's Film.*

10. The term *identity enclosures* appears in Trinh T. Minh-ha's essay "Difference: A Third World Woman's View."

11. Dash alludes to her orisha models in several scribbled notes throughout the screenplay.

Works Cited

Ashcroft, Bill, Gareth Griffths, and Helen Tiffin. *The Empire Writes Back: Theory and Practice in Post-Colonial Literature.* London: Routledge, 1989.

Brodber, Erna. *Jane and Louisa Will Soon Come Home.* London: New Beacon Books, 1980.

Cooper, Carolyn. "Afro-Jamaican Folk Elements in Brodber's *Jane and Louisa Will Soon Come Home." Out of the Kumbla.* Ed. Carol Boyce Davies and Elaine Savory Fido. Trenton, N.J.: Africa World Press, 1990. 279–88.

Dance, Daryl Cumber. "Go Eena Kumbla: A Comparison of Erna Brodber's *Jane and Louisa Will Soon Come Home* and Toni Cade Bambara's *The Salt Eaters." Caribbean Women Writers: Essays from the First International Conference.* Ed. Selwyn Cudjoe. Wellesley, Mass.: Calaloux, 1990. 169–184.

Dash, Julie, Toni Cade Bambara, and bell hooks. *Daughters of the Dust: The Making of an African American Woman's Film.* New York: New Press, 1992.

Drewal, Henry, John Pemberton, and Rowland Abiodun. *Yoruba: Nine Centuries of Art and Thought.* Exhibition Catalog. Ed. Allen Wardwell. New York: Center for African Art, 1989.

Mbiti, John S. *African Religions and Philosophy.* London: Heinemann Books, 1990.

Minh-ha, Trinh T. *Woman, Native, Other.* Bloomington: Indiana University Press, 1989.

Morrison, Toni. "Rootedness: The Ancestor as Foundation." *Black Women Writers 1950–1980.* Ed. Mari Evans. New York: Doubleday, 1984. 75–97.

Salaam, Kalamu Ya. "Searching for the Mother Tongue." Interview. *First World* 2.4 (1980): 48–53.

Wasikhongo-High, Freida. "Afrofemcentric: Twenty Years of Faith Ringgold." *Faith Ringgold: Twenty Years of Painting, Sculpture, and Performance, 1963–1983.* Exhibition Catalog. New York: Studio Museum in Harlem, 1984. 17.

CONTRIBUTORS

Omisola Alleyne (formerly Zain A. Muse) graduated from Spelman College in 1994 after creating an independent major in Literature, Art, and Culture of the Caribbean and Afro-America. As part of this work, she studied at the University of the West Indies in Jamaica and conducted research in Cuba.

Paula C. Barnes is an associate professor of English at Hampton University in Virginia. Her current research and writing examines spirituality in contemporary African American women's fiction as well as the slave narrative tradition. She has published in *Belles Lettres, Black Women in America: An Historical Encyclopedia,* and *The Oxford Companion to African American Literature.*

Brenda F. Berrian teaches in the Department of Africana Studies at the University of Pittsburgh, specializing in women's writing from the Caribbean and Africa. She is the editor of *Bibliography of African Women Writers and Journalists* (1984) and the co-editor of *Bibliography of Women Writers from the Caribbean* (1989). Her critical essays have appeared in scholarly journals and books across the globe.

Erna Brodber is the author of two novels set in her home, Jamaica, *Jane and Louisa Will Soon Come Home* (1980) and *Myal* (1988). She worked as a children's caseworker and later earned her doctorate in sociology at the University of the West Indies, Mona, where she taught for several years. She has published monographs and case studies on Jamaican children, women, and urban life.

Jane Bryce, born and raised in Tanzania, worked as a freelance journalist and editor in England and Nigeria before taking the post as lecturer at the University of the West Indies at Cave Hill, Barbados, in 1991. She is a specialist in African women's writing, contemporary Nigerian writing, and African popular culture and film. Her critical essays appear in numerous anthologies, most recently *Writing and Africa* (1997), *Readings in African Popular Culture* (1997), and *Caribbean Portraits* (1998).

Carolyn Cooper teaches literature at the University of the West Indies, Mona, Jamaica. She is the author of *Noises in the Blood: Orality, Gender, and the "Vulgar" Body of Jamaican Popular Culture* (1996). She contributed to *Motherlands: Black Women's Writing from Africa, the Caribbean, and South Asia* (1991) and *Out of the Kumbla: Women and Caribbean Literature* (1992).

Kari Dako is a senior lecturer in the Department of English, University of Ghana, Legon. She is currently working on a dictionary of local variety markers. She has recently edited and published the original manuscript of the early Gold Coast (Ghanaian) novel *Eighteenpence* by R. E. Obeng.

Yakini Kemp is a professor of English at Florida A & M University. She served as chair of English/Communications for over a decade and as dean of Humanities at Talladega College (Alabama). Her articles have appeared in *Sage: A Scholarly Journal on Black Women, Obsidian II, AfroAmerican Literature Forum, Belles Lettres,* and *African Literature 1988: New Masks.*

Janice Liddell presently serves as special assistant to the provost at Clark Atlanta University, where she chaired the English Department from 1988 to 1998. Her essays on Africana women's literature appear in *As the Curtain Rises: Black Female Visions on the American Stage* (1998), *Out of the Kumbla: Caribbean Women and Literature* (1991), and *Caribbean Commentary.* She is also author of the children's book *Imani and the Flying Africans* (1994), a children's play, *Amy's Beauty,* produced in April 1999, and Hairpiece, an African American women's play.

Carol P. Marsh-Lockett is an associate professor of English at Georgia State University. Her areas of research/publication include African

American, Caribbean, and seventeenth-century English literature. She is editor of *As the Curtain Rises: Black Female Visions on the American Stage* (1998).

Naana J. Opoku-Agyemang is a senior lecturer in the Department of English, University of Cape Coast, Ghana. She was an exchange professor at Eastern Washington University and a Fulbright scholar at Northwestern University. Her essays appear in *Asemko* and *The Afro-Centric Scholar,* and she contributed chapters to *Nwanyibu: Womanbeing and African Literature, Images of African and Caribbean Women: Migration, Displacement, Diaspora and Writing African Women.* She is also the author of *A Handbook of Writing Skills* (1998).

Australia Tarver is associate professor of English at Texas Christian University. She has contributed entries to *The Dictionary of Literary Biography, Black Women in America,* and *The Dictionary of Literary Biography.* Her critical articles appear in *Contemporary Literature in the African Diaspora* and *Winds of Change: The Transforming Voices of Caribbean Women Writers and Scholars.* She is currently co-editing a volume of essays, *New Voices in the Harlem Renaissance,* with Paula Barnes.

Thelma B. Thompson-Deloatch, a native of Jamaica, is professor of English and interim vice president for academic affairs at Norfolk State University. She is author of *The Seventeenth Century Hymn: A Mode for Sacred and Secular Concerns* (1989). She has published in the *College Language Association Journal,* the *Mid-Atlantic Writers Association Review,* the *Journal of Negro Education,* the *Zora Hurston Forum, The Dictionary of Literary Biography—Afro-American Volume, Studies in the Literary Imagination,* and *Afro-Americans in New York Life and History.* She is also past president of the College Language Association.

Emma Waters-Dawson is former chair and professor of English in the Department of English at Florida A & M University. Her literary analyses on the works of African American women writers have been published in *Alice Walker and Zora Neale Hurston: The Common Bond, The Aching Hearth: Family Violence in Life and Literature, Obsidian II: Black Literature in Review,* and *The Florida A & M University Research Bulletin.* She is currently co-authoring *Toni Morrison: A Bibliography* and is president of the College Language Association.

Gay Wilentz is director of ethnic studies and coordinator of the multi-cultural literature at East Carolina University, as well as adjunct faculty at the University of Belize. She is author of *Binding Cultures: Black Women Writers in Africa and the Diaspora* (1992) and has published in *College English, Research in African Literatures, African American Review,* and *MELUS.* She is also co-editor of the African World Press series, *Emerging Perspectives on Ama Ata Aidoo.*

Wei-hsiung (Kitty) Wu teaches in the Department of English and Foreign Languages at Bowie State University. Born in China and educated in both Taiwan and the United States, Wu brings her bilingual and bicultural experiences to her teaching and research. She conducted research in Senegal and Ghana in 1991 as a Fulbright-Hayes scholar and has contributed two essays to *The Oxford Companion to Women Writers in the United States.*

INDEX